The Dillinger Days

•

Merce
Little Bohem
Dillinger and
gang escape FBI
trap, Apr. 22, '34

MINNESOTA

WISCO

Harry Sawyer's
"Sanctuary for Criminals";
Bremer and Hamm kidnaped
by Barkers; Touhy tried for
Hamm kidnaping but freed

Minneapolis

SO.
DAK.

St.
Paul

Dillinger escapes
trap, Mar. 31, '34, but
Eddie Green killed
three days later;
Hamilton mortally
wounded, Apr. 23, '34;
Van Meter killed,
Aug. 23, 1934

Rochester

Sioux Falls

Mason City

Baby Face Nelso
kills two FBI ager
Nov. 27, '34

Sioux City

Tommy Carroll killed,
June 5, 1934

Waterloo

Cedar Rapids

IOWA

Dexter

NEB.

Buck Barrow mortally
wounded by posse as
Clyde Barrow and
Bonnie Parker escape,
July 24, 1933

MISSOURI

IL

KANSAS

Topeka

Kansas City

Kansas City
Massacre,
June 17, 1933

St. Lou

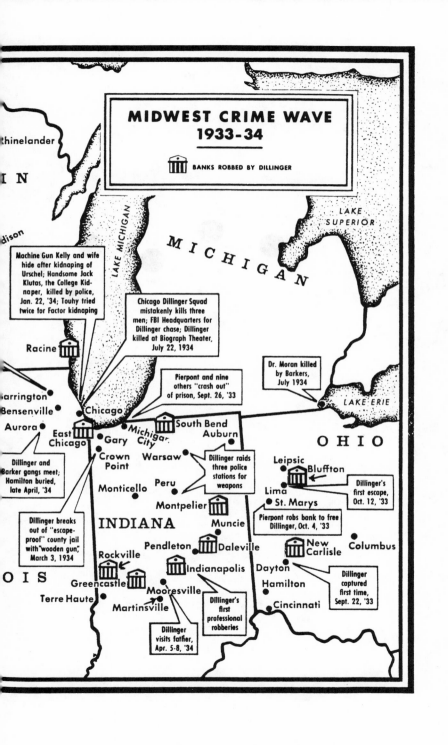

MIDWEST CRIME WAVE 1933-34

🏛 BANKS ROBBED BY DILLINGER

Rhinelander

WISCONSIN

Madison

LAKE SUPERIOR

LAKE MICHIGAN

MICHIGAN

Machine Gun Kelly and wife hide after kidnaping of Urschel; Handsome Jack Klutas, the College Kidnaper, killed by police, Jan. 22, '34; Touhy tried twice for Factor kidnaping

Chicago Dillinger Squad mistakenly kills three men; FBI Headquarters for Dillinger chase; Dillinger killed at Biograph Theater, July 22, 1934

Racine

Dr. Moran killed by Barkers, July 1934

LAKE ERIE

Barrington
Bensenville
Aurora

Pierpont and nine others "crash out" of prison, Sept. 26, '33

Chicago
East Chicago
Gary
Michigan City
South Bend
Auburn

OHIO

Crown Point
Warsaw

Dillinger and Barker gangs meet; Hamilton buried, late April, '34

Dillinger raids three police stations for weapons

Leipsic
Bluffton

Peru

Monticello

Lima
St. Marys

Dillinger's first escape, Oct. 12, '33

Montpelier

Dillinger breaks out of "escapeproof" county jail with "wooden gun", March 3, 1934

INDIANA

Pierpont robs bank to free Dillinger, Oct. 4, '33

Muncie

ILLINOIS

Rockville

Pendleton
Daleville

New Carlisle

Columbus

Indianapolis

Dayton

Dillinger captured first time, Sept. 22, '33

Greencastle

Mooresville

Hamilton

Terre Haute

Martinsville

Cincinnati

Dillinger's first professional robberies

Dillinger visits father, Apr. 5-8, '34

THE
DILLINGER
DAYS

John Toland

DA CAPO PRESS • *New York*

Library of Congress Cataloging in Publication Data

Toland, John.
  The Dillinger days / John Toland.—1st Da Capo Press ed.
    p.   cm.
  Originally published: New York: Random House, 1963.
  Includes index.
  ISBN 0-306-80626-6
  1. Dillinger, John, 1903–1934. 2. Criminals—Middle West—Biography. I. Title.
HV6248.D5T6 1995
364.1′ 523′ 092—dc20
[B]   94-48000
                                                                  CIP

First Da Capo Press edition 1995

This Da Capo Press paperback edition of *The Dillinger Days*
is an unabridged republication of the edition originally published in
New York in 1963. It is reprinted by arrangement with the author.

Published by Da Capo Press, Inc.
A Subsidiary of Plenum Publishing Corporation
233 Spring Street, New York, N.Y. 10013

Quotation on page 10: from "Oh, What a Pal Was Mary." Copyright
1919 by Mills Music, Inc. Copyright renewed 1947. Used by
permission of the copyright owner.

Contents

The Dillinger Days

●

Leading Gangs of the Dillinger Days
(women companions listed in parenthesis)

•

FIRST DILLINGER GANG, *September 1933–January 1934*
John Dillinger (Evelyn "Billie" Frechette)
Harry Pierpont (Mary "Shorty" Kinder)
Charles Makley
John "Red" Hamilton (Elaine Dent)
Russell Clark (Opal "Mack Truck" Long)
Harry Copeland
Ed Shouse

SECOND DILLINGER GANG, *March 1934–July 1934*
John Dillinger (Evelyn Frechette and Polly Hamilton)
"Baby Face" Nelson (his wife, Helen)
John Hamilton (Patricia Cherrington)
Homer Van Meter (Marie Conforti)
Tommy Carroll (his wife, Jean)
Eddie Green (his wife, Bessie)
Pat Reilly

BARROW GANG
Clyde Barrow (Bonnie Parker)
"Buck" Barrow (his wife, Blanche)
Raymond Hamilton
William Daniel Jones
Henry Methvin

THE BARKER-KARPIS GANG
Kate "Ma" Barker
Arthur "Dock" Barker
Fred Barker (Paula "Fat Witted" Harmon)
Alvin Karpis (his wife, Dolores)
Volney Davis (Edna "The Kissing Bandit" Murray)
Fred Goetz (his wife, Irene)
Dr. Joseph Moran; *and numerous associates and aids*

KANSAS CITY MASSACRE
Verne Miller
Adam Richetti
Charles "Pretty Boy" Floyd

KIDNAPERS OF CHARLES F. URSCHEL
George "Machine Gun" Kelly (his wife, Kathryn)
Albert Bates; *and numerous aids*

PART ONE

CHAPTER 1

Dream World

1

IT WAS MAY 20, 1933.

Some forty-five miles from Chicago's Loop, just behind the deserted dunes of Lake Michigan, on the outskirts of the pleasant town of Michigan City, 2,500 men lived in cramped solitude at the Indiana State Prison. Within the high gray walls, an area of twenty-three acres, was a silent city of outcasts. Many were already professional criminals when they entered but just about as many were misfits who were merely amateurs in crime. Almost all had been degraded and embittered and, despite the state's avowal that the purpose of imprisonment was rehabilitation, they would come out far greater threats to society.

Early that afternoon Warden Walter H. Daly was handed a telegram from a prisoner's father:

JOHN DILLINGER NO. 13225 MOTHER NOT EXPECTED TO LIVE CAN YOU SEND HIM AT ONCE ANSWER.

Daly told an assistant to finish processing Dillinger's papers and inform the father he could pick up his son in two days. Governor Paul V. McNutt had already paroled Inmate #13225 on May 10 under Executive Order No. 7723, but paper work took time. Besides, what difference did a week or so make to a man who had already spent nine years behind bars?

Within a few minutes John Herbert Dillinger heard the news over the grapevine—that mysterious telegraph system that operates in every prison—while setting collars in the shirt factory. He was a short, stocky man of twenty-nine, greatly resembling a then unknown young actor, Humphrey Bogart. Only one crime was listed on his record: a clumsy attempt to rob an elderly grocer.

His victim and almost two hundred of the leading citizens of his adopted home town, Mooresville, Indiana, had signed a petition for parole. In a letter to the Clemency Board written ten days after President Franklin D. Roosevelt's inauguration, J. W. Williams, the judge at Dillinger's trial, said:

I believe if this prisoner is paroled, that he has learned his lesson and that he will go straight in the future and will make a useful and honorable citizen. . . .

J. E. Comer, a respected physician of Mooresville, expressed the opinion of many of his neighbors when he wrote Governor McNutt:

. . . He is a bright man and so far as I know was never in trouble until this unfortunate circumstance placed him in the condition he is now in.

I believe the community at large would sanction his release and think all would help him to become the man he should. . . .

After two days Dillinger was released with a cheap suit of clothes, a five-dollar bill, and a handshake from the warden. His half brother, Hubert, was waiting. They drove south toward Mooresville, a quiet Quaker farming community of about 1,800, some eighteen miles southwest of Indianapolis. When they reached home—a small white farmhouse just out of town—another car was pulling into the driveway. In it was a local funeral director. Dillinger had arrived a few minutes too late.

He was greeted warmly at his first appearance in downtown Mooresville; many shook hands with him. Friends were amazed at his new, trim figure. He had gone away—nine years before—a porky, sleepy-looking boy.

While being driven to Crown Hill Cemetery in Indianapolis to the burial of his stepmother, Dillinger told the undertaker, "I'm sick of it. I'm going to go straight." A few Sundays later—it was Father's Day—he attended the local Friends Church for the first time and heard the pastor, Mrs. Gertrude M. Reiner, preach on the Prodigal Father and the Prodigal Son. She noticed that Dillinger, sitting next to his father, openly wept. After the sermon the young man told her, "You will never know how much good that sermon has done me."

By now even the doubters in Mooresville were convinced that he would become a credit to the community. They did not know, of course, that in the few weeks since his release he had already robbed two super markets, a drugstore, and a small bank. Long before his parole John Dillinger had chosen crime as his career.

2

He was born in a middle-class residential section of Indianapolis called Oak Hill late in the sultry evening of June 22, 1903. Three years later his mother, Mollie, suffered an apoplectic stroke and, after an operation, died. Mr. Dillinger—he pronounced the name with a hard "g" in the German style—was an unemotional, somber man. Though kindly, he believed any masculine display of emotion, even to a three-year-old son, was weakness.

John Wilson Dillinger, a charter member of the Hillside Christian Church, was a hard-working grocer who scrupulously gave penny-for-penny value. He tried to instill in the youngster his own stern religious and moral principles, punishing him for the slightest misbehavior, yet he could also be indulgent. It was Johnnie Dillinger who had the first new bicycle in the block, who spent the most on fireworks, who always had enough money to treat the other children to candy.

At first Dillinger's red-haired sister, Audrey, thirteen years older, took the place of his mother. But she married within a year and soon moved out of the snug, two-story house on Cooper Street. In the next few years Mr. Dillinger spent most of his time in the grocery store, sometimes locking his son in the house for safekeeping, sometimes letting him roam the neighborhood till after dark. It was a strange world of extremes; and, to make it worse, the youngster had only one close friend—Fred Brewer, another child with an unhappy home life. The two boys, bound by loneliness, became inseparable and it was a common sight in Oak Hill to see them strolling down the street, Dillinger's right arm around Fred's shoulder, occasionally pulling the lobe of his friend's ear.

Fred's father was a whiskey salesman who regularly came home on Saturday night for the week end—drunk. Once the two boys secretly piled large rocks on the front-porch roof and, as Mr. Brewer staggered up the steps, dumped them on his head. But Dillinger's war with his father was far subtler. When he was old enough to wait on customers he sometimes gave the neighborhood children overgenerous portions of candy. One day Mr. Dillinger saw him surreptitiously slip a pretty girl a bonus package of "Kiss Me" chewing gum. The grocer snatched the gum from the girl, then knocked his son over a large coffee container. Dillinger didn't cry, just wiped the blood from his mouth and stared up at his father.

When the boy was nine Mr. Dillinger married Elizabeth Fields, a quiet, self-effacing country woman in her late twenties. Though neighbors and relatives always insisted theirs was a warm relationship, Dillinger from the first regarded his stepmother as a stranger. As time went on and he saw his father giving her the affection he longed for, he grew increasingly resentful, developing a sarcastic, lopsided smile.

Not long after his father's second marriage he became the ringleader of The Dirty Dozen, a neighborhood gang. At first it was just another kid gang but by the time Dillinger was in the sixth grade he was leading the more daring members in raids against the Pennsylvania Railroad. They were stealing tons of coal from gondolas of the belt line that ran through Oak Hill, finding plenty of buyers among the neighbors. One day several women asked Dillinger if he would sell the coal cheaper if they helped haul it from the tracks. Since the boys were eager to go to Riverside Park that day they agreed. While the wagons were being loaded, Fred Brewer spotted a railroad detective coming around the bend and whistled. The boys disappeared; the women were caught.

That night Dillinger and the other young conspirators were hauled out of bed by police. At Juvenile Court everyone was frightened except Dillinger. He stood arms folded, slouch cap over one eye, staring steadily at the judge—and chewing gum. When the judge ordered him to take off the cap and remove the gum, Dillinger grinned crookedly and slowly stuck the gum on the peak of his cap.

"Your mind is crippled," said the judge.

About this time his stepmother gave birth to a boy, Hubert. Whenever Mr. Dillinger showed the slightest affection for the baby, Dillinger would sulk. Once he told Fred that when he was rich and famous his father would wish he'd been nicer to him.

By now Fred Brewer's parents were divorced and his mother had remarried a man named Whiteside. Both boys felt they were outcasts from their own homes and became almost like brothers. One of their favorite playgrounds was Drinkard's Veneer Mill, next to the Dillinger store. When the mill closed, the two would often sneak in and operate the saw. One late afternoon, after they tied another boy on the carrier, Dillinger threw the switch propelling the terrified victim toward the large buzzing circular saw. Only when the boy was a yard from death did Dillinger stop the carrier.

Most of the neighbors knew nothing of this side of young Dillinger, but his father became increasingly worried by his son's conduct. Lecturing had never helped nor had beatings with a barrel stave been effective. Now he went so far as to chain him to the wheel of the horse-drawn delivery cart parked in back of the store.

But vindictive punishment only made John Dillinger more rebellious. He commandeered an untended switch engine and ran it into a line of coal cars; then stole three cases of whiskey from a boxcar and wound up at school drunk. He also began to take an extremely precocious interest in sex.

In the summer of his thirteenth year, 1916, he was digging a cave with Fred and several friends near the railroad tracks when a girl approached with a coal cart. Dillinger suggested they "have some fun" with her. The boys grabbed the girl, who apparently put up only a token protest, and took her into a nearby abandoned house. Dillinger gave a brief lesson in sex to those who needed it, allotted so much time to each boy, then stood guard in front of the door while each in turn had intercourse with her.

After finishing Washington School, Dillinger, now sixteen, announced that he was going to get a job. Mr. Dillinger replied that anyone wanting to go to work when he could attend Arsenal Technical High School was a fool. It should have been a most important discussion between father and son but neither was able to listen to the other. Everything that Mr. Dillinger said only irritated the youth. He was tired of school and, more important, wanted independence.

He got a job at Drinkard's and amazed the workers with his mechanical aptitude. No one knew he had been operating the saws for years. After a while the mill, like school, proved boring and he became a mechanic at the Reliance Specialty Company, a west side machine shop. From the first he showed remarkable manual dexterity. He worked hard, kept regular hours, and was, said the owner, "very fast and accurate . . . sober, honest, and very industrious."

At last it appeared as if he had found himself. His father was delighted but did not praise the young man, feeling this might "break the spell." Before long, however, Dillinger began coming home in the early hours of the morning. Asked for an accounting, he would smile crookedly and answer evasively.

Mr. Dillinger was convinced his son was not only getting out of hand in general but becoming seriously involved with women in particular. One solution would be to get him into the country; such a youth with money could get into serious trouble in a city. Since Mr. Dillinger had already reached the point where he wanted to retire, his son's wildness was only an added reason to act at once. He sold his store and four houses —contrary to later popular belief, he was relatively well-off— and moved to his second wife's home town, Mooresville. What Johnnie needed, he thought, was healthy life on a farm, far from the temptations of Indianapolis.

In his first days at Mooresville Dillinger was accepted into a group of young people from the Christian Church. He became popular with the boys because he was generous and drove them around in his father's Apperson "Jack Rabbit"; with the girls because he was quiet, polite, and always neatly dressed. Then one day, while taking several young people for a ride in the big, open Jack Rabbit, his coat tail blew up. When a girl grabbed it he thought she was ridiculing him. Furiously yanking free, he drove the car "like a madman" the rest of the way into town. The crowd, including a girl named Mary he was presently dating, promptly dropped him.

That fall Dillinger, against his will, entered Mooresville High School. Though well-behaved, he never studied and received failing grades in almost every subject. Mr. Dillinger was asked to come to school and discuss his son's poor marks but claimed he was "too busy." Yet he was furious when Dillinger quit before Christmas vacation.

In spite of his father's vigorous protests, Dillinger now went back to work at the Reliance Specialty Company, commuting the eighteen miles to Indianapolis by motorcycle. Night after night, upon returning from work, he would clean up, stand outside the house where Mary was staying with a girl friend, and hopefully sing one of the popular songs of the day:

> Heart of my heart was Mary,
> Soul of my soul divine.
> Though she is gone, love lingers on
> for Mary, old pal of mine.

But she never came out.

Delbert Hobson, who lived next door to Dillinger, now became his closest friend, even though two years younger. The two hunted squirrels, went on double dates, and talked at length in the hayloft of the Dillinger barn. Excessive in everything, Dillinger began to read volume after volume of Wild West stories. His favorite hero was Jesse James and he would bore Hobson with involved accounts of the famous gunman's Robin Hood qualities; he seemed obsessed not only by Jesse's courage and daring but also by his kindness to women and children.

Within a year it was obvious that the move to the country had had little effect on young Dillinger. In fact, he had become only more maverick. He would stay out late, sometimes all night, and then refuse to tell where he had been. As a result, the arguments between father and son grew so open and bitter that Hobson dreaded visiting the farm, and saw Dillinger less and less.

Dillinger was spending most of his spare time these days in Martinsville, the county seat, sixteen miles away—mainly because he'd had such poor luck with local girls. Here he loitered around Gebhardt's pool hall, played baseball, and seduced those girls who didn't resist his direct approach. He wasn't interested in courting them, only in sleeping with them, and seemed almost driven to incessant conquests. As he later confided to a fellow prisoner: when he didn't make love for any length of time it felt as though an iron band around his head was "squeezing" his brains out.

But there was one girl who attracted Dillinger in a different way. He fell in love with his uncle's stepdaughter, Frances
Thornton. Out of all the girls he knew she was the only one he
looked on as something more than a sexual partner and he
asked her to marry him. His uncle thought they were too young
and persuaded Frances to refuse him.

Believing his father responsible for this rejection, he grew
more insolent and mutinous. By now he had tired of or been
thrown over by the available girls in Martinsville and had gone
back to Indianapolis. His tastes had also changed; he preferred older, more experienced women who would not abruptly drop him—in other words, prostitutes whose loyalty
could be bought. After a year of this life he had gonorrhea
and had become so dissipated he was forced to quit his job.

On Sunday evening, July 21, 1923, Dillinger had a date
with a young woman in Indianapolis who, according to stories,
was pregnant by him. But he didn't have the carfare and
his father wouldn't let him borrow the family car. He walked
to the Friends Church, where services had just begun—he
had changed denominations during an unsuccessful campaign
to seduce the pastor's daughter—and took the newest car in the
parking lot.

In the early hours of the following morning a policeman
found him aimlessly strolling the streets of Indianapolis.
Suspicious even after Dillinger's explanations, he grabbed the
young man's coat collar and escorted him to a call box. Suddenly Dillinger ducked down, leaving the policeman with an
empty coat.

The break with his father was now complete. He couldn't
go home nor did he want to. Frightened, he hid in a barn, and
the next morning enlisted in the Navy, giving his real name but
a fictitious St. Louis address.

But Dillinger soon learned that naval life suited him no
better than life on the farm. He hated the regimentation, went
AWOL for "about twenty-three hours," and was sentenced to
solitary confinement for ten days, his first imprisonment. The
following month, when his ship, the *Utah*, docked at Boston,
he simply walked off.

Several weeks later his old friend, Fred Brewer Whiteside, met him in downtown Indianapolis. Dillinger lied about his recent experiences, claiming he'd been "kicked out of the Navy." After boasting that he had ridden the "blinds" of the Twentieth Century baggage car from New York, Dillinger insisted that Fred come to an apartment and meet his "wife." Whether this was a legal relationship or not, no one will probably ever know. "Mrs. Dillinger" carried a baby in her arms and there was another, about a year old, in a play pen. Dillinger said he was working at a machine shop on Kentucky Avenue, and then displayed the tools he had stolen. "I have half the shop up here," he said proudly.

Early that March Dillinger finally returned to Mooresville —alone. The Navy, he explained, had given him a dishonorable discharge. He talked little of the past eight months but did tell his father he hated being a sailor because there were "too many people" ordering him around. At home he was moody, often wandering alone in the hillocks and gullies behind the farm. Occasionally he went hunting with a neighbor but most of his time was spent in Martinsville with sixteen-year-old Beryl Ethel Hovius, an attractive girl who came from a poor, hard-working family.

On April 12, 1924, Dillinger suddenly walked into the farmhouse with Beryl on his arm and told his father they'd just been married. He was "grinning and proud."

But Beryl had no better influence on him than the "wife" in Indianapolis. Within a few weeks he and two companions were arrested for stealing forty-one chickens from Homer Zook of Lawrence Township. The day after the trial Mr. Dillinger brought Zook a document from the judge and said if Zook would sign it, his son would be given a suspended sentence. Zook refused.

In spite of Zook's lack of co-operation, however, Mr. Dillinger somehow managed to get the case quashed. But even this did not bring father and son together. Their quarrels only continued until Dillinger, already cramped from living with Beryl in his little room, decided that he couldn't stay under the same roof with his father. The newlyweds now moved in with

Beryl's parents in Martinsville. Although he got a job as an upholsterer in a Mooresville furniture factory and was rated an expert and affable employee, he tired of family life and began staying out nights again.

That summer he played on the Martinsville baseball team, usually as shortstop. One of his new cronies was a querulous umpire, Ed Singleton, an employee of the Mooresville Electric Light Company and a relative of Dillinger's stepmother. Ten years older, Singleton was a weak, tortured man with webbed fingers who drank heavily.

The two learned that B. F. Morgan, the proprietor of the West End Grocery store, usually carried the day's receipts when he went uptown Saturday nights for a haircut. They decided to rob Morgan, though the grocer had shown kindness to Dillinger in the past; years before he had caught the boy stealing pennies from the counter and had merely lectured him gently on honesty.

At about 8:30 P.M. on the evening of September 6, 1924, Morgan—a well-built man, six feet tall—pocketed the receipts and locked up. But this time he first left the money in his home before going on to the barber shop. As he was walking past the Christian Church on his way home, Dillinger accosted him.

The young man had been drinking to get up nerve. In one hand was a .32 revolver, in the other a bolt wrapped in a handkerchief. He struck the grocer on the head with the bolt. Morgan's straw hat saved him from serious injury and he fought back as Dillinger hit him again. The grocer shouted the Mason's cry of distress and several neighbors ran to his assistance. When Morgan grabbed the gun it discharged and Dillinger, thinking he had shot his victim, ran down the street where Singleton was to be waiting with the getaway car. No one was there.

Two days later the deputy sheriff of the county drove to the farm. Though Dillinger said he knew nothing about the brutal assault, he was taken to Martinsville and jailed. The county prosecutor promised leniency if he would plead guilty but he refused. A few days later Mr. Dillinger visited the jail and the young man broke down, sobbing out the truth. Persuaded by his father, he confessed the whole story to the prosecutor, who then convinced Mr. Dillinger that the expense of a lawyer was unnecessary. He was certain the court would be lenient.

The next day Dillinger was tried without a lawyer. His father, who had once been "too busy" to consult his son's high school teachers, was now too busy to attend the trial. The young man pleaded guilty, believing the prosecutor's assurance of a light sentence, but the judge reflected the indignation of the people of Mooresville and sentenced him to Pendleton Reformatory for ten to twenty years.

When he passed through the gates of Pendleton he was confused and full of hate—his father, the county prosecutor, and the judge had all deceived him. His bitterness was so apparent he was brought before Superintendent A. F. Miles.

Dillinger said he had been tricked into confessing, then added quietly, "I won't cause you any trouble except to escape. I can beat your institution."

Miles, a stern disciplinarian, had met a thousand Dillingers before. "If you have the notion to escape," he said in a grimly parental manner, "we'll play that game with you." Curiously enough, he even looked somewhat like Mr. Dillinger.

The young man's mouth twisted into its sarcastic grin and he said, "I'll go right over the Administration Building."

CHAPTER 2

Buried Alive

1

SOME THIRTY MILES NORTHEAST OF INDIANAPOLIS IS PENDLETON, a small community surrounded by prosperous farms and fertile rolling fields. One and a half miles south of town lay the Indiana Reformatory. Its buildings, uniformly finished in tan brick, trimmed with white stone and roofed with red tile, were surrounded by reinforced concrete walls as high and formidable as those of the state prison.

The reformatory was dangerously overpopulated with 2,340 inmates, and the guards, who were paid only about $100 a month, were burdened with extra duties. When Dillinger ate his first dinner in the big, bare dining room—pungent with the mixed smell of disinfectant, sweat, and food—the only sound was the jangle of knives and forks on tin dishes. He ate the usual evening stew. Every night this unsavory concoction of meat and potatoes had a different name on the menu board— Hungarian Goulash, Baked Hash, Irish Stew, Chili.

The thirty-one acres in which the inmates were penned was a permanent battleground. Here the unceasing war between prisoners and "screws"—guards—was waged. Every time an inmate successfully broke a rule, he struck a blow for the entire inside population.

The two sides clashed most often over illegal smoking. Each man got a bag of Duke's Mixture on Saturday night for use in his cell at a specified time. The more experienced somehow managed to smoke in the shops, at the athletic field, even at the movies. During the weekly showing of the usual two-reel silent Westerns, scores of men would duck down and light rolled cigarettes with buzzers—homemade lighters. In a few minutes the auditorium was full of smoke but by the time one of the sleepy, overworked guards noticed great clouds obscuring the ray from the projector and turned on the lights, every cigarette had disappeared.

The first three weeks of caged living were like a nightmare, which was at its worst when the lights went out—a newcomer would weep and a few old hands would begin shouting for quiet. Finally Dillinger felt he could stand it no longer.

On October 10, when the evening count was made at G Cell House, he was missing. Immediately the duty officer struck the large steel triangle hanging in the officers' dormitory. Every available guard and even the employees dressed and rushed into the walled area, where they began a building-by-building hunt. Dillinger was finally found hiding in the foundry and six months were added to his sentence.

Five days later he enjoyed a few hours of freedom on the drive to Franklin, where his partner in crime was being tried. Singleton, after claiming he was drunk and had taken no part in the actual robbery, was sentenced to a term of two to fourteen years. Dillinger's bitterness at this more lenient sentence to a man ten years older was understandable but hardly justified. It was he, after all, who had struck the grocer. On the return to Pendleton, Dillinger broke away from his guard in Indianapolis but was soon recaptured.

About a month later he smuggled a saw into his cell, hacked through the grillwork and, with two other men, escaped into the corridor. All were caught while still in the cell house and another half year was tacked onto Dillinger's growing sentence.

For the first few months he paced sullenly in his cell. At

work he was surly and unco-operative. There were four factories inside the walls run by civilians for profit. Inmates worked eight hours a day making shirts, underwear, trousers, fiber furniture, kettles, and other metalware. The most unpopular shop was the foundry with its almost constant 130-degree heat. Dillinger worked here making manhole covers. Then he tried another kind of escape: he poured hot steel into one of his foundry shoes. This was by no means the first case of self-injury and he was kept on the job. But Dillinger, more persistent than most malingerers, poured acid on his injured heel, which became so ulcerated he had to be transferred to yard duty. This was his first victory at Pendleton over the "management."

Instead of being inspired to more rebellion, he suddenly became a model prisoner and even began to make friends. He learned that most of the inmates had, like himself, drifted into crime through "bad luck," association, or chance. His first comrades came from this group of misfits but his admiration slowly settled on that small handful of professionals who had deliberately chosen crime as a career. Such men belonged to the hierarchy of American criminals listed in the FBI's special file of 10,000 Public Enemies—those who had to be captured by force of arms. The one Dillinger looked up to most was Harry "Pete" Pierpont. He was a slender, good-looking young man, an inch over six feet, with light brown hair and extremely blue eyes, which appeared to darken when he grew angry. Though only a year older than Dillinger, he was already classed as an incorrigible.

At nineteen he had tried to steal a car in Indianapolis. When the owner grabbed him, he fired four times, fortunately only slightly wounding the victim. Pierpont's mother was a big, determined woman, fully convinced her boy had meant no harm and should be freed at once. She visited the reformatory superintendent, revealing that her Harry had been hit on the head with a baseball bat and was released conditionally from a hospital for the insane.

Pierpont also had a physical deformity: the second and third toes of his feet were grown together. As a child he must have wondered why he should have been so peculiarly afflicted. When a lawyer from Indianapolis wrote regarding his parole, the superintendent answered:

> . . . He is in a measure, mustang and must be curbed. I think it can be done with kindness and time better than with force and an early release.

Mrs. Pierpont protested, but the superintendent replied:

> This young fellow has been as wild as a March Hare. . . . I only wish I could write a different letter to you, but this boy has put a 10 rail fence up for me and it is hard to climb.

The mother persisted and Pierpont was finally paroled but within a year he was arrested after robbing a Kokomo bank and, since he was still so young, returned to the reformatory.

When Pierpont arrived at Pendleton he was surrounded by a sheriff and a dozen heavily armed deputies. He gave the wrong name; refused to recognize Superintendent Miles; declined to make a statement or have his picture taken; and spit at a guard. Two months later he drilled the bars of his cell in an escape attempt and was transferred to the Michigan City penitentiary. But by that time the handsome Pierpont, who had almost classic features and walked among his fellows with quiet authority, had made an indelible impression on Dillinger.

Dillinger's own behavior, however, was so exemplary that he was taken off yard duty and put to work in the #2 shirt factory. Here he became very close to a young man who was not at all like Pierpont. Homer Van Meter was just under six feet but weighed only 125 pounds. He had a comedian's face and would throw himself out of joint, hobbling around like a paralytic to amuse the other inmates. Though Pierpont already disliked Van Meter and in a few years would detest him, Dillinger never lost either his affection for one or his admiration for the other.

In the shirt shop Van Meter spent so much time entertaining the other workers that he often failed to "make task." An inmate assigned to a shop was given a week or so to learn his operation and then was required to turn out a specific amount of work each day—a task. Those failing to make task were sent to the guard house for special punishment. After breakfast each man was forced to stand until evening in his socks on a small mat, about two feet square. If he stepped off he was beaten. A man could be excused only to go to the bathroom and then the prisoner could not flush the toilet until the guard had been assured it had been a genuine call of nature. If there was no evidence, the guard rapped him sharply with the loaded end of his cane.

Dillinger, a seamster, worked at the end of the line yoking down the sleeves. With his remarkable manual dexterity he made double task easily and several times accomplished the incredible feat of triple task. Almost every day he helped less adept comrades, although this was punishable by several days on the mat. The civilian in charge never reported him but finally a guard caught him. On that same day Van Meter, as usual, failed to make task and the following morning the two reported to the guard house.

The prisoners didn't mind the physical discomfort of the mat as much as the boredom. There seemed to be nothing to do except count the bricks in the wall. But Van Meter—according to fellow inmate Willard Kelley—had done so much mat time he finally devised a unique way to keep his sanity. He brought several three-inch-long pieces of thread looped at one end. When the guard wasn't looking, says Kelley, who stood on the next mat, Van Meter tried to catch flies by hand. He got his first after an hour. Unfortunately it was crushed and he had to catch another. This took a second hour. Now he slowly, carefully lowered the loop end of a piece of thread over the fly and drew it tight. When he opened his hand the fly clumsily headed for the ceiling with its burden. Late that afternoon the startled guard finally noticed several pieces of thread flying mysteriously near the ceiling.

Most of the inmates enjoyed the antics of the tall, skinny, sallow young man, those afraid to show their own hostility especially delighting in his open insolence.

Van Meter's father, a railroad conductor, had been a heavy drinker whose death was attributed to a "general nervous collapse." When Homer was in the sixth grade he ran away from home in Fort Wayne, went to Chicago, and found work as a bellboy and waiter. At the age of seventeen he was convicted of "disorderly conduct and intoxication" and fined $200. That same year he stole a car, was caught and sent to Southern State Prison at Menard. By then his forearm was tattooed with an anchor bearing the word HOPE—and he had syphilis.

After serving thirteen months, he was paroled. Two months later in Toledo he ran into a fellow prisoner and together they robbed the passengers of a New York Central train of several hundred dollars.

Van Meter was again arrested and this time sent to Pendleton. "This fellow," warned an officer of the Gary police force, "is a hardened criminal and would not hesitate to shoot and kill in order to accomplish his purpose."

In January 1926 he agreed to go to Chicago under guard to testify against a man being falsely tried as his accomplice in the train robbery. He only went to get away from Pendleton for a few days, since he knew his partner was already dead. While William Taylor, a parole agent, was asking directions in Union Station, Van Meter suddenly dashed into the crowd. Hiding handcuffs in his overcoat sleeves, the thin young man threw himself out of joint and hobbled to the corner of Van Buren Street and Wabash Avenue. Here he began begging money. When he was discovered and returned to the agent he only said, "Mr. Taylor, there you are. I've been looking all over Chicago for you!"

A few weeks later he and his cellmate sawed their way out of their cubicle after the evening count. Just then an elderly guard, Charles Stewart, who was well liked by all the inmates, returned for a second count. Van Meter hit him over the head with a lead pipe and, when Stewart struggled, slugged him again and again until he fell, senseless. The two escapees ran to a window whose basket bars were loose and soon were in the yard.

Van Meter was caught near the flagpole and beaten by the night captain until he dropped and had to be carried off to the hospital. He spent the next two months in the "hole," where, according to inmate witnesses, he was blackjacked regularly every night.

Upon his return to the cell block he looked like a skeleton; several teeth were missing; and his body was covered with bruises. Instead of complaining, he gave comic imitations of the guards. The Director of Research examined him and reported:

> This fellow is a criminal of the most dangerous type. Moral sense is perverted and he has no intention of following anything but a life of crime. . . . He is a murderer at heart and if society is to be safeguarded, his type must be confined throughout their natural lives.

A few weeks later Van Meter, like Pierpont, was transferred to Michigan City. Apparently Dillinger took it almost as a blow aimed at himself, for he began acting like a spoiled child. But after being punished for a series of juvenile offenses —"braying like a jackass" was one—he made another abrupt about-face, and kept out of trouble for the next year and a half.

His wife, Beryl, visited him regularly and he wrote her letters filled with longing and studded with extravagant sentiments, but in the summer of 1928 her visits began to be punctuated by misunderstandings and quarrels. After one of these fights he wrote:

> . . . You were mad now weren't you and I came very near not writing at all last time. I hope you are not worrying about how your going to keep me home with you after I get out as sweet as you are you can let me do the worrying. Dearest we will be so happy when I can come home to you and chase your sorrows away and it won't take any kids to keep me home with you always for Sweetheart I love you so all I want to do is just be with you and make

you happy. I wonder if I will get an interview Monday. I
sure hope so for I am dying to see you. Darling have some
pictures taken. Everytime I see you you look dearer and
sweeter to me so I want late pictures. Now say rassberries
but Honey when I am expecting to see you soon everything is hunky dory so you can imagine what a disappointment it was to me when you didn't come your birthday.
I've been cross as a bear ever since, so Dearest don't tell
me you are coming unless you are sure you can for Sweetheart it's an awful disappointment to not get to see you
when I am expecting you. I know though Darling that you
come as often as you can. Give my love to your Mother. I
hope you and her are well. I guess I will say by for this
time. Lots of love and kisses to the sweetest little wife in
the world. . . .

In spite of his efforts to patch up their growing differ-
ences, Beryl's visits became less frequent and finally stopped—
and in the spring of 1929 she filed for divorce. At first Dillinger
would sit on his cot for hours, hand in chin, brooding. Then he
sought a different kind of escape, this time, a more construc-
tive one. He asked permission to enter the eighth grade of the
reformatory school, where he studied diligently, led classroom
discussions, and soon was the outstanding student in the class.
His teacher, young Ernest Ellingwood, had never seen such an
intense desire for learning.

On June 20 the same judge who had sentenced him
granted Beryl a divorce. Though Dillinger once more lapsed
into a depressed mood, he kept out of trouble, continuing to
work diligently at the shirt shop. In a few weeks the parole
board would meet to discuss his case and he was positive he
would then be freed.

On the afternoon of the hearings he played shortstop in a
baseball game with a semiprofessional team from a nearby
city. In the large crowd were Governor Harry Leslie, a member of the parole board, and William "Tubby" Toms, State
House reporter for the *Indianapolis News*. Although Dillinger
could hit the ball savagely—as he showed in practice—he

rarely did well in games, but this day was an exception. He fielded perfectly and hit like a professional.

The governor, himself a well-known athlete while a student at Purdue, told Toms, "That kid ought to be playing major league ball."

But he was not as impressive at the hearings. After some discussion the chairman said, "Young man, you've served only a small part of your term and apparently you aren't amenable to prison life. Perhaps you'd better go back for a few years."

Dillinger was stunned. He had already served nearly five years for a minor robbery and his behavior the past two years had been perfect. What more did they want? Hiding his bitterness, he asked if he could be transferred to Michigan City. The trustees had never before heard such a request and one asked why anyone would possibly prefer a state prison.

"I want to go up there and play baseball," said Dillinger with a crooked grin. "They have a real team."

There was a burst of laughter and he was excused.

"I don't see any merit in that," said a trustee stiffly.

Governor Leslie interrupted. "It might be an occupation for him later. I'd be in favor of his transfer."

On July 15, 1929, John Dillinger was en route to Michigan City and would soon be inside the same walls as the two men he admired most—Harry Pierpont and Homer Van Meter.

2

Dillinger had seen little reformation at the reformatory and would see even less penitence at the penitentiary. There was no regret for having committed a crime, only for being caught. Almost every inmate thought himself wronged, pushed into crime by poverty, companions, police, or bad luck. Yet in the same breath he would brag of his deeds.

Dillinger was shocked to see so many gray heads. It was hard to believe that men as old as his father could have once done the wild things that led to jail. The older men, their faces

often branded by prison time, were more subdued than the reformatory inmates. Here there seemed to be ready acceptance
of authority.

Dillinger quickly learned, however, that this acceptance
was sometimes a mask assumed by the more mature. The most
dangerous criminal might be the calmest and most tractable—
until the moment of revolt. Dillinger had entered a new world
where a small core of unbroken spirits known as "red shirts"
had learned how to cope with the guards on a more equal
basis, how to combat deadly boredom, how to endure beatings
and privations. These determined men had learned how to
harden themselves to long stretches of time in the hole, even
though they were often made to sleep naked on the cement
floor. Instead of eating their daily half loaf of bread, some of
them molded it into a pillow. The pangs of hunger were great
at first but by the third day an almost pleasant state of eupho-
ria would numb them and they didn't care whether the door
opened or not. They had proved they could punish themselves
more severely than the management.

They also devised other ways to endure solitary confinement. One was a game called "Battleship." Two men in different cells would mark off one hundred squares, numbered one
to ten horizontally and A to J laterally. Each man had five
ships valued from one to five points, which could be placed on
any square. One contestant "fired" by calling out, for example, "A-9." If his opponent had a ship on that square, it was
sunk. For years the more obtuse guards wondered what was
being plotted when they heard men calling: "B-7." "Miss."
"C-8." "Destroyer sunk!"

When Dillinger arrived the Silent System was in effect.
Men ate, marched, worked in silence, raising their hands like
children if they had to go to the toilet. They learned to talk to
each other without moving their lips. Each prisoner lived in a
cell six by nine by seven feet, lit by an unshaded twenty-five-
watt bulb. On the bare wall was hung a card listing the
twenty-seven rules that restricted life. There were no books,
magazines, or newspapers and a man was only allowed one
piece of soap, a corncob pipe, tobacco, and a towel. He could

smoke three times an evening in the cell, his pipe or cigarette lit by a trusty who carried a torch from range to range.

At Pendleton the professional criminal was rare; here there were experienced forgers, holdup men, confidence men, and even several gangs of bank robbers. The beginners in crime from the reformatory could, if accepted by these "older heads," get an education available nowhere else.

Dillinger, who was soon caught toasting sausage and bread in D Cell House over a fire eighteen inches high, was considered far too scatterbrained to be admitted into the Michigan City school for crime. He was merely a choir boy—a rank beginner.

Though Pierpont had been several years younger upon arrival, he had been instantly accepted by the professionals and was now leader of an elite group of former bank robbers. He had already become a legend at Michigan City. A declared rebel, he was not one who wore a mask, but openly hated all law and every lawman; he had tried to escape four times. His ability to endure hunger and to absorb beatings was so exceptional that he won the awed respect of all the prisoners.

Soon after Dillinger's arrival a rumble of revolt stirred within the walls. With the population swollen to 2,801, the guards were forced to tighten restrictions and, when the rebellious spirits protested, swing their loaded canes more freely. By early September 1929 an alarming number of individual attempts to escape were frustrated only because of the constant state of alert. Then, not long after the great stock market crash, five inmates went from shop to shop openly urging a strike. A number of men stopped work but Deputy Warden H. D. Claudy, responsible for security inside the walls, quickly isolated the ringleaders and ended the trouble. He was the most disliked man in the prison and had been nicknamed by some inmates "I, God" because of the way he said "My God."

Though Dillinger admired the strikers, he didn't join them, for he felt certain he would soon get a parole. But as the months went on and each petition for clemency was summarily turned down, he became depressed. He had come to Michigan City at his own request, partly as an escape, partly from pique, but now he knew he had made a mistake. At Pendleton he had been somebody—and he became almost nostalgic when he thought about the reformatory. His letters home in the spring of 1930 were dispirited, full of self-pity:

> Well, baseball season is nearly here but I don't care to try for the team here although I love to play, if I hadn't played on the team at the reformatory I don't think I would have been sent up here; and I'm sure I would have made a parole there this Winter, so you can see why I am not so enthusiastic about making this team.

Not long after this he was caught gambling in C Dormitory and sent back to D Cell House and a few weeks later a guard found him "in bed with George 13529 on E Range." To one so highly sexed, homosexuality obviously was better than nothing. In prison the "old ladies," the partners of such as Dillinger, were regarded almost as prostitutes.

For the second year in a row, autumn seemed to inspire revolt. There was another long series of frustrated escapes, climaxed on the evening of December 29 when Pierpont let himself out of his cell with a homemade key and freed eleven others. They took apart their iron beds to make a ladder and were caught while sawing out the bars of one window.

Dillinger was just as resentful as Pierpont but he could not bring himself to try escape, merely manifesting his rebellion in another callow outburst. He was punished because he "broke into the garden house and stole all the melons and tomatoes," and then was twice put into solitary for "having razor in his cell and shaving with it," and possessing several books of cigarette papers and a lighter. ". . . It just seems like I can't keep out of trouble here," he dejectedly wrote his half brother, Hubert.

But when he left solitary, following this last offense, the older inmates noticed that he had changed, almost overnight, from a "harebrained, good-natured kid to a real man." After almost seven years of imprisonment, the petty rebellion had abruptly ended, never to be resumed. At Shop 8A where Blue Yank work shirts were made he became so skillful with the

Tomcat, the sewing machine, that he regularly began turning out a double task setting collars. In addition, as at Pendleton, he often secretly assisted the slower men.

One day that summer a lifer who desperately needed two dollars went to Dillinger's cell after dinner. Dillinger knew the man only by name but took a five-dollar bill from a hiding place in his shirt. "Half of it's mine," he said. "Can you change it?"

The lifer didn't have time for this complicated transaction, but Dillinger told him to take it all anyway and not to "strain" himself about paying it back.

There were many such incidents in the next few months and Dillinger's reputation for helping others began to spread around the yard.

3

In the summer of 1932 there were three men close to Pierpont. None of them had gone beyond the eighth grade and all three had had gonorrhea. All were bank robbers with little chance of parole who were determined to escape and resume their professional careers.

John "Red" Hamilton, like so many others, had started as a rumrunner before turning to bank robbery. The only black mark on his record in five years was for skipping rope in the shirt shop but, because he was considered such a dangerous character, his pleas for clemency were repeatedly turned down.

Pierpont's other chief lieutenant, Charles Makley, also had an almost perfect inside record. He was forty-three, short and stout. Outside the law since his teens, he too had gone from petty thievery and bootlegging to bank robbery in at least three states. He was noted for his ability to bluff his way out of trouble. In appearance he could pass as a bank president or prosperous businessman and often bragged that he once addressed a civic luncheon just before robbing the town's bank. In a few months Makley would steal a furnace salesman's car, trade it in on a new Terraplane and, using a pamphlet left by the salesman, sell the Terraplane dealer a furnace for cash.

The third man was Russell "Boobie" Clark, a big, good-looking young man serving a twenty-year sentence for his single bank robbery. When he had learned that many inmates were doing far less time for the same crime he had brooded, then exploded into violence. One of the leaders of the 1929 strike, he had attempted escape three times.

This unlikely quartet—the explosive, volatile Pierpont and Clark and the stable, more mature Makley and Hamilton—began to make plans for the greatest prison break in Indiana history. Makley insisted that impulsive escape plans were senseless, complicated schemes no better. Most practical would be a simple, workable plan based on bribery of a few key guards and possession of three or four guns.

Such a plan, of course, depended on accomplices outside the walls who had enough money for guns, bribery, and a hideout. Pierpont had several close outside friends who had offered to help but none was capable of engineering the entire operation; none of them, for instance, knew how to smuggle guns into the prison. Someone on the inside who was about to be released and was completely dependable had to be found.

Pierpont approached Dillinger, who had served most of his sentence. If he helped them escape, he could be the wheelman, the driver, in their bank-robbing team. Of course, such an escape would cost a large amount of money and they would have to teach him how to get it. They promised to give him a list of the best banks and stores to rob, and the names and addresses of reliable accomplices. He would be told where to fence stolen goods and money; how to get rid of bonds. He would, in short, know almost as much about bank robbery as they did.

Excited by Pierpont's tales of successful robberies, by the dream of a life of freedom and luxury, he agreed. It is doubtful if any amateur was ever offered a better opportunity. He insisted, however, that James Jenkins be included in the prison break. Young Jenkins was serving life for first-degree murder —a murder, he claimed bitterly, he never committed. Like

Pierpont and Clark, his record was filled with disobedience, insolence, and refusal to work. There was some hesitation because of rumors that Jenkins was Dillinger's "old lady" but Pierpont finally consented.

For the first time in his life Dillinger not only had a goal but a sense of responsibility. The shirt shop foreman praised him for his work, and once reported to the warden that he had contributed to the general welfare by inventing an ingenious gauge. Dillinger wrote home that he was now staying out of trouble and would soon be eligible to submit another plea for clemency. He said he was at last becoming mature. And in a sense, he had matured. For the first time in his life, he belonged.

Sometime late in 1932 Walter Dietrich, one of the two survivors of a Clinton, Indiana, bank robbery, was allowed to join Pierpont's group. In return he promised to reveal the detailed technique of a most remarkable bank robber, Baron Lamm.

Just before World War I a young Prussian officer, Herman K. Lamm, was caught cheating at cards and forced to resign from his regiment. He emigrated to Utah, determined to put his military training to the best commercial use, and became a holdup man. He was caught and spent 1917 in Utah State Prison, where he devised a system designed to take the guesswork out of bank robbing. Up until then it had usually been a hit-or-miss, improvised project, but it was his contention that a bank robbery should be planned as carefully as a battle campaign and carried out with timing and precision. Upon release he put his plan into practice. First he would spend several days investigating the bank he planned to rob until he could draw an accurate floor plan of its interior, knew how the petes—safes—operated and who was responsible for opening them.

Then came Step Two, a series of rehearsals with his carefully selected confederates, sometimes using an actual mockup of the bank as a stage setting. Every man in the gang was given a definite job and told, to the second, how long

it should take. One of Lamm's principles was to leave a bank
at the scheduled time no matter how little money had been
collected.

For the getaway, Step Three, a high-powered, nondescript
car was essential. The driver, often a veteran of the race tracks,
had pasted in front of him a chart indicating, block by block
by speedometer readings, the git road—escape route. This was
also clocked to the second and rehearsed by the driver under
different weather conditions.

For almost thirteen years the Lamm plan worked—until
December 16, 1930. On that Tuesday morning Lamm walked
into the Citizens State Bank of Clinton, Indiana, followed
by a seventy-one-year-old, wizened gentleman who looked
like a retired clerk, G. W. "Dad" Landy. Next came a dapper,
good-looking young man of twenty-six, Walter Dietrich, and a
chunky man in overalls and lumber jacket, James "Oklahoma
Jack" Clark. No quartet could have looked less like a team of
experienced robbers. In minutes they filled a paper shopping
bag and several typewriter covers with $15,567, then calmly
walked outside to a new Buick sedan which had just pulled
up in front of the bank.

As the robbers were getting in the car, the driver, an
ex-rumrunner with a hawklike nose, saw a man carrying a
shotgun walk toward the bank. It was a local barber, one of
the thousands of Indiana vigilantes organized to help local
police combat the increasing bank holdups, who had been
sitting in one of his chairs watching a friend follow the robbers into the bank. When this friend, a very methodical man,
didn't reappear and continue as usual to the post office for his
morning mail, the barber became puzzled, then suspicious.

Even the Lamm plan could not have foreseen one man's
extraordinary alertness. A series of unpredictable misfortunes
quickly followed: the ex-rumrunner panicked at the sight of
the armed barber and, attempting a fast U-turn, drove the
getaway car over a curb, blowing out a tire; the car to which
they transferred could go no faster than thirty-five miles an
hour because of a governor secretly installed by a son to pre-

vent his elderly father from speeding; their next transportation, a truck, had almost no water in the radiator.

The chase ended in Illinois, when the last car they commandeered turned out to have only one gallon of gas in the tank. In a gun battle with almost two hundred police and vigilantes, Lamm and the driver were killed. "Dad" Landy committed suicide rather than face prison but Clark and Dietrich were captured and sent to Michigan City for life.

In the spring of 1933 Lamm's ingenious plan was reborn and, if all went well, it would be put into practice again in a few months.

4

By this time, of course, Dillinger had also resumed his friendship with Homer Van Meter, who, next to Pierpont, had probably given more trouble to the guards in his first three years at Michigan City than any other inmate. He smuggled saws into his cell, wrote notes which were kited—illegally mailed—to friends on the outside, and twice was caught trying to escape. (In spite of their common passion for freedom, Pierpont detested Van Meter: he was a clown.)

Then abruptly Van Meter made up his mind to get a parole and spent every available hour in the library studying law, history, and literature. He volunteered for extra duties; he even stopped ridiculing the guards and became one of the most co-operative prisoners in Michigan City. The man who had once brutally beaten a guard at Pendleton and was labeled "a confirmed criminal of the most dangerous type" seemed to have made a most incredible conversion.

Still more incredible was Van Meter's success in making officials believe in his sincerity. The prison doctor rated him "an industrious, quiet and peaceful" worker in the tubercular ward of the hospital. The chaplain, Robert Hall, was so impressed that he wrote the Parole Board:

I verily believe that Van Meter #11561 is ready to prove that he is no longer the man who got off on such a bad start. He has put off the old man. Judge him by the new man.

Van Meter added his own plea to the Board in a meticulously handwritten letter.

Through self education, I have become aware of life as a social minded man sees it. The more I read, the more I become convinced that a man has a purpose in life with his duty towards society. That a life dedicated to humanity is far more important than to be a Croesus. I began to age and mellow like a fine old wine. I rebuilt a new philosophy and ethics; and when I felt sure I could give a promise and honorably keep it—I went to see Mr. H. D. Claudy, Deputy Warden. I respected him as a square-shooting man and I told him I was ready to be trusted. He did not hesitate. He was shrewd enough and big enough to stake his judgement on men, and transferred me to a position of trust. . . .

All I ask of you, is to get in touch with Mr. Claudy and feel sure he will substanuate this. I want you to judge the —reformed man of today—who has developed into a self-educated, honest, mature man; from the ignorant, wild boy of yesterday.

Two years earlier Van Meter had written a friend, "I am sure I have not lost my formula of salesmanship." Nothing could have better demonstrated this than his second letter to the Board:

My plea is—be big enough to cast aside the musty archives dealing with the follies of an unthinking boy before the needs of a clean matured man. If reformation is the theme of penology, then I am ready to become a useful citizen. If it be not, then society defeats itself along with the reformed felon, and adds an extra tax burden upon a tax ridden public. This is the age of the new deal. I place my destiny in your hands. You can restore a sterling citizen and a sound matured man to freedom.

Favorable action at the coming meeting of the Parole Board looked certain. While waiting for the verdict, Van Meter frequently chatted with Dillinger, promising to show him how to make "the big money" once they were released. Dillinger agreed to meet him in Indianapolis; he could use every contact.

His own plea for clemency was also progressing favorably. Though he lacked Van Meter's flowery language, he impressed prison censors with the sincere affection he felt for his family. In a letter to his niece, Mary, he wrote:

I expect you think your Uncle Johnnie has forgotten you but I haven't, I've just been getting even with you for neglecting me. So after writing you this nice long letter I am expecting you to mend your ways. Doggone it I've been your sweetie for sixteen years and you've been trifling with me something scandalous. You sorry? Well, you had better be young lady and I don't mean probably. Gee! Honey I would sure like to go to your graduation excercises. I am so glad you are better. And say, how is that red headed Sis of mine? I havn't heard from her in ages and I'm beginning to think I'm an orphan.

After three long paragraphs filled with anxious discussions of his parole the letter concluded:

. . . I have asked Dad several times why he doesn't see Howard Phillips and Rev. Fillmore and get their help, but he doesn't say anything about them and I am sure they would help me out. People like them are the one that count and we can't afford to miss any opportunity. So Norman is helping Dad cut wood is he? Well he will have a hard time keeping up with Mom. Ha! Ha! Gee Honey I would like to see all of you this Spring. I hope you and the kids are all well. I guess I will ring off for this time and listen hear young lady give me a break will you for about an hour a week. You can surely stay away from him that

long, use your will power kid. Well Honey by for this time.
Love to all and write soon. Love and kisses from Johnnie.

On May 10 Governor McNutt signed Dillinger's parole
papers and nine days later did the same for Van Meter. It
was May 22, 1933, when Dillinger passed through the last two
steel gates of the turnkey's cage and into the outer lobby.
He must have experienced, like so many others, a feeling of
tremendous elation. He was free. And he felt superior to every
person outside, having gone through experiences they could
not even imagine. He also felt that he should now be paid
for the nine lost years—that anything he stole he had already
bought with his time in prison.

CHAPTER 3

Underworld—'33

1

BEFORE WORLD WAR I PROFESSIONAL CRIMINALS WERE MOSTLY men with little education, almost no organization, and often recognizable by their appearance and speech. But with the advent of Prohibition, crime began to come of age. Since Americans refused to give up their drinking habits, rumrunners were regarded with open sympathy, and thousands in the grandstand at Charlestown Race Track would even rise to cheer their favorite bootlegger, Al Capone, as he walked in with his bodyguard.

America became such a nation of scofflaws that bribery was commonplace, the "fix" operating in every big city. Out of immense bootlegging profits emerged a group of businesslike crime empires. Crime no longer had a distinct face.

Public apathy, the automobile, the tommy gun, the Mafia, and the mushroom growth of cities contributed to this crime explosion. Urban centers were becoming so immense that local law enforcement had grown unwieldy and inefficient. Because state and federal laws had not yet caught up with the development of crime the more intelligent criminals could move from city to city and from state to state with comparative safety.

. . .

At the time of Dillinger's release from Michigan City, 13,000,000 Americans were jobless, and the national income was less than half of that in 1929. Bread lines stretched around the New York Times Building and late subway riders picked their way among the paper-covered bodies of homeless sleepers.

Hundreds of banks had already failed, a bitter army of war veterans had marched on the capital—and been dispersed by force. America was never closer to collapse, perhaps revolution. Radicalism was such a growing tide that many prominent writers, including Theodore Dreiser, Erskine Caldwell, Sherwood Anderson, and John Dos Passos, had endorsed William Z. Foster, the Communist candidate for President in the 1932 election.

Even bootlegging suffered from the Depression. Moreover, since it was also evident that President Roosevelt would soon be able to effect the repeal of the Eighteenth Amendment, many criminals were already turning to other fields. Bank robbery was becoming so commonplace that some communities formed their own vigilante committees, and kidnaping, inspired by the still unsolved kidnap-murder of the Lindbergh baby, was increasing at an alarming rate.

Significantly, as repeal drew near and the Depression deepened, there appeared—especially in the cities and towns of the Midwest—a different type of criminal. These were men who, unlike Capone, actively participated in robberies and kidnapings. Theirs was a philosophy of personal action. Some were even descendants of the outlaws from the Ozarks and Cookson Hills: the James brothers, the Youngers. Almost all were native-born Americans.

Instead of horses, these modern bandits used fast cars and the intricate system of highways was their escape route. This was crime based on the earlier frontier pattern of strike and run. Armed with machine guns, these new prototypes of the old outlaw breed operated openly, insolently. They could rob a federal bank, gun down the tellers, and flee to the next state for sanctuary.

They shuttled between distant cities like commuters. Local police were helpless. They had few machine guns; their cars were old and often broke down during pursuit; they were undermanned and underpaid, often even having to buy their own guns and provide their own transportation. In addition, police chiefs were frequently changed by new political administrations at the cost of efficiency and morale.

County officials were equally helpless. Most of them had no training in law enforcement and some were completely incompetent. And the state police, with few exceptions, were little more than paper organizations.

The most potentially effective law organization was the Federal Bureau of Investigation, known as the Division of Investigation until 1935. Since 1924 its youthful director, J. Edgar Hoover, had been building a force of increasing efficiency. After studying the methods of Scotland Yard, the Royal Canadian Mounted Police, the Prefecture of Paris, and other famous law enforcement agencies, he had collected a group whose prime function, within the limits of their federal authority, was to assist local police officers without violating states' rights. He realized that his special agents—subject to no politics or local pressure—had to lead the way.

No other lawman had ever been required to be so versatile and so disciplined. The special agent learned to shoot a pistol, submachine gun, shotgun, and rifle; he became adept at defensive tactics; he was trained in fingerprint identification, scientific crime detection, and the preservation of evidence at the scene of crime. An applicant had to be a lawyer or an accountant between twenty-five and thirty-five, and was expected not only to apprehend a criminal but to gather conclusive evidence for a court conviction.

In the spring of 1933, however, there were only 266 special agents and these were often hamstrung by restrictions. They were not allowed to carry guns except in extraordinary cases and often had to call local police to make a simple arrest. To make matters worse, they received little or no cooperation from a number of police officials, who derisively labeled them "Boy Scouts" and "College Cops."

These 266 agents, handicapped as they were, led the battle against the new outlaws.

The crime wave of 1933 was centered—not far from John Dillinger's home—in great Midwestern cities such as Chicago, St. Louis, and Kansas City. Here were the fences for stolen goods, the buyers of kidnap money, the doctors who never reported gunshot wounds, the right lips—lawyers—who knew how to evade the law, the police who could be bribed, the tailors who made clothes with concealed pistol pockets, the garage men who provided special bulletproof cars, the mob markers who advised which places to rob, and the gun molls who not only helped their men to escape but were housewives and mistresses as well.

There were other, smaller cities and towns almost as important: the underworld heavens, sanctuaries specializing in "cooling-off joints," where a criminal with money could find safety. Three of the most popular were Joplin, Missouri, St. Paul, Minnesota, and Hot Springs, Arkansas.

Although relatively small, Joplin had been a favorite criminal hangout since the late 20's because of its strategic location at the southwest corner of Missouri. Liquor flowed freely in this bootlegging headquarters and customers from the traditionally dry states of Oklahoma, Arkansas and Kansas flocked to the gaudy little metropolis. Only fifty miles to the southwest lay the timbered, wild Cookson Hills, the storied hideaway for desperadoes since the days of Jesse James, and still without a single paved road.

That spring Clyde Barrow and his girl friend, Bonnie Parker, already wanted for several murders and numerous robberies, decided to take a holiday in Joplin. They were a strange pair. He was a small twenty-three-year-old man of medium build with wavy, dark brown hair slicked down and parted in the middle. He had pixie ears, a weak chin, soft hazel eyes and appeared quiet, even effeminate. He was convinced that the police had hounded him into crime, and while in prison he had chopped off two toes of his right foot with an axe to avoid work.

Clyde had known Bonnie only a year. Soon after his parole from the Huntsville, Texas, prison he had passed her on a Dallas street. Fascinated by her striking yellow hair, he stared; she smiled and they began to talk. She was tiny, boyishly slender, and had a hard, determined mouth. She was a waitress with a husband, although she was currently juggling dates with several men. In a few weeks the couple left Dallas, picked up a boy friend of Bonnie's, Raymond Hamilton, and embarked on a series of violent holdups in a dozen states.

Bonnie and Clyde were fascinated by speedy cars and all kinds of firearms. Their automobile soon became loaded with submachine guns, automatic rifles, shotguns, and several dozen pistols and revolvers. Clyde, with Bonnie's help, even worked out a quick draw with a sawed-off shotgun. It was blatantly theatrical but effective and the shotgun, concealed in a zippered compartment down his right trouser leg, could be drawn almost as rapidly as a pistol.

When Hamilton was captured in Michigan the Barrows began to look for another man, not only to assist in the robberies but to help satisfy Bonnie's sexual abberations. Clyde, who had homosexual tendencies, didn't object to her peculiar tastes. In fact, he enjoyed sharing her pleasures. Near the filling station run by Barrow's father in Texas they encountered a seventeen-year-old car thief, William Daniel Jones.

"How would you like to take a ride with us?" asked Barrow. When the awed Jones discovered he was talking to two notorious bandits he agreed to join them. A few days later he and Barrow stole a car. When the owner jumped on the running board, Barrow stuck a revolver against his neck and fired. Now young Jones was an accomplice to murder, and though he wanted to quit, didn't dare.

Not long after this the three were joined by Clyde's older brother, Buck, recently released from Huntsville, and his wife, Blanche. All five drove to Joplin, where they rented a two-story garage apartment in a respectable neighborhood.

They lived quietly, sleeping late, playing cards, and admiring the Kodak pictures they had taken of their amazing arsenal. Many of the snapshots featured Bonnie, now red-headed, posing dramatically with machine guns and rifles and in one photo even smoking a cigar.

A week passed uneventfully. Then a nervous man came to the Joplin station of the Missouri State Highway Patrol and told Sergeant G. B. Kahler that two cars with Texas license plates were behind a garage apartment and people were "darting in and out of the living quarters above the garage like frightened animals."

After several interviews with neighbors Kahler was sure the suspects were bootleggers and decided on a raid. About 4:00 P.M., April 13, Kahler, with a highway patrolman, a constable, and two Joplin police detectives, drove past the stone building in two cars. Clyde and Jones, who were standing outside, jumped into the garage and slammed the door. The police car behind Kahler swung into the driveway, blocking the gangsters' two cars.

Upstairs Blanche was cooking dinner, Buck was reading, Bonnie was writing a poem, "The Story of Suicide Sal." As soon as they heard shots from the garage, Buck grabbed a submachine gun and Bonnie ran into the bedroom for two pistols. Blanche, a newcomer to crime, could only scream.

The constable was already stretched out on the street, dead, with ten shotgun slugs in his neck and left shoulder. Near him one of the Joplin detectives lay dying, his face blasted with buckshot. Jones suddenly ran out and struggled with the hand brake on the police car blocking their escape. He clutched his head, shouted in pain, then staggered back into the garage.

Now one of the Barrow brothers ran out, released the brake and pushed the police car, which slowly coasted down the driveway, crossed the street, and crashed into a red oak tree. Blanche, still screaming, burst out of the building and ran down the street. Just then a Marmon sedan, gears clashing, roared out of the garage with the rest of the gang. The car turned left, chasing Blanche. Kahler saw a man lean out and pull Blanche into the car but the sergeant's gun was empty and all he could do was write down the Marmon's license number. Then it disappeared. A few minutes later reinforce-

ments arrived, half of the men giving chase. The rest cautiously
went into the upstairs apartment, where they found an arsenal
of rifles. On the dining-room table was Bonnie's unfinished
poem.

THE STORY OF SUICIDE SAL

By "BONNIE" PARKER

We, each of us, have a good alibi
    For being down here in the joint;
But few of them are really justified,
    If you get right down to the point.

You have heard of a woman's glory
    Being spent on a downright cur.
Still you can't always judge the story
    As true being told by her.

As long as I stayed on the island
    And heard confidence tales from the gals,
There was only one interesting and truthful,
    It was the story of Suicide Sal.

Now Sal was a girl of rare beauty,
    Tho' her features were somewhat tough,
She never once faltered from duty,
    To play on the up and up.

Sal told me this tale on the evening
    Before she was turned out free,
And I'll do my best to relate it,
    Just as she told it to me.

I was born on a ranch in Wyoming,
    Not treated like Helen of Troy,
Was taught that rods were rulers,
    And ranked with greasy cowboys. . . .

That night Ed Portley, the Joplin Chief of Detectives,
swore he would never rest until he caught the murderers of

the two lawmen. Miles away, in the Texas Panhandle, the Barrow brothers were also making a vow, swearing never to surrender or desert each other.

2

About the same time another gang, unknown to the newspapers but soon to be hunted by the FBI, was leaving the St. Paul area, the most notorious of the underworld vacation lands. This was the group presided over by Ma Barker. In America's long criminal history probably no more varied, bizarre, and desperate cast of characters had ever been assembled. And they would return to St. Paul shortly, not to rest but to work.

If the two O'Connor brothers—originators of the St. Paul layover system whereby criminals from all over America could come for a rest provided they behaved themselves within the city limits—had been alive, it is doubtful if the Barker gang would have dared to violate the rules of sanctuary.

The O'Connors had been a remarkable, talented pair, responsible for the crime-free record of their city for more than twenty years; in St. Paul no thief dared to steal as much as a lawn mower, and an unescorted woman could walk any street on the darkest night without fear.

When John J. O'Connor became Chief of Police near the turn of the century, out-of-town criminals soon got the word they would be welcome to visit St. Paul and spend their money freely. First they reported to "Paddy" Griffin, owner of a lodging house on Wabasha Street, who kept in constant touch with the chief and assigned the newcomers temporary homes at a suitable rent. These visitors were under constant surveillance by O'Connor spies and if they even became rowdy in public, would be brought to The Big Fellow.

John O'Connor's operation was successful largely because of the political influence of his younger brother, Richard, better known as The Cardinal. Not only was he the leader of the Democratic Party in St. Paul and Minnesota, he was one of the Big Four in national party circles, a personal friend of the legendary railroad tycoon, James J. Hill, and of several Presidents, including Grover Cleveland. He was a tall, imposing man of magnetic personality, loved in the poor districts for his liberal contributions to charity.

None of the protection fees paid by visiting criminals found its way to O'Connor pockets; their money came from other sources, such as the string of saloons owned by The Cardinal. During the O'Connor years prostitution flourished in a well-regulated manner. The most famous of the numerous whorehouses was Nina Clifford's—located just behind the police station—celebrated for its plush rooms, beautiful girls, and illustrious patrons.

St. Paul was an Irish Catholic town quite similar in political and ethnic structure to Boston. It followed naturally that in politics it was Democratic. In 1920 The Big Fellow resigned as chief of police because of ill health and The Cardinal began to take more interest in national politics and less in local St. Paul matters. Although the succeeding chief of police was against the O'Connor system, it continued, being ingrained in the city's economics, politics, and police department.

Soon after World War I, Paddy Griffin was replaced by an even more colorful character, "Dapper Danny" Hogan. Italian in spite of his name, Hogan was short, dark, pudgy. He was quiet, dressed immaculately, and never permitted any rowdyism in his headquarters, the Green Lantern saloon at 545½ Wabasha. Here, in sight of the state capitol, was the new checking-in station for incoming underworld characters.

The reign of Dapper Danny came to a violent end on December 5, 1928, when he stepped on the starter of his car and a bomb exploded. His successor was his partner, an emigrant from Russia, Harry Sandlovich, commonly called Harry Sawyer. But he was no Hogan. In spite of a formidable appearance, Sawyer was far too soft to control his inherited hoodlum empire and, though visiting gangsters still checked in, he was finding it increasingly difficult to keep them in hand. He even had trouble with his own men and before long St. Paul was plagued with a series of unsolved gangland killings, something unheard of in the old days.

An inefficient police department added to the confusion. There had been some competent chiefs and many dedicated and able police officers, but honest detectives were often shackled by a chief "on the pad" and, conversely, honest chiefs sometimes were betrayed by corrupt subordinates. As a result the once neatly regulated haven for tired criminals was ripe for a local crime wave.

The Barkers, who arrived in the spring of 1933 intent on starting one, came from the Southwest. Arizona "Kate" Clark was born in the Ozarks of poor Scotch-Irish parents, though some early friends insist she also had a touch of Indian blood. In 1892, when she was twenty, she married George Barker, a quiet, mild man who was equally poor but a good worker. Their four sons—Herman, Lloyd, Arthur, and Fred—were born in a ramshackle mining cabin near Joplin. Kate was fiercely protective of her young brood, and when neighbors complained to George that his boys had broken a window or swiped apples he would invariably say, "You'll have to talk to Mother. She handles the boys." Ma, when approached, would self-righteously and indignantly call the neighbors liars. Even when the police began picking up Herman for petty thievery she would insist that any son of hers had to be innocent—and invariably get him released. Some thought Ma actually believed her sons were the dupes of jealousy and police persecution; her fierce defense appeared too real to be assumed.

During these years Ma took the boys to church almost every Sunday and to every revival meeting. "I don't know why," George said later, "because when I'd try to straighten them up she'd fly into me. She never would let me do with them what I wanted to."

In 1915 Herman was arrested by Joplin police for highway robbery. Ma stormed down to the station and, with a strange combination of offensive tirades and motherly pleading, once more convinced the police that Herman was innocent. After this episode, Ma told the neighbors she couldn't stand living in such a suspicious town and moved her family to Tulsa, Oklahoma, a booming, wide-open oil and cattle center. Almost immediately after settling in a two-room shack near the railroad tracks on the north side, the four boys helped form the Central Park gang. If one of the members got into trouble with the police, he would run to the protection of Mother Barker, who stuck up for the boys as stanchly as she did for her own sons. It was, she claimed again and again, police persecution. "All these boys," she told one chief of police, "would be good if you cops would just let them alone."

In 1918 Arthur—nicknamed "Dock," not "Doc," as popularly believed—was sent to jail for stealing a car. He was small, about five feet four inches, and weighed only 119 pounds; he had high cheekbones and extremely intense eyes. He escaped, was caught, and escaped again. Then he was arrested for the murder of an elderly night watchman at a Tulsa hospital.

Ma worked out an ingenious alibi for him. Several months previously, twenty-year-old Volney Davis, born in the Cherokee Nation and just freed from a three-year term for stealing a pair of shoes, had joined the Central Park gang. Young Davis had spent the night of the killing in an apartment with two girls but Ma persuaded them to testify that Dock was the man who had been in the apartment. In spite of this, Dock was convicted and sent to Oklahoma Penitentiary for life.

When Davis was arrested and charged with participation in the same crime Ma told him she had appealed Dock's sentence. If Davis used the two girls as witnesses, she argued, they would not only be tried for perjury but Dock's petition would be denied. If Davis would stand trial offering no defense, she promised to get him a parole in case he were convicted.

The gullible Davis agreed and was sentenced to the penitentiary—for life. Ironically it is probable that neither he nor Dock was guilty, for a man in California later confessed to a priest that he was the murderer. At any rate Ma became still more bitter against the law and, since she needed money to fight Dock's case, now began to help her remaining boys and their friends actually plan robberies. To her this was only justice. In 1922 Lloyd was sent to Leavenworth for robbing the

United States mails. There was no question about his guilt to anyone but Ma, who began a tireless campaign for his parole and wrote scores of letters representing herself as a woman bereft of support.

The following year Fred, according to his mother's own words, "made a mistake." That is, he made the mistake of being caught stealing and was sent to the reformatory for five years. When Ma's appeals got him out on parole he almost immediately robbed a bank, was arrested, and let out on a $10,000 bond provided by her. He fled town, forfeiting the bond, but for the next few years he must have led a somewhat successful life of crime, for neighbors noticed that the old shack near the tracks was being refurnished with lavish bad taste.

Herman, the oldest, was also a good son all these years, sending home part of his earnings as a minor holdup man and petty swindler. But the Barker fortunes took a bad turn in 1927. Young Fred was caught while committing a burglary in Kansas and sentenced to the state prison at Lansing, and Herman committed suicide after a holdup, rather than face arrest.

Ma now left George Barker, moving to another old shack on North Cincinnati Avenue which she soon filled with new, garish furniture. In the next few years she hounded parole boards with appeals for her imprisoned sons and on March 30, 1931, her youngest and dearest, Freddie, was finally released from the Kansas State Prison. Two months later Fred's best friend at Lansing, Alvin Karpis, christened Francis Albin Karpaviecz, was also paroled. He was tall, slender, thin-featured and, though young, had the eyes of an old man. His cheeks sagged; his mouth was narrow and hard.

Born in Canada in 1907 of Lithuanian parents, he became city marbles champion soon after moving to Topeka, Kansas. In 1926 he was implicated in a robbery and sent to the Kansas Reformatory. Like Homer Van Meter he violated so many rules he spent much of his time in solitary. These lonely hours were apparently spent in fruitful plotting and in 1929 he escaped to his parent's home in Chicago. Young Karpis got work in several bakeries for almost a year, then returned to

Kansas, where he was picked up for auto larceny and safe blowing. He was sent back to the reformatory, but almost immediately graduated to the penitentiary at Lansing.

Kate Barker took an instant liking to the sallow, pimply-faced Karpis and treated him as if he were another son. A few days after they arrived in Tulsa, Alvin and Fred were arrested on suspicion of robbing a jewelry store. Upon their release Ma and the two young men moved to a cottage in Thayer, Missouri, rented by her current lover, Arthur V. "Old Man" Dunlop. She made plans for large-scale operations in the Missouri area but these were thwarted when, late in 1931, the two young men killed a sheriff and had to flee to St. Paul.

After reporting to Harry Sawyer at the Green Lantern, they were assigned a rented house at 1031 South Robert Street in West St. Paul, where they lived quietly, using the house as a base of operations for robberies in the Northwest. But their landlady became suspicious, wondering why one of the young men always carried a violin case, and late one night her son noticed pictures of Fred and Alvin, wanted for murder of the Missouri sheriff, in a copy of *True Detective Magazine*. At about 1:00 A.M. on April 25 the landlady phoned the St. Paul police and said the suspects were sleeping. Unfortunately the call was taken either by one of Sawyer's bribed policemen or by an exceedingly lax one. When a raid was made six hours later the house was empty.

The next morning a nude body shot three times was found on the shores of Lake Freasted near Webster, Wisconsin—next to a woman's bloodstained glove. The corpse was subsequently identified as Dunlop's, and FBI agents deduced that Fred, Alvin, and Ma had falsely assumed the Old Man had betrayed them in St. Paul.

The investigation of Dunlop's murder grew so intense the trio fled to Kansas City. By now Ma had learned that the simplest way of avoiding police attention was to rent an apartment in an exclusive or upper-middle-class residential area. They moved to the Country Club Plaza district, joining forces with several notorious bank robbers they had met in St. Paul through Harry Sawyer. The new gang robbed a bank in Fort

Scott, then returned to Kansas City to relax and play golf.

A few weeks later agents of the FBI located two of the gang members, Francis Keating and Thomas Holden, whom they were seeking as escaped federal prisoners, on the Old Mission golf course. Special Agent Raymond Caffrey and police officers surrounded the two fugitives and bank robber Harvey Bailey, all attired in sporty knickers. They were arrested without a struggle. A fourth gangster, a poor player, was on another part of the golf course and fled to warn Ma Barker. She, Fred, and Karpis hastily quit the apartment, leaving a fully cooked meal on the table.

They hurried back to the safety of St. Paul but it was so sweltering in town that Harry Sawyer advised them to take a house at a nearby summer resort, White Bear Lake. On July 9 "Mrs. Hunter and two sons" moved into a spacious two-story frame house on the shores of the lake in the wealthy Dellwood section, where they spent a leisurely summer, arousing no suspicion. Often they were visited by a small, bald-headed man who walked with a limp; he lived in a cottage a mile down the road. This was Frank "Jelly" Nash, one of the country's leading bank robbers. On July 26 Nash, Fred, and Alvin left their hideouts and, with a few associates, held up the Cloud County Bank at Concordia, Kansas, returning to White Bear Lake with $240,000 in bonds and some cash.

That September Ma Barker's attempts to win a parole for Dock finally succeeded and he was freed on condition that he leave Oklahoma forever. As promised, the Barkers were also working on Volney Davis's freedom. When Davis, partly through their efforts, was released he was so grateful he immediately joined the gang in St. Paul and offered to do anything to repay their kindness.

A few days later Ma took Davis to visit her sister in California. While she was gone, the gang robbed the Third Northwestern Bank in nearby Minneapolis. Her careful planning was sorely missed. Two police officers and an innocent civilian were shot in the getaway and the gang was forced to flee the Twin Cities and retire temporarily, but several months later, coun-

seled by Ma, they robbed the National Bank at Fairbury, Nebraska, of $151,350.

The Barkers, with plenty of money for protection, were
now ready to plunder St. Paul itself—with the help of Harry
Sawyer, the city's supposed protector from crime. They arrived
on May 29, just a week after Dillinger's parole. That same
day Karpis and the two Barker brothers were called to a meeting at Jack Peifer's night club, the Hollyhocks. Also present
were Harry Sawyer, Peifer, and three men from Chicago: an
ex-convict with a long record; a golf professional turned criminal; and a good-looking, clean-cut man who looked like a successful businessman, Fred Goetz. An enlisted flier in the World
War and a former student at the Engineering School of the
University of Illinois where he managed his fraternity house
and was an outstanding athlete, Goetz had been arrested in
1925 for the attempted rape of a seven-year-old girl when he
worked as a life guard at a Chicago beach. His mother, convinced he had been wrongly accused, put up a $5,000 bond
but Goetz disappeared and she forfeited her money. He joined
Capone and became a proficient gunman. His greatest moment
—according to a later confession by his stooge, the golf professional—came on St. Valentine's Day in 1929 when, in a policeman's uniform, he won the gratitude of Capone by helping to
mow down six of George "Bugs" Moran's gang in a garage.

Peifer said he had an idea for a quick, safe, and clean job
—the kidnaping of a wealthy brewer, William A. Hamm, Jr.
Then Sawyer, whose profits from supplying sanctuary to visiting criminals had become so small that he had drifted into the
planning of crime itself, promised to provide the protection.
He said that a St. Paul detective on his payroll, one of the investigators of any kidnaping, would keep them advised of the
progress of the police.

The proposition looked foolproof to the Barkers and Karpis. An equitable split was arranged and the meeting broke up.

3

Seventeen days later, on June 15, William Hamm stepped out of his office adjacent to the brewery and started up the steep hill to the imposing family home on Cable Avenue to have lunch with his mother. He was a tall, good-looking man of thirty-nine, probably the most eligible bachelor in the Twin Cities. After a block two men approached. One held out his hand and said, "Mr. Hamm?"

The other abruptly grabbed Hamm, turned him around, and quickly escorted him into the back seat of a large black sedan. He was shoved face down on the floor and, as the uniformed driver headed east, a white hood was slipped over his head and shoulders.

Hamm did his best to keep track of time and direction. The car, he guessed, kept going east for about thirty miles, then stopped. The hood was lifted slightly so he could look downward at four folded pieces of paper and he saw the first line of one of the notes: "You are hereby authorized to pay . . ."

"Sign these papers and sign quick," said someone. "Everything will be all right."

Hamm took a fountain pen and, still kneeling, signed the notes.

"Who do you want as a contact man?" asked someone. "We want a hundred grand."

Hamm suggested William W. Dunn, sales manager for the brewery.

At 2:40 P.M. Dunn was in his office when the phone rang. Alvin Karpis said gruffly, "I want to talk to you and I want you to listen to what I'm going to say and don't butt in. We have Mr. Hamm. We want you to get $100,000 in twenty-, ten-, and five-dollar bills. And goddamn you, see that they aren't marked." Dunn thought it was a joke. "If you tell a soul about this or call in the police, it will be too damned bad for you and you will never see Hamm again."

Dunn asked where he was going to get $100,000 but he was talking to a dead line. Dunn checked Hamm's home. He had not returned for lunch. It was no practical joke. After some time, Hamm's three brothers-in-law were located and it was decided that they should go up the hill and break the news to Hamm's mother. When she was told of the kidnaping, a little after 6:00 P.M., she insisted the police be informed in spite of the warning and a meeting was arranged with Chief of Police Thomas Dahill in a room at the Lowry Hotel. There Dunn revealed all the details to Dahill.

After dark the hood over Hamm's head was replaced by goggles stuffed with cotton and he was allowed to sit upright. Near midnight the car stopped some twenty miles northwest of Chicago and Hamm was helped out. Then an icy hand—it felt like a woman's—guided him up a flight of stairs to a bedroom. Here he was allowed to take off the goggles but warned to keep his back to the door. It was a plain, small, square room with boarded windows containing a bed, chair, and small table and lit by a single unshaded electric light. He was a prisoner in a prosperous-looking house on a main street of Bensenville, Illinois, the home of Edmund Bartholmey, who would soon become the local postmaster.

An hour or two later the phone in Dunn's home at 1916 Summit Avenue rang. "Well, Dunn, you have carried out instructions pretty good so far," said Karpis. "You realize now that we have got your boy friend and it isn't any joke." Dunn was told that he would receive a note in a few minutes signed by Hamm.

He called the police. As Detectives Charles Tierney and Tom Brown turned into Summit Avenue at about 2:00 A.M., they saw a taxi slowly passing houses as its driver threw a spotlight on porches. The driver told the detectives he had been given a note to be delivered to a Mr. Dunn.

According to the note, Dunn was to have $100,000 ready the next day. Some ten hours later Dunn received a second note saying he needn't think he was so smart. The kidnapers had trailed the taxicab and seen the police.

4

On that same day an event that was another piece of the vast jigsaw puzzle of Midwest crime took place many miles to the southwest—in one of the underworld's favorite resting places, Hot Springs, Arkansas. The local police department was operated very laxly by Chief Joseph Wakelin, whose mistress was the madam of a house of prostitution and whose chief of detectives was known in underworld circles as an officer who would hide any criminal if paid enough. These two lawmen not only conveniently closed their eyes to crime but themselves engaged in the wholesale theft of cars which they sold to criminals.

At noon a small man with a bushy mustache and wearing nose glasses was drinking beer in the doorway of the White Front cigar store and chatting with several men. Though he had been in town only a few days, he was already well known as a wealthy but democratic Chicago businessman with a marked generosity toward beggars. He insisted that everyone call him George and was fond of showing his credentials as a Mason.

Suddenly a car drew up. Its three occupants waited until the men talking with George left, then walked up, guns in hand. "Put your beer down and come on," said one. George allowed himself to be herded into the car. One of the abductors took off his hat and pulled his hair. It came off. George was the famous bald-headed bank robber, Frank "Jelly" Nash, the Barkers' limping neighbor at White Bear Lake, his crooked nose straightened by plastic surgery. His abductors were two FBI agents from Oklahoma City and a local law officer.

The FBI car headed toward the federal prison at Leavenworth, from which Nash had escaped several years previously, then doubled back toward Little Rock to throw off possible pursuers. The relaxed bank robber offered Special Agent Frank Smith, who was impressed with his good manners, the toupee as a souvenir. "I paid $100 for it in Chicago." Smith had no use for it. Nash also displayed a Blue Lodge Masonic card. "I've humbugged enough people with this," he said and offered it to his captors, but this too was declined.

A few minutes after Nash was picked up, the Hot Springs police learned there had been "trouble" at the White Front and telephoned for information. Dick Galatas, who ran a horse-racing and baseball book inside the cigar store, told them that a businessman from Chicago named George had been kidnaped.

While Galatas was giving further details at the police station, a call came in from the Benton, Arkansas, police department. Their officers had just stopped the wanted car and learned the kidnapers were federal agents and "George" was the notorious bank robber, Jelly Nash. When Galatas heard this he hurried to the Oak Park tourist camp where Nash had been staying with his attractive wife, Frances, and a young daughter by her first marriage. Upon learning that her husband had just been picked up, Mrs. Nash became hysterical. She had no idea why he had been arrested, insisting she only knew her husband was a businessman nicknamed "Jelly" whom she had met at Stacci's O.P. Inn, a favorite hangout for gangsters near Chicago. She suspected Jelly was a bootlegger but asserted he was wonderful to her and the child.

Galatas, later claiming that he helped only because Nash was a brother Mason, drove Frances and the girl to his home; then he called the Little Rock police, who revealed that they too had stopped the car. The agents were taking Nash back to Leavenworth. What route were they taking? The Joplin road.

A little later Galatas and Mrs. Nash were at the Municipal Airport dickering with the operator, John Stover. Mrs. Nash wanted to pay him only $50 for the flight to Joplin, about two hundred air miles away, but Stover held out for $100. Mrs. Nash finally agreed but as soon as her bags were placed in the plane she became nervous. Was the plane safe? When Galatas explained it was a sister ship of the one Lindbergh had flown across the Atlantic, she insisted that he accompany her.

They were met in Joplin by Herbert "Deafy" Farmer, a gentlemanly gambler, ex-con man, and pickpocket who conducted, with exceptional discretion, a shelter for criminals and also operated one of the most efficient underworld post offices in the country. Farmer, a big, blue-eyed, soft-spoken man, drove them in a Cadillac to his twenty-three-acre farm six miles south of town.

That evening Mrs. Nash, the Farmers, and Galatas discussed their problem, and someone suggested telephoning Verne Miller. He would know what to do. Miller, one of the leading criminals in the Midwest, had been a parachute jumper at county fairs, a wrestler, a boxer, and an expert machine gunner in the army. Because of his good World War record, he was elected sheriff of his home town, Huron, South Dakota, but was soon caught embezzling and sent to prison. After his release he became a bootlegger, then a bank robber with the Barkers and others. Because of his exceptional skill with the submachine gun he was also occasionally hired by Chicago and Detroit gangsters as a torpedo—gunman.

The two women went into the bedroom and just before midnight put in a call to the Miller home in Kansas City. A moment later Mrs. Nash was tearfully telling of Jelly's arrest.

"Don't take it so bad," said Miller. "Is Dick there?"

After Galatas told him that the FBI was taking Nash to Fort Smith by car and then to Kansas City by train, Miller called New York and Chicago for help, but nobody could be found and flown out in time. He called the Barkers in St. Paul and learned they were too involved with the Hamm kidnaping. It was up to him alone.

He and two others with machine guns could easily free Nash at Kansas City's Union Station, since the guards would only have shotguns and pistols. He asked local gang leaders to lend him two "typers" but they refused to become involved in the venture.

Late that night, however, Miller got word from one of the

leaders of the north side that two out-of-town hot rods who needed money urgently had just arrived. About an hour later Miller brought two strangers to his neat Dutch colonial home. One was chunky with powerful shoulders, Charles Floyd. He hated his nickname, "Pretty Boy," but it had stuck through the years. The other, Adam Richetti, was short, slight, with liquid brown eyes and straight black hair thinning at the crown. Both were exhausted. That morning, after barely evading capture in a garage, they had kidnaped a sheriff and kept him hostage in a wild 175-mile chase over back roads until they reached Kansas City.

Miller explained what had to be done the next morning, then drove to Union Station to check the train arrivals from Fort Smith. There he telephoned the Farmer home and asked Mrs. Nash what she was going to do. She began to cry—she didn't know. He told her to go to her mother's but she "couldn't do that."

"Don't carry on so," he said. "You'll see Jelly again." When she continued sobbing, he hung up in disgust.

The next morning, June 17, was bright and pleasantly cool, 71 degrees. At about 6:45 A.M. Mrs. Lottie West, a capable, motherly case worker for the Travelers Aid Society, walked into Union Station. Her office, an old-fashioned roll-top desk and two chairs, was in the concourse near the Fred Harvey Restaurant.

A nice-looking man with big shoulders was sitting in her chair. Since it was her business to identify people, she automatically memorized that he wore a fairly expensive blue serge suit, a beautiful panama hat, and two-tone shoes.

"Is there something I can do for you?" she asked.

Pretty Boy Floyd said nothing. Mrs. West was also silent but she thought: What kind of a character are you? Floyd finally got up without saying a word and walked out the east gate of the station and across the plaza.

Mrs. West had come early to meet a boy arriving on a Missouri-Pacific train and at 7:00 A.M. she met the train and brought the youngster back to her desk. When six nuns from the same train asked if there was some place they could wait all day, Mrs. West called St. Benedict's Church and was told to send the sisters there.

Just then, about 7:20 A.M., the manager of Harvey's restaurant, who was standing back near the train doors, motioned. She joined him. It was an ordinary June scene. Women in summery dresses made clicks on the marble with their heels as they walked through the station. A voice announced a new train arrival and there were the usual pleasant breakfast noises from Harvey's. The manager pointed to a group of eight men heading toward the east gate.

In the center was Frank Nash wearing an open white shirt, his handcuffs poorly concealed by a handkerchief. The men who had captured him in Joplin the day before—Special Agents Frank Smith and Frank Lackey of Oklahoma City and Otto Reed, Chief of the McAlester, Oklahoma, police department—were augmented by Raymond Caffrey, the young FBI agent from the Kansas City office who had captured the three friends of Ma Barker on the Old Mission golf course; his chief, R. E. Vetterli; and two city detectives, W. J. "Red" Grooms, only a year on the force, and Frank Hermanson, a veteran of thirteen years. Lackey and Reed carried shotguns, the others pistols.

When Mrs. West saw the prisoner she said to the Harvey manager, "That must be Pretty Boy Floyd," then returned to the desk and led the nuns out the east gate to a row of waiting cabs.

The seven lawmen shepherded Nash across the plaza toward a parked Chevrolet belonging to Caffrey. The four agents and Chief Reed were to drive Nash to Leavenworth in the two-door Chevrolet. Grooms and Hermanson would follow in another car.

Caffrey unlocked the right door of the Chevrolet. Nash started to get in the back but when Lackey told him to get in front he obligingly shifted over to the driver's seat while Lackey, Smith, and Chief Reed began clambering into the rear. The two Kansas City detectives stood at the right of the car near the hood with Vetterli, the Special Agent in Charge, who was waiting to get in. By now Caffrey had walked around the back of the car to the driver's door and was about to open it.

At that moment Mrs. West's attention was drawn to the parking lot about twenty-five feet beyond the FBI car—two men were standing on the running board of her Oakland. One was blond and hatless, Verne Miller. The other was short and dark, Richetti. Both were staring over her car at the Chevrolet. Then she saw the man in the blue serge suit who had been sitting at her desk, Pretty Boy Floyd, move behind the officers. He was cradling some object in his arms.

Pretty Boy raised his machine gun and suddenly shouted, "Put 'em up! Up! Up!"

One of the men on the Oakland running board, probably Miller, called, "Let 'em have it!"

Nash, still sitting behind the wheel, cried out, "For God's sake, don't kill *me!*"

There was sudden chaos as shots rang out. Vetterli looked up and saw a man—he seemed to be standing on something, perhaps a running board of another car—blazing away with a machine gun. Vetterli crouched as bullets knocked Grooms and Hermanson to the pavement. He heard the windshield of Caffrey's car shatter and knew the four men inside were helpless targets. As Vetterli dropped to the pavement, he felt a stinging pain in his left arm.

Lackey, the thirty-two-year-old agent sitting behind Nash, heard the cry, "Up! Up!" Then he saw Nash, evidently mistaken for an agent since he sat in the driver's seat, slump back, his toupee hanging askew. Lackey felt a paralyzing pain and dropped to the floor. A few seconds later he felt another pain.

Next to him Agent Frank Smith, a veteran of sixteen years' service, drew his pistol when he heard firing "from all sides." As he looked up, he saw the barrel of a machine gun spitting flame at him. Smith could feel the heat of the firing, hear the thuds of bullets. He dropped to the floor and "played dead." Seconds later when he felt Chief Reed fall on top of him, he looked up and saw Nash. The top of his head seemed to have been shot off, and blood was trickling down the back of his bald head.

One of the killers leaned into the car and shouted, "He's dead! They're all dead!" Only thirty seconds had passed since the first shot.

Smith put his arm under Reed's head. His friend, who had volunteered his help, was dead. Then he heard Lackey groan. He noticed that the handle of Lackey's revolver, still on his hip, had been splintered and guessed correctly this had saved the young agent's life. "Steady, now," said Smith, "you'll make it all right."

At least twenty-five people saw the killings. A few thought there were two gunmen; others three or four. Somebody cried out, "My God, is this Chicago?"

Mrs. West probably had the best view. She turned, ran back toward the east gate, and shouted, "Bandits! Everyone in the station! Bandits!" The nuns were ahead of her. All but one fled inside. The last, an elderly sister, was paralyzed. Mrs. West pushed her into the station, then phoned the police, "They're killing everyone at Union Station! Get help down here."

She started back toward the east gate, noticing that the Harvey manager, also a witness, had staggered into the restaurant and fainted. As she burst outside, she was followed by Patrolman Mike Fanning. When she saw the killers getting into a car in the parking lot, she shouted, "Shoot, Mike!"

Fanning stood behind a column and fired his .38. Near the rear of the FBI car Vetterli, though still stunned by the bullet that had creased his arm, managed to get to his feet. Fanning ran across the plaza. "Who are you?" he suspiciously asked Vetterli.

It was a shocking scene. The Chevrolet was riddled with bullet holes, the divided windshield shattered. Nash was dead in the front seat. In the back Reed lay dead. Next to the car Caffrey was dead. So were Grooms and Hermanson, their hats blown many feet away by the blast of the machine guns. Only

Smith was completely unharmed and he was wishing he could take Reed's place. How would he tell Mrs. Reed?

All the dead men left wives.

5

No other gang killing aroused Americans as much as the Kansas City Massacre. To many people the endless stories of underworld murders in the past ten years had become a source of entertainment, since the victims were almost invariably mobsters, and the site of the notorious St. Valentine's Day killings—a dingy garage in Chicago—had even become a tourist mecca. But now four law officers had been murdered in the open plaza of a great railroad station. Crime was suddenly everyone's business. Angry editorials all over the nation demanded new laws, stronger police measures. It was the turning point in the education of the people to the reality of the growing crime wave.

That same morning the public also learned, for the first time, of the Hamm kidnaping and there were immediate demands for even more stringent kidnaping laws. Later in the day Karpis telephoned the final instructions. Hamm's friend, Dunn, was to drive a Ford or Chevrolet coupé with doors off and rumble seat cover removed so that a red lantern could be hung in the back. He was to travel north on U.S. Highway 61, past White Bear Lake, at twenty miles an hour. "You will meet two cars. They will pass back and forth several times, and then you will be given the signal." When one of the cars blinked its lights five times Dunn would throw the money bag on the highway and proceed to the New Duluth Hotel to pick up Hamm.

At about 10:00 P.M. Dunn left St. Paul in a doorless coupé. On the floor in a briefcase was $100,000. He passed White Bear Lake and continued north. It was chilly with the doors removed. Suddenly a big car roared by at about seventy miles an hour, then a smaller car. Both cars turned off the highway, letting Dunn pass, then moments later raced past again.

This routine was repeated several times, with Dunn growing more and more tense. Finally, about sixty miles north of St. Paul, he saw a car's lights flash five times. He dropped the briefcase onto the highway and continued north. At the New Duluth Hotel Dunn called his home, expecting to reach Brown and Tierney, but they weren't there. To his surprise, apparently through a misunderstanding, the two detectives soon joined him at the hotel. The three sat up waiting for Hamm.

He was far from Duluth, still in the home of Bensenville's future postmaster. He had been well treated and fed adequate, simple meals. Only Fred Goetz talked to him, though he never saw Goetz's face. They chatted about Prohibition and Roosevelt and once Goetz said in an amused tone, "You know, I'm a man with a champagne appetite and a beer income."

Goetz kept informing Hamm of the ransom negotiations. No threats were made but Hamm felt uneasy one day when Goetz said in a snarling tone, "They're very slow at the other end."

When food was brought in, Hamm was told to put his head between his knees so he wouldn't see Goetz. He was also warned to keep his face to the wall so he couldn't see the guard who always sat on a chair in the doorway. Whenever he wanted to use the bathroom he informed the guard, who would disappear and Hamm would walk unescorted down the hallway, then return to his room and face the wall. There were no newspapers or books to relieve the dragging hours, only one magazine which Hamm read over and over. Curiously he later forgot what it was.

The day after the ransom was paid, Goetz came to the doorway and said, "Face the wall. Take off all your clothes."

It was the first time Hamm had undressed since his arrival and he got an ominous feeling. Goetz carefully searched the clothes, then handed Hamm a clean white shirt and a razor, told him to shave and put on the shirt.

"We have good news for you," said Goetz a few minutes

later. "The ransom's been paid and you're going home." He would be released in Duluth.

It was dark when Hamm, wearing goggles, was led to the car. After a ride of some ten hours the car stopped.

"We're going to get some sandwiches and coffee," said someone. Hamm was led to a field. "Wait here. We're coming back for you."

Hamm's captors walked off, but he didn't hear the car drive away. After waiting about two minutes he took off the goggles. It was daylight, about 5:30 A.M. He was in a vacant lot just off a road—alone. He walked to a nearby farmhouse, told the owner his name, and learned he was two miles from Wyoming, Minnesota, a town on Highway 61 about halfway between St. Paul and the point where Dunn had dropped the ransom.

Since there was no telephone, he walked to another house where he called his mother and was told the police would come for him. A few minutes later he heard a car speed past, then stop at the point where he had been left. After a moment's wait, it roared off. The kidnapers, he guessed, had really gone off for sandwiches.

A large crowd of newsmen, photographers, and curiosity seekers blocked the Hamm estate's main entrance but the car bringing him home entered the grounds through a back road. When reporters were finally admitted into the house for a news conference, the Ramsey County Attorney suggested that Hamm tell them "what the fellows said when they turned you out."

"They said that if I ever want anything or they ever can do anything for me, just to let them know." A reporter facetiously asked if they had left a forwarding address. "No," said Hamm. "They neglected to do that."

This was the mosaic of crime, the interwoven underworld of Midwest America in the spring of 1933—the world John Dillinger was about to enter.

PART TWO

•

CHAPTER 4

"Desperate Dan"

1

IN INDIANAPOLIS ON JUNE 4, 1933, JOHN DILLINGER AND NOBLE
Claycomb parked their car a short distance from a group of
young men playing scrub softball in Spades Park. It was a
balmy evening and the light was just beginning to fail. Claycomb, an ex-convict on Pierpont's list of possible associates, got
out of the car and walked over to one of the ballplayers.

Claycomb had promised to rob a super market that evening with Dillinger if they could get a third man. But it was
soon evident to the waiting Dillinger that he was having trouble convincing the ballplayer to join the venture. The two

walked into a drugstore, still arguing, and several more minutes passed before they finally approached the car.

Dillinger stuck his hand out the window. "I like you, kid," he said. "You're smart to check on a guy like me."

The ballplayer, William Shaw, shook Dillinger's hand unenthusiastically. He was nineteen, slender, good-looking and came from a respectable, middle-class family. For the past few months he and Claycomb had led the White Cap Gang in a series of small local robberies.

Though Shaw made it obvious he wasn't too eager about admitting Dillinger into the gang, it was agreed that they would steal a car, then pick up Claycomb at a neighborhood poolroom. An hour later Dillinger and Shaw found an unlocked Dodge sedan with out-of-state license plates. Shaw casually raised the hood as if he owned it, and attached a jumper —a coil with three wires—to the motor. It took only a few seconds to clamp one wire on the starter cable, the others on the distributor. Now no ignition key was necessary and he drove Dillinger to a saloon known as "Shorty" George's, where Shaw introduced Dillinger as "Dan." After Dillinger looked over the stock of weapons and selected a .32 with an extremely long barrel, they picked up Claycomb at the pool hall.

Dillinger, whose only previous robbery had been the clumsy attempt in Mooresville, felt that at last he was to take part in a smooth professional operation. And this feeling was strengthened when Shaw calmly stole a pair of Indiana plates to replace the more conspicuous out-of-state tags.

A patrol car spotted them and gave chase, but Shaw eluded the police and after several blocks pulled into an alley to change the plates. As he finished, a prowl car turned into the alley. Shaw extinguished the lights, speeding off before Claycomb could close the rear door. There was a loud crash as it smashed against a telephone pole. After losing the police, they stopped, wired the door shut, and headed east toward one of the new super markets. By now Dillinger was having some doubts about his partners.

They circled the market, then parked, and Dillinger was handed colored glasses and a white cap. He thought it was "kid stuff," but his partners explained that witnesses would be too impressed by the glasses and caps to notice faces. He put them on reluctantly.

"I'll go in first and get close to the office door," said Shaw, "so they can't lock it when we show our guns." He and Dillinger started into the market while Claycomb was double-parking near the front entrance.

As Shaw neared the office door, a girl inside told the manager, "Here comes the White Cap Gang." Shaw pushed his way into the office, pulled out his automatic, and rifled the cash register of about $100.

Out front Dillinger was ordering the customers and clerks to move to the rear of the store. All did so except a terrified elderly man. Dillinger told him to move several times, then panicked and hit him in the mouth with his gun.

At that moment Shaw came out with the money and when he saw the old man spitting out blood, looked reproachfully at Dillinger. On the drive back to Shorty's place Dillinger suddenly told Shaw almost apologetically, "I'll never go back to the Pen. They're not going to catch me—not if I have to kill someone."

When he returned to Mooresville that night his father told him that a parole officer had called for the first time and would return later—and then almost shyly asked if he had found a job yet. Dillinger only shook his head and for the first time his father accepted the situation without argument.

In town Dillinger was quiet and amiable, strengthening the impression he wanted to create. Both Pierpont and Van Meter had warned him that his parole officer would make inquiries in the neighborhood and he should appear to be well-adjusted, unresentful, and eager to begin a respectable life.

Almost everyone in town was friendly and sympathetic. The majority now were convinced Singleton had plotted their crime and some wondered whether Dillinger would avenge himself on his partner, who had served only two years. It was rumored that Singleton had built a special place in his house to hide from Dillinger and that he always carried a knife.

Their first encounter came in front of a local gas station. As Dillinger approached, Singleton stood uneasily in the street. Dillinger ignored him and called out to the gas station owner that he was going up to the lakes "for a little vacation."

Instead of going north, however, he picked up two men recommended by Pierpont and headed east. Their destination was New Carlisle, Ohio, a small town near Dayton. For the first time John Dillinger was going to rob a bank.

Horace Grisso, bookkeeper of the New Carlisle National Bank, unlocked its front door at eight o'clock on the morning of June 10. It was Saturday and business would be brisk. As he entered the teller's cage, three men, faces covered with handkerchiefs, jumped him. They had sneaked in through an unlocked window.

"All right, buddy," said Dillinger, "open up the safe."

Grisso reached for the drawer to get the combination book. Dillinger stopped him, then let him slowly pull out the drawer. Glancing at the book, Grisso tried to open the safe but twice failed, and one of Dillinger's companions said nervously, "Let me drill him, he's stalling."

Dillinger waved him back and told Grisso, "Take your time and open it."

Now the bank clerk entered. Dillinger told her to come in and lie down, then gallantly spread a banker's smock on the floor. Saying apologetically he didn't want to hurt her, he wired her hands and feet, and after Grisso opened the safe, tied him with wire also.

Two more men—the cashier and a customer—entered the bank and were herded behind the cage. Dillinger bound both, then grinned and told the customer, "You hadn't ought to come in the bank so early."

Dillinger was pleasantly surprised when he and the others counted $10,600 in cash, a large amount in the Depression for a small-town bank. But for him the day had only begun. He returned to Indianapolis and persuaded Shaw to help him stage two more robberies that same evening. While their

wheelman, Paul "Lefty" Parker, who had never driven a getaway car before, double-parked outside a Haag's Drugstore,
Shaw donned his glasses and white cap. Dillinger refused to
wear the gang's costume and instead put on a sailor straw hat.
He and Shaw entered the store with drawn guns, Shaw heading toward the main cash register. Dillinger took the smaller
one at the soda fountain.

He stuck his gun at three employees and several customers, telling them to look the other way. They submissively
turned toward Shaw, who ordered them to stop looking at him,
then obediently looked back at Dillinger, who angrily repeated his order.

The farcical pattern continued when the two robbers ran
outside with the contents of the registers only to find that the
neophyte Lefty had neatly reparked the getaway car flush
against the curb, wedging it tightly between two other cars.

After Lefty at last butted his way free they headed for the
next robbery site, a super market, with Dillinger and Shaw
warmly lecturing him on the technique of parking a getaway
car.

Shaw had robbed the super market recently but said he
hadn't, so when the two walked in, the manager said, "Oh-oh,
here they are again," and told Shaw there was no money in the
cash drawers. "You guys have started the company collecting
and the collector just left."

Dillinger was disgusted and headed for the door but Shaw
took a moment to gather up an armful of tin cigarette boxes.
As soon as Dillinger got in the Ford, Lefty stepped on the accelerator, leaving Shaw behind. Dillinger shouted to him to
stop, but it took Lefty a block to obey. They backed up, got
the hard-breathing Shaw and his cigarettes aboard, but Lefty
was so nervous he ran through the next stop sign, then a block
later slowed the car to a crawl.

"If you can't drive," shouted Dillinger, "let the kid have
the wheel!" He was fed up. In the past hour he could have
been caught twice and he realized that if he didn't avoid amateurs like Lefty and improve his own technique, he would soon
be back at Michigan City.

After returning to his apartment, he counted out almost $3,600. In spite of the wasted, almost catastrophic, evening it had been a good day. But he knew it would take many more such good days before he had enough to free the Pierpont gang, since stolen money often had to be fenced at only a fraction of its value.

He contacted more men on Pierpont's list and joined still another bank-robbing team. In spite of this busy schedule, he found himself with several free days and returned to Indianapolis on June 23, the day after his thirtieth birthday. After locating Shaw, the two examined Pierpont's list, finally picked out an Indianapolis bank—and learned it was closed. Inside prison the Depression had just been a word, but now Dillinger was learning that at least half the establishments on his list were closed. They headed for another prospect in the same neighborhood, a gambling resort, only to be refused admittance by the doorman.

There was nothing else listed in Indianapolis, and Dillinger was forced to select Marshall Field's Thread Mills in Monticello, some eighty miles to the northwest. According to notations on the list, the payroll there was fairly large and the next day was pay day.

Shaw stole a car, a 1932 De Soto sedan, and they started north after dark, stopping overnight at tourist rooms. The next morning they drove into Monticello, a pleasant, prosperous town, soon to become a popular resort center. After parking the car about two blocks from the mill, they put on straw hats —Dillinger's new personal trademark—and strolled around till they found a place where they could observe the mill entrance. Soon, Dillinger knew, Fred Fisher, the assistant manager, a man with a noticeable limp, would come out and walk up the hill to the bank. When he returned with the payroll, they would be waiting at the end of the street.

Finally a short, stocky man wearing a light blue dress shirt came out of the mill office. He limped. But instead of going up the street they were watching, Fisher turned and disappeared up a side street. They walked briskly up the long hill expecting to see him when he emerged on the main street. He didn't.

They waited a few moments, then went into the bank. To their surprise he was at a window getting the payroll.

They started back toward the mill to intercept Fisher, openly discussing how Fisher could have gotten past them without being seen and why he had so unexpectedly changed his routine. For men about to stage a holdup they were making themselves surprisingly obvious.

They had been so since their arrival. Half an hour earlier Fisher's wife had seen them wandering around the neighborhood and had become so suspicious she telephoned her husband to be careful. Consequently Fisher had walked up a different street to his home and driven his car the rest of the way to the bank.

After a few minutes Dillinger and Shaw were amazed to see Fisher drive past them down the hill. Their original plan was useless; now they would have to raid the mill itself. Dillinger said he would go in and apply for a job—and try to find out if Fisher had picked up the money. He walked into the main entrance of the mill. Immediately to the right was a door to a large office and, through a long glass window which extended down the corridor, he could see two girls counting out money and putting it in envelopes. Without waiting to talk to anyone, he turned and tiptoed out. Perhaps he lost his nerve. At any rate he now told Shaw to go back in alone as if applying for a job. Shaw, he said, should knock on a door only a step from the main entrance and when a girl opened it, he was to draw his gun and walk her back into the office, slamming the door behind him as a signal for Dillinger to come in. Dillinger said he had to wait outside; if the office help saw him again, they would get suspicious.

Shaw knocked on the door Dillinger had indicated but nobody answered it. Instead, a door twenty-five yards farther down the corridor opened and a stenographer, Mildred Wilson, peered out. Shaw walked up to her, said he'd like to see the manager of the mill. As the girl started toward Fisher, who was working at a long payroll table with the bookkeeper and filing clerk, Shaw put his .45 in Mildred's back and said, "Act natural and you won't get hurt." He slammed the door.

Since this door was too far from the main entrance, Dillinger did not hear it close. He waited outside near the car, wondering why Shaw took so long.

Shaw was paying for Dillinger's carelessness. Fisher, instead of putting his hands up as expected, grabbed the gun and, in an effort to yank it away from Shaw, pulled it under his own chin. Shaw grimly held onto the automatic, expecting Dillinger to burst in and save him but when no help arrived, grew desperate. It was either kill Fisher or give him the gun. He thumbed the safety and released his grip.

Dillinger still waited impatiently outside. Suddenly the main door burst open and Shaw ran out past him, into the car. "Come on, the man has my gun," he said, starting the motor.

As the car was pulling away, Fisher burst out the doorway with the gun. "Stop!" shouted Dillinger. After Shaw obeyed, Dillinger leaned out and fired. Although he had aimed several feet from Fisher, the bullet ricocheted off the building and hit the assistant manager in the left leg.

When Fisher jumped back, Dillinger said a bit shakily, "I either got him or scared him half to death." The factory whistle began shrieking, then the alarm at the city hall sounded.

Half an hour later the two inept bandits were on a dirt road several miles out of town. It had never occurred to them to map out an escape route and they were lost. Finally after about fifty miles they came onto a paved highway and were dismayed to learn they were still only twelve miles from Monticello. Just ahead was an ambulance. As they drew closer, Dillinger said, "The fellow inside looks like the mill manager." He was right; Fisher was on his way to the Logansport Hospital.

Late that afternoon, after a fruitless trip to Muncie to rob a bakery long since closed by the Depression, they returned to Indianapolis, bought a paper, and went to Spades Park to find out how badly Fisher had been hurt. There was no mention of their holdup.

Dillinger suddenly laughed. "We drove all over northern Indiana and didn't make a penny. I'll be better off listening to you than trying to go by my notes." He convinced Shaw they should try to salvage the day with a successful robbery and a few hours later walked into an open-air fruit market.

But the mishaps of the day were not over. As they drew their guns, Shaw saw a boy who lived almost directly across the street from him. He ducked his head and said they'd better leave. They scooped the money from the register and ran to their car. The day ended as it had begun—on a ridiculous note. Someone threw a milk bottle at them.

"You didn't even make expenses today," said Dillinger sarcastically when they split about $175. "You've got to pay for a .45." Then he told his young partner to try to set up something more lucrative while he was away. He went to Muncie, Fort Wayne, the East Chicago area, and even Kentucky, arranging bank robberies with at least three different gangs, including Homer Van Meter's. Probably no other robber in history was more industrious. In the next three weeks he helped loot some ten banks in five states.

In the middle of July Dillinger rejoined Shaw in Muncie and, together with Claycomb and two others, made plans to rob the nearby Daleville bank. On the eve of the proposed robbery, they impulsively held up a local tavern, the Bide-A-Wee. Early the next morning they woke up at their apartment and began to prepare for the day's robbery. After breakfast Dillinger left to park his car in the rear garage and drove down the alley behind the apartment, but as he was about to turn into the back yard, he saw Shaw and Claycomb standing near the back stoop, hands in the air—surrounded by half a dozen policemen.

Dillinger threw the clutch in reverse, shoved the accelerator to the floor. Just a week ago, still not yet used to late-model cars, he had run off the road and rammed a fence. Now, in a crisis, he deftly backed out of the narrow alley, full speed.

Two days later—Monday, July 17—Dillinger and two others drove in his sporty Chevrolet coupé to the tiny unincorporated town of Daleville, parking near the Commercial Bank which was located in a small two-story brick building. At about 12:45 P.M. Dillinger, wearing a dark gray coat, light gray trousers, and a straw hat, walked into the little bank. The only one inside was the teller, Margaret Good, who had worked in the bank for about five years. She had twice been held up but suspected nothing when Dillinger, who looked like a businessman, politely asked if the president was in. She told him the president wasn't active in the bank. And the cashier was out to lunch.

"Well, honey, this is a holdup." Dillinger brought up his long blue-barreled gun. Suddenly, using the ledge of the cage as a step, he vaulted lightly over the six-foot barrier. She wondered why, when he could have simply walked through the door. Necessary or not, an original twist had just been added to the art of bank robbing. Dillinger, an admirer for years of Douglas Fairbanks, straightened his straw hat and asked where the vault was.

The leap did what Dillinger secretly must have wanted— it called attention to himself. It also brought him to the attention of a man who would spend more time trailing him than any other. News of the athletic bank robber reached Captain Matt Leach, head of the Indiana State Police, almost simultaneously with word from Muncie that Noble Claycomb had confessed that he, Shaw, and "Dan" Dillinger had held up the Bide-A-Wee.

The intuitive Leach, who would attempt to outwit Dillinger many times in the months to come, guessed he might also be the vaulter. Pictures of Dillinger were sent to Daleville, and he was tentatively identified as the man who had made the remarkable jump over the barrier. Muncie reporters nicknamed him "Desperate Dan," bringing fame, on a local scale at least, to John Dillinger.

When Leach ordered him brought in for questioning it was the modest start of one of the most remarkable personal duels ever waged between lawman and criminal. Leach—his original name was Lichanin—was a tall, wiry, raw-boned man who wore a perpetually dissatisfied look. He was born in Croatia while his mother, a naturalized American, was there visiting relatives. In America he was adopted by a family whose name coincidentally was Leach. He started as a wood finisher in an Illinois factory, served in the World War, and then decided to be a lawman.

He soon became one of a small group of crime fighters convinced that psychology could be an important aid in catching criminals. Studying the most modern police methods, he applied them to his own theories so assiduously and effectively that he was promoted over the heads of older and more experienced men. By the spring of 1933 Governor McNutt was so impressed with Leach's ability that he often talked directly to him on police matters without bothering to go through his superior, the Commissioner of Public Safety.

Leach was a man of conflicts: hot-tempered and yet capable of unusual self-control; intense, nervous, yet one who could accept setbacks with stoicism. He was a self-educated, self-polished man whom many assumed to be a college graduate. At moments of excitement or anger he sometimes stuttered badly—and it was typical of the man that he even made use of this impediment. Once a reporter watched him interview a prisoner who had refused to talk to anybody. Leach purposely stuttered so badly that the suspect, in spite of himself, pronounced several words Leach couldn't seem to get out. Leach smiled and reached for a pack of cigarettes but his fingers fumbled so nervously that the prisoner offered his own pack. Leach now tried to light a match. It was hopeless and the suspect produced his lighter. By this time he was feeling such sympathy toward Leach he began to talk as if to a friend and in a few minutes Leach had a full statement. This was his concept of the third degree.

Since there were only forty-two men, including clerks, in the entire Indiana State Police, the job of bringing Dillinger in for questioning was given to Frank Hope, the parole officer who had not yet repeated his original call, a month previously, to Mooresville. As sole parole officer of three counties for both the reformatory and the prison, he simply hadn't had the time.

On July 2 Hope drove alone to Mooresville, since there were no deputy sheriffs available in Morgan County. At the farm he learned Dillinger was visiting his older sister, Audrey

Hancock, and in Maywood Mrs. Hancock said he was taking her two daughters for a ride—they might be in Indianapolis at a gas station run by her two sons. By now Hope was getting so suspicious he picked up two deputy sheriffs at the Marion County jail, posted them near the Hancock home and instructed them to arrest Dillinger in case he brought his two nieces back home. Then Hope headed for the gas station.

At this moment Dillinger was leaving Indianapolis. When he dropped off his nieces at Maywood the two deputies, who might have terminated a notorious career before it began, were dozing in their car.

All that afternoon Dillinger, armed with a gun, hid in the orchard of his father's farm. Near dusk he saw Hope drive up, look around, then leave. It was the first and last time he would see his parole officer.

2

When Dillinger was at Michigan City, Jim Jenkins—the impetuous young man he had asked Pierpont to include in the prison break—talked incessantly of his sister, Mary. She had married a man named Longnaker but was now in Dayton suing for divorce. From the time Dillinger first saw Mary's picture in prison he had been determined to meet her.

Soon after his parole he drove to Dayton where she lived. His excuse for calling was to discuss ways and means of bribing certain guards. She and Jenkins were much closer than most brothers and sisters, since they had grown up together in an orphanage, and she was deeply grateful to Dillinger for trying to help Jimmy escape from an almost certain life sentence. She was twenty-three, good-natured and fairly attractive.

Dillinger at once felt completely at ease with Mary. Because he had shared life in prison with her brother he knew he was already something special to her and, considering his nine years of confinement, it was not at all surprising that he became infatuated with her and, a week later, offered to pay for her divorce. He was a persistent companion between bank robberies, within a month renting a room in her boarding house, an impressive three-story mansion with tall columns.

On the evening of July 20 Dillinger, Mary, and her girl friend, Mary Ann Buchholtz, left for the Chicago World's Fair. On the way they visited the farm at Mooresville, even though Dillinger knew he was wanted by the state police.

Dillinger had become what his father had always feared, a professional criminal—yet there were no lectures, no recriminations. It was as if Mr. Dillinger finally realized his son was a man. Dillinger's attitude was also far different. He was no longer at odds with his father; now he was at odds with the law. His sarcasm had vanished and he treated his father affectionately, almost with respect. For the first time, there was an understanding between them. Dillinger next drove to Maywood, where he left $10 with a filling-station attendant to give to his half brother, Hubert. He liked his new role as family breadwinner.

He and the girls arrived in Chicago early the following morning, checking in at the Crillon Hotel. They spent three leisurely days at ball games or the Century of Progress, where Dillinger was particularly fascinated by the Colonie Nudiste and the General Motors assembly line. He took numerous snapshots of blimps, exhibitions, and the girls. Another favorite subject was policemen, and he seemed to get a special kick out of asking them to smile.

On the morning of July 24 the three headed back home and, when Mary suggested they stop off at Michigan City to see her brother, Dillinger readily agreed. He thought Jimmy would appreciate seeing a pretty girl like Mary Ann. Besides he wanted to give him a present.

After buying some fruit, Dillinger parked in front of the prison. Turning his back on Mary Ann, he drilled a hole into the top of a banana with a pen knife, rolled up a $50 bill, wrapped it in dark paper, and slid it into the hole. As he was stopping up the hole with banana pulp, he instructed Mary to have Jenkins split the money among several guards.

Then he waited outside as the girls walked into the prison.

Near the reception room Mary slipped another $50 bill to a prison employee and told him it was "to fix my brother's teeth." During the interview with Jenkins she read from a small piece of paper lying in front of her.

Mary Ann sat, only half listening, but she thought it curious when Mary reread the contents of the paper and said, "Sit tight." Just before leaving, Mary handed her brother the bag of fruit and advised him to "eat the banana first."

Only a day after Dillinger returned the girls to Dayton, he wrote Mary:

. . . Honey, I miss you like nobody's business and I don't mean maybe. You know I must be thinking of you for I just got up. My trip to Illinois and Missouri was postponed a few days but I am leaving for the east in an hour. I hope I can get fixed so I can spend more time with you, for baby I fell for you in a big way and if you'll be on the level I'll give everybody the go by for you and that isn't a lot of hooey either. I know you like me dear but that isn't enough for me when I'm as crazy as I am about you. You may never get to feel the same toward me as I do you in which case I would be better off not to see you very much for it would be hell for me.

I hope you seen the kids yesterday. I'm just crazy to see them. I only wish I had you and two or three sweet little kids and was in South America with Jimmy with us. . . .

If that lousy husband of your bothers you any more just let me know and he will never bother you again.

Well, sweetheart I guess I'll ring off for this time, love me a little or do you love me a lot? Well, baby, ta ta for this time hope I hear from you soon.

                                    Lots of love from Johnnie

After five days he finally received an answer, special delivery. It was friendly but little more, and that night Dillinger visited a Fort Wayne house of prostitution. Two days later he got another noncommittal letter. Desperate for a permanent relationship, he wrote that he was "crazy" to see her and would like to take her with him if she cared enough for him. They could have good times together, he said, if she was always "on the level." He also asked if she had seen her children.

Gee! I would sure like to see the little darlings. Baby if I can only get Jimmy out we will get the kids and leave the country. Jimmy and I have planned on going to South America but of course we werent thinking of you with us, how in hell did I know I would fall for you. . . .
Honey I wish you would get your hair fixed up and put on your black gown and have your picture taken especially for me how about it?

He asked her to write him a long, sweet letter telling how much she loved him and that she couldn't live without him.

Ha! Ha! Kid you've sure got me tied up in a knot but dont leave me dangling for I want to know something when I see you again.

Lots of love from Johnnie

CHAPTER 5

"They Wouldn't Give Up Till They Died"

1

ON THE EVENING OF JULY 19, THE DAY BEFORE DILLINGER TOOK
the two girls to the Chicago fair, the Barrow gang was close
to disaster. They had been discovered in a long brick tourist
cabin; and a posse armed with machine guns, protected by
steel shields and spearheaded by an armored car, was about
to attack. The lights in the cabin were out and the lawmen
were sure the gang was asleep.

Since shooting their way out of the garage in Joplin three
months previously, the Barrows had fled from town to town,
from state to state, committing a series of petty holdups. Unlike
the better-organized gangs they had no political or legal connections nor did they have enough money to check into the
safe retreats such as Hot Springs or St. Paul. Moreover
they were now unwelcome in underworld circles. They were,
in short, not only outlaws but outcasts.

Bonnie and the Barrow brothers thrived on the daily
tension, but Buck's wife, Blanche, and the seventeen-year-
old Jones were near collapse. In Louisiana, Jones ran away
from the gang, stole a car, and fled to his mother's but Clyde
and Bonnie found him a few weeks later and forced him to

return. The next month was a nightmare to the young man: he was in a flaming car wreck in which Bonnie was badly burned; he helped kidnap two lawmen and assisted at a dozen robberies during which there was another murder. When it seemed that the gang was finally trapped on a mountain, they stole a doctor's car, broke through the cordon, and raided a National Guard Armory for automatics and ammunition. For a week they remained out of sight but on July 18 several Iowa filling stations were robbed by three men and two women, one wearing bandages on her arms. It was obviously the Barrow gang.

At 10:00 that same evening they drove up to the Red Crown Cabin Camp near Platte City, Missouri, and rented a double brick cabin separated by two garages. Bonnie, Clyde, and Jones moved into the room on the left while Buck and Blanche took the other one.

The manager's curiosity was aroused when they paid him in silver and the next day he mentioned his suspicions to the owner, who, in turn, related the incident to the Missouri State Highway Patrol. The lawmen, guessing it was very likely the Barrows, called Kansas City for reinforcements.

That evening the posse was ready to attack, confident the gang was asleep. And they would have been except for an overheard conversation. About an hour earlier, while Jones was buying bandages and salve for Bonnie at a local drugstore, he heard a customer casually remark that he had seen "a lot of officers out near the Red Crown Cabins."

Jones had alerted the gang and they were presently all huddled in Buck's darkened room watching every move of the lawmen. They saw the armored car drive up, watched two men with machine guns set up steel shields. A moment later there was a knock at the door and someone called, "Officers. We want to talk to you."

Bonnie said, "As soon as we get dressed," adding, as the Barrow brothers crept to the front window with their guns, "The men are on the other side."

"You had better come out," called the lawman.

"Let the bastards have it," cried Clyde.

There was a burst of fire. Bullets bounced off the heavy shields of the two machine gunners but surprisingly punctured the armored car, and before the men inside could back up the vehicle a bullet short-circuited the horn, which began a steady blast. The rest of the posse thought it was a signal and rushed forward.

Suddenly Buck burst from the building, two pistols cracking, followed by Bonnie and Blanche, who held up mattresses —their incessant target practice had taught them that stuffing made a good shield. Clyde now opened the garage doors and jumped on the running board of a Ford, which shot out of the garage, then stopped. The women dropped their mattresses and began firing pistols until Buck, hit in the head, fell. Blanche helped him to his feet.

As the attackers closed in, Buck was pushed into the car, which then roared onto the highway. Police bullets shattered the windshield and a piece of glass went into Blanche's left eye. The Ford careened wildly, finally straightened and escaped toward Platte City. It was Joplin all over again.

FBI agents requested all neighboring hospitals to hold anyone with gunshot wounds and the radio station of the *Kansas City Star*, WDAF, broadcast descriptions. Four days later, after a smoldering campfire and bloody bandages were found by a farmer at a deserted amusement park near Dexter, Iowa, a member of the county vigilantes hid in bushes nearby and waited. Later that afternoon he saw two cars drive up. Three men and two women got out. The vigilante crept away and phoned the local sheriff, who, convinced that these were the Barrows, called the sheriffs of nearby counties, and the Iowa National Guard. Within a few hours a small army had congregated at Dexter, its ranks swollen by dozens of local citizens armed with squirrel rifles and shotguns.

Before midnight every possible escape road had been blocked and the motley law force began to surround the camp-fires. At dawn the posse quietly moved in, going from tree to tree, Indian fashion. Bonnie was cooking coffee, and Jones —chained to a tree the previous night so he couldn't escape—

was roasting frankfurters, while the others stood smoking cigarettes. Blanche wore riding breeches and boots; dark goggles hid the injury to her left eye. Buck was clad only in a one-piece suit of underwear.

Clyde, seeing something move among the trees, shouted, "The law's coming!" All five went for guns as a withering fusillade showered them from all sides. Clyde told Jones to start the car but the youth was hit by a load of buckshot and fell, momentarily stunned. Clyde picked up Jones, threw him in the back seat, and tried to drive off with Bonnie squatting next to him but in a few seconds he was hit in the arm and the car smashed into a stump. They all scrambled to the second car but there was another thunderous volley and its windows were shattered. Bonnie, Clyde, and Jones plunged into the woods, half the posse on their heels, and, after a wild chase, again escaped, almost miraculously.

The other lawmen had trapped Buck and Blanche behind a stump. Blood was pouring from his old head wound but for a few minutes he held off the attackers with a pistol—then his head dropped limply and Blanche began to cry hysterically. A national guardsman, a doctor, dashed forward and knocked Buck's gun from his hand. He was bleeding from seven wounds.

"Don't die, Daddy," Blanche screamed. "Don't die!"

At a local hospital doctors said there was no hope for Buck. Blanche, who had been living on the brink of hysteria for months, was almost incoherent and her few understandable words were unprintable. But when she learned her husband would die her bitterness turned against Clyde. He had broken his word—deserted his brother.

That night the three survivors were about fifty miles south of Minnesota. In the next few days, as the chase continued, Bonnie became obsessed with the idea of composing one final poem which she would send to a newspaper so the world would know why they had been forced into a life of crime. She called it "The Story of Bonnie and Clyde" and it took her only a few hours to finish the first stanzas:

You have read the story of Jesse James,
Of how he lived and died.
If you still are in need of something to read,
Here is the story of Bonnie and Clyde.

Now Bonnie and Clyde are the Barrow gang.
I'm sure you all have read
How they rob and steal,
And how those who squeal,
Are usually found dying or dead.

There are lots of untruths to their write-ups,
They are not so merciless as that;
They hate all the laws,
The stool-pigeons, spotters and rats.
They class them as cold-blooded killers,
They say they are heartless and mean,
But I say this with pride,
That I once knew Clyde
When he was honest and upright and clean.

But the law fooled around,
Kept tracking him down,
And locking him up in a cell,
Till he said to me,
"I will never be free,
"So I will meet a few of them in hell."
This road was so dimly lighted
There were no highway signs to guide,
But they made up their minds
If the roads were all blind
They wouldn't give up till they died. . . .

2

George Kelly, his wife Kathryn, and Albert Bates were about
as different from Bonnie, Clyde, and Jones as could be im-

agined. Almost the only thing they had in common was the desire to live on other people's money. At the time Bonnie was beginning her new poem, the Kellys and Bates were turning from bank robbery to kidnaping, encouraged by the success of the Barkers in St. Paul, and had already selected a wealthy mark—victim—in Fort Worth, Texas.

George "Machine Gun" Kelly was big, blue-eyed, good-looking, and rather good-natured; and an acquaintance once said he must have bitten off a big chunk of the Blarney stone. He had started as a hip-pocket bootlegger in Memphis and, after serving a few months at the New Mexico State Penitentiary, resumed bootlegging in Oklahoma. Soon he was making good money and spending it with a flourish.

One evening he was introduced to an attractive, well-mannered young woman, Kathryn Thorne, whom two husbands had found irresistibly charming. She divorced the first and the second, bootlegger Charlie Thorne, had been discovered dead with a revolver at his side. A typewritten note said, in language that Thorne's friends had never heard him use, "I can't live with her or without her, hence I am departing this life." Although it was also revealed that the day before the shooting Kathryn had told a gas station attendant, "I'm bound for Coleman, Texas, to kill that goddamned Charlie Thorne," the coroner's jury called it suicide.

Kathryn's association with the underworld was not accidental. One aunt was a prostitute; a cousin operated a still; one uncle was suspected of counterfeiting; another was in Leavenworth for car theft; and her mother was a bootlegger. Apparently she thought she could make a successful criminal out of the talkative Kelly and began to build him up among her underworld friends, passing out cartridges as souvenirs from Machine Gun Kelly.

But she couldn't prevent him from getting involved in ridiculous situations. The amiable Kelly was caught smuggling liquor into an Indian reservation and shipped off to Leavenworth, where he was liked by everybody, including the guards. After three years he was released and Kathryn, who apparently could find no one else as malleable, was still waiting. She married him and, like Bonnie Parker, took over the family destinies, so ingratiating herself with other criminals and their women that Kelly was at last allowed to help rob banks in Mississippi and Texas. Before long Kathryn was able to buy a home in Fort Worth, expensive jewelry, and fashionable clothes. But hers wasn't an idle life; she didn't trust Kelly out of her sight, and went with him on all his trips. Who could possibly suspect that an attractive, well-groomed woman driving up to a bank in a Cadillac had come to memorize details of the institution's interior?

As the Depression deepened, Kathryn's mind, like Ma Barker's, finally turned to thoughts of kidnaping, but her first attempt in South Bend, Indiana, failed through inexperience. The kidnaped man simply didn't have the money. When she learned that the Barkers got $100,000 from Hamm she decided to try again, and this time an old friend, Albert Bates, was asked to help. He was a middle-aged man with a thickening waist and a silver plate in one shoulder from an old wound. A thief since his teens, he had done time at three different state penitentiaries and was presently wanted in four states for bank robbery. They selected Guy Waggoner, son of a millionaire Texas banker, as their first mark.

About this time Kathryn gave a party at her home on Mulkey Street in Forth Worth. Two guests were local police detectives, Ed Weatherford and J. W. Swinney, who had cultivated her, hoping to get information about the underworld. Kathryn, assuming they were open to graft like so many lawmen, suggested they help kidnap young Waggoner. When the detectives declined, protesting it would be too dangerous since the victim came from Fort Worth, Kathryn didn't get suspicious. She even asked a favor. In case her husband or their partner, Albert Bates, ever got in trouble out of the state, would the detectives wire that they were wanted for bank robbery in Texas? "And you boys come and claim them. Is that a go?"

They agreed, left the party to warn the FBI, and Waggoner was placed under special guard by local authorities. Shrewd as she was, Kathryn never realized the detectives had betrayed her and only thought that this new profession was much more complicated than it appeared. But she and her partners were undaunted and wasted no time in selecting an even more lucrative target, a wealthy Oklahoma oil man.

It was hot and dry in Oklahoma City on the evening of July 22. On the screened sun porch of their mansion at 327 Northwest 18th Street, Charles Urschel and his wife, Berenice, were playing bridge with neighbors, Mr. and Mrs. Walter Jarrett. There had been considerable publicity about the Urschels since their recent marriage. Berenice was the widow of the fabulous Tom Slick, famed as King of the Wildcatters, and the combined fortunes of this personable couple made them a logical subject for numerous newspaper stories in these days of Depression.

At 11:25 the screen door suddenly opened and Machine Gun Kelly and Bates entered.

"Stick 'em up," said Kelly nervously. "We want Urschel. We mean business. Don't bat an eye, any of you, or we'll blow your heads off. Which man is Urschel?"

When there was no reply, Kelly said they would take both men. For a moment Urschel, who was portly and about six feet tall, thought of resisting, but after looking at his wife, allowed Bates to take him outside with Jarrett. Kelly warned the women not to move until they heard a car start in the driveway.

"Hurry," whispered Mrs. Urschel a moment later. "Fly upstairs." The two women locked themselves in upstairs and phoned the chief of the Oklahoma City police department, who advised Mrs. Urschel to call J. Edgar Hoover.

It was a few minutes after midnight in Washington, D.C., when her call came into the FBI switchboard on a special line set up because of the recent kidnapings. It was transferred to Hoover's home and the Director of the FBI reassured Mrs. Urschel that his department would do nothing to endanger her husband's life. Even the question of paying ransom would be left up to her. Hoover then phoned the Agent in Charge of his Oklahoma City office, ordering him to contact the local police and go to the Urschel home.

While Hoover was talking, the car carrying Urschel had reached the edge of the city, where it turned right on a dirt road for about twelve miles. Here Jarrett was put out of the car, which then disappeared to the south. Now one of the kidnapers blindfolded Urschel with a bandage of cotton and adhesive tape, and said, "We don't want to hurt you." They stopped twice for gas and once to transfer into another car. About 2:30 the next afternoon they drove into what Urschel guessed was a garage and after dark he was led, still blindfolded, into the bedroom of a house. He was at the comfortable Paradise, Texas, ranch of bald, hawk-nosed Robert K. G. Shannon, the second husband of Kathryn's mother. After one of the men told him there were two beds and he could have either one, he heard a woman talking to another man in an adjoining room, then cotton was stuffed in his ears and taped down with adhesive. He tried to sleep on the narrow iron bed but couldn't.

The following morning, Monday, the blindfolded Urschel was given a light breakfast. He knew he was in the country for he could hear barnyard noises: chickens, guinea hens, cows, and dogs. That afternoon one of his captors read aloud the newspaper headlines, remarking that since Urschel's family and friends had called in the Federals, negotiations would be difficult.

In the meantime Kathryn drove to Fort Worth in her Cadillac to find out if the law had any leads—and unwittingly provided the first. She telephoned one of the two local detectives she supposed were her friends, inviting him to her home. A few minutes later she was telling him she'd just come from St. Louis but the observant detective noticed that even after such a long drive she wasn't tired. When he saw an Oklahoma City paper on the front seat of her Cadillac and noticed that the car's tire rims were covered with the red soil peculiar to Oklahoma, he reported his suspicions to the FBI.

That same evening Urschel was put in a small coupé but it stopped in several minutes and he was led into another house, which had no carpeting on the floors. After he lay down on an old quilt he was handcuffed to a baby's high chair.

He could hear the voices of another man and woman. The man was the owner of the shack, twenty-three-year-old Armon Shannon, son of Kathryn's stepfather. Kelly had just talked young Shannon into letting Urschel be jailed there.

The next morning Urschel was told that there were so many FBI agents in Oklahoma City it would be safer to make contact in some other town. Did he have a trusted friend in Tulsa? Urschel suggested John G. Catlett, an oil man.

The kidnapers gave him a tablet and a pencil and then dictated a note to Catlett. They also let him write a letter of his own composition to Mrs. Urschel, even allowing him to say, "If the demand is too great, just forget it, it will be O.K. with me." Apparently Kathryn felt such language would only make a wife more willing to co-operate.

While Fort Worth detectives placed the Kelly home on Mulkey Street under surveillance, FBI Director Hoover ordered discreet inquiries into the activities of the two suspects. Then he instructed Special Agent Gus T. Jones to leave Kansas City, where he was in charge of the massacre investigation, and take over the case. Jones, a former Texas Ranger, arrived on July 25 and learned that the Urschels had already been the victim of many fake ransom demands. After examining all the spurious notes he said, "When the real contact comes there will be no doubt as to its authenticity."

The next day in Tulsa, John Catlett was shaving when a messenger delivered a large envelope containing three sealed letters. In one addressed to himself he was asked by Urschel to follow instructions and not to discuss the matter "with anyone other than those mentioned." He was to deliver personally the other two letters—one to Mrs. Urschel and one to E. E. Kirkpatrick, a family friend.

Catlett took them to the Urschel home in Oklahoma City and Kirkpatrick—a newspaperman, rancher, and oilman—was called in. His note was typewritten and it instructed him to collect $200,000 in $20 bills:

It will be useless for you to attempt taking notes of SERIAL NUMBERS MAKING UP DUMMY PACKAGE, OR ANYTHING ELSE IN THE LINE OF ATTEMPTED DOUBLE CROSS. BEAR THIS IN MIND, CHARLES F. URSCHEL WILL REMAIN IN OUR CUSTODY UNTIL MONEY HAS BEEN INSPECTED AND EXCHANGED AND FURTHERMORE WILL BE AT THE SCENE OF CONTACT FOR PAY-OFF AND IF THERE SHOULD BE ANY ATTEMPT AT ANY DOUBLE XX IT WILL BE HE THAT SUFFERS THE CONSEQUENCE.

As soon as you have read and RE-READ this Carefully, and wish to commence negotiations you will proceed to the DAILY OKLAHOMAN and insert the following BLIND AD under the REAL ESTATE, FARMS FOR SALE, and we will know that you are ready for BUSINESS, and you will receive further instructions AT THE BOX ASSIGNED TO YOU BY NEWSPAPER, *AND NO WHERE ELSE* SO BE *CERTAIN THAT THIS ARRANGEMENT IS KEPT SECRET* AS THIS IS OUR FINAL ATTEMPT TO COMMUNICATE WITH YOU, on account of our former instructions to JARRETT being DISREGARDED and the LAW being notified, so we have neither the time or patience to carry on any further lengthy correspondence.

RUN THIS AD FOR ONE WEEK IN DAILY OKLAHOMAN.

"FOR SALE—160 Acres Land, good five room house, deep well. Also Cows, Tools, Tractor, Corn and Hay. $3750.00 for quick sale . . TERMS . . BOX #——"

After a conference the ad was inserted. Now there was nothing to do but keep the matter secret and wait for an answer. Two days later, on July 28, a special delivery letter unsigned and postmarked Joplin was received at the *Daily Oklahoman.*

It instructed Kirkpatrick to board The Sooner bound for Kansas City on the night of July 29. When he saw two successive fires on the right side of the railroad track he was to throw a light-colored leather bag containing the money from the observation platform.

Mr. Urschel will upon our instructions attend to the FIRES and secure the BAG when you throw it off, he will open it and transfer the contents to a sack that he will be provided with, SO, IF, you comply with our demand and do not attempt any subterfuge as according to the News reports you have pledged, Mr. Urschel should be HOME in a very short while.

REMEMBER THIS—IF ANY TRICKERY IS AT-TEMPTED YOU WILL FIND THE REMAINS OF URSCHEL AND INSTEAD OF JOY THERE WILL BE DOUBLE GRIEF—FOR, SOME-ONE VERY NEAR AND DEAR TO THE URSCHEL FAMILY IS UNDER CONSTANT SURVEILLANCE AND WILL LIKE-WISE SUFFER FOR *YOUR ERROR.*

If there is the slightest HITCH in these PLANS for any reason what-so-ever, not your fault, you will proceed on into Kansas City, Mo. and register at the Muehlebach Hotel under the name of E. E. Kincaid of Little Rock, Ar-kansas and await further instructions there however, there should not be, IF YOU COMPLY WITH THESE SIM-PLE DIRECTIONS.

THE MAIN THING IS DO NOT DIVULGE THE CONTENTS OF THIS LETTER TO ANY LAW AU-THORITIES *FOR WE HAVE NO INTENTION OF FURTHER COMMUNICATION.*

By the next night, Saturday, the Urschel home was be-sieged by reporters, cameramen, and even newsreel photog-raphers. Not since the kidnaping of the Lindbergh baby had there been such nation-wide interest in a crime. At 8:00 P.M. a car drove up to the Urschel home. Mrs. Urschel turned on a floodlight and recognized the comptroller of the First National Bank of Oklahoma City. Then she saw a guard walk to the car, get a Gladstone bag, and return to the house.

In the new, light-colored bag were $200,000 in used $20

bills, their serial numbers recorded. Two hours later Kirkpatrick and John Catlett, carrying two identical bags, boarded
the train. One was filled with $200,000; the other, in case of
hijacking, with an equal weight of magazines and papers. To
his surprise and consternation, Kirkpatrick learned from their
porter that two extra Pullmans, loaded with tourists bound for
Chicago's Century of Progress, had been attached to the observation car.

The two men threaded their way through the extra Pullmans to the rear vestibule of the last car. At about 10:10 P.M.
as the train slowly pulled out of the station, the two men
found campstools and sat down. Whenever the train approached a town Catlett would step inside the Pullman, while
Kirkpatrick stood under the vestibule light smoking a cigarette,
anxiously searching for the signal flares. They passed through
Witcher, then approached Luther.

It was here that the kidnapers had planned to build the
two signal fires but they had trouble with a new Buick and
arrived at the rendezvous too late to do anything—they
were unable to follow their own elaborate and uncompromis-
ing instructions.

By dawn, July 28, Kirkpatrick was exhausted. He had
lit fifty-one cigarettes, futilely stood under the lights fifty-one
times. He and Catlett were sure they had been hoaxed and
wondered if they themselves would be kidnaped if they continued to the Muehlebach Hotel as ordered.

When they debarked at the Kansas City station and walked
onto the plaza Kirkpatrick thought of the recent massacre.
Near the spot where five men had died, the two got in a
taxi and started for the hotel. Kirkpatrick registered as E. E.
Kincaid and the two men began another wait. Finally at
10:00 A.M. a Postal telegram arrived.

UNAVOIDABLE INCIDENT KEPT ME FROM SEEING YOU LAST
NIGHT WILL COMMUNICATE ABOUT 6:00 O'CLOCK.

E. W. MOORE

That Sunday was the longest day in Kirkpatrick's life, an
unforgettable nightmare, for he felt he held the life of a friend

in his hands. He wondered if he had blundered by carrying two suitcases instead of one and bringing Catlett along. From somewhere in the hotel he could hear a pianist playing Mendelssohn's "Spring Song."

The vigil lasted almost ten hours until the phone rang at 5:45 P.M. Kirkpatrick was told to take a Yellow cab to the La Salle Hotel and walk west with the suitcase in his right hand. Kirkpatrick asked if he could bring a friend along.

"Hell, no! We know all about your friend. You come alone and unarmed."

Kirkpatrick stuck an automatic in his belt, put on his hat, and picked up the Gladstone bag containing the money. "Godspeed and good luck," said Catlett.

A few minutes later Kirkpatrick reached the La Salle Hotel and began walking leisurely along Linwood Boulevard. Almost immediately he noticed two big cars across the street, each containing three men, and recalled Walter Burns's "The One Way Ride." Then a heavy-set man about six feet tall approached in a nervous shifting stride, and when Kirkpatrick saw his furtive glances he guessed the moment for pay-off had come.

Machine Gun Kelly kept walking, eyes straight ahead, then stopped a few feet to Kirkpatrick's right. "I'll take that grip," he said.

Kirkpatrick took a few seconds to memorize everything about the man so he could later identify him—he had black hair, dark skin, and wore a stylish summer suit, two-toned shoes, and a turned-down Panama hat.

"Hurry up," said Kelly.

"How do I know you're the right party?"

"Hell, you know damned well I am."

Kirkpatrick said $200,000 was a lot of money and he wanted assurance.

"Don't argue with me," said Kelly, on edge. "The boys are waiting."

Kirkpatrick stalled, asking when Urschel would be home. He put the bag on the sidewalk between his legs. "Tell me definitely what I can tell Mrs. Urschel."

Kelly, growing red-faced as he nervously shifted his feet, promised that Urschel would be home within twelve hours. Kirkpatrick, leaving the bag, walked away without looking back and a few minutes later was talking to Mrs. Urschel in Oklahoma City. "I closed the deal for that farm. It will require about twelve hours for the lawyers to examine the abstracts, then title will pass."

3

Urschel was still handcuffed in the shack but now a chain had been attached to the cuffs and he was able to move about to some extent. He was pestered by chigger bites and his blindfolded eyes ached. Since his arrival he had kept mental notes on everything: actions, sounds, the vaguest scraps of conversations. One day Bates talked at some length about the Barrow brothers and their recent wild fight in Iowa in which Buck had been mortally wounded.

"They're just a couple of cheap filling station and car thieves," he said. "I've been stealing for twenty-five years and my group doesn't deal in anything cheap. I wouldn't hesitate to rob the Security National Bank."

Kelly was even more talkative. "This place is as safe as it can be," he once told Urschel. "All the boys use it. After they pull a bank job or something they come down here to cool off."

At the moment three escapees from prison were paying Boss Shannon several hundred dollars for the privilege of hiding in the main house. This worried and exasperated Bates, who told Kelly it was stupid to endanger a $200,000 operation for a few dollars. When Kelly kept postponing a showdown with Kathryn's stepfather, Bates took the initiative and warned the escapees that the ranch was hot and they had better get out.

This was the same day that Bates and Kelly had left to negotiate with Kirkpatrick. Shannon and his son replaced them as guards but Urschel only knew that one was called "Boss," the other "Potatoes." He also noticed that the water he drank had a mineral taste and was drawn with considerable noise from a well near the house. He planted his fingerprints on the planked walls, window sills, corners of the floors. Most important, he noted a plane passed over every day at 9:45 A.M. except on the one day it rained, Sunday, July 30. Though he didn't have a watch, he had determined the time by a ruse. After a plane passed he would mentally count off five minutes before casually asking one of the guards what time it was.

Kelly and Bates returned with the ransom at 2:00 P.M., July 31, and went into the front room to divide the $200,000. The Kellys were to get half, Bates half. The expenses were $11,500, leaving each a profit of $94,250.

Bates packed his money and went out to the back porch to clean up. There was Harvey Bailey, one of the three prison escapees. The other two had taken Bates's advice and fled but Bailey, a notorious bank robber, said he was still recovering from a leg wound. Bates gave Bailey $500 of the kidnap money and Kelly also handed over $500.

A few minutes later Bates, Kelly, and Kathryn began to argue bitterly about the fate of Urschel. One went so far as to say, "Kill the bastard. Then we won't have any trouble with him."

But murder was finally overruled. Bates now drove the mile and a half to the kidnap shack and told Urschel he was going to be released. Then after his nine-day beard was shaved off, Urschel was led to a car.

An hour later the car stopped and Kelly joined them, warning Urschel to say nothing about the kidnaping when he got home. Otherwise he and his entire family would be killed. They headed north. Kathryn, wearing only a house robe, preceded them in her Cadillac.

Nineteen miles from Oklahoma City both cars stopped. Urschel was given a hat, a $10 bill, and was told to walk to a gas station where he could call a taxi. Then he was let out of the car. His legs were so weak he staggered down the road in the drizzling rain.

Since early that morning Mrs. Urschel had been waiting anxiously, her alarm growing with each passing hour. At

about 8:30 P.M. Kirkpatrick knelt down and set a trap to catch
a mouse he had seen scooting under the divan in the sun-
room. When it suddenly snapped, he violently threw it to the
ceiling and swore, and Mrs. Urschel laughed for the first time
in nine days. Twenty minutes later Urschel, eyes blinking,
wearing wrinkled, dirty clothes, came to the back door.

Within an hour Agent Gus Jones arrived and Urschel
described his capture briefly before going to bed. The next
morning, under Jones's expert guidance, Urschel gave a detailed description of the kidnap shack and his conversations
with the kidnapers.

The hat the kidnapers had given Urschel was labeled
"Newmans—Joplin's Greatest Store," but, since the second
letter had been postmarked from Joplin, Jones was suspicious
and said, "Too much Joplin." Nevertheless, it was believed the
kidnap cabin was located in that general area.

A team of agents began to assess the clues, checking
weather reports and plane schedules. Jones drew a detailed
map of the kidnap cabin and its surroundings from Urschel's
descriptions, then flew over the peaks of the Arbuckle Uplift,
the Kiamichi Mountains of southeastern Oklahoma, and the
Ozarks. The next day he skimmed low over the Osage bad-
lands, the classic desperado territory, but still did not find
Armon Shannon's shack.

It was far to the south.

And the kidnapers were far to the northeast, in the Twin
Cities, selling some of their ransom money at cut-rate prices.
The Kellys left Minneapolis August 5, the day that four local
hoodlums involved in the money-passing operation were arrested by FBI agents.

By then the FBI had made a systematic check of all air
schedules within six hundred miles of Oklahoma City, and
discovered that American Airways planes left Fort Worth daily
at 9:15 A.M. and Amarillo at 3:30 P.M., flying over a town
named Paradise, Texas, between 9:40 and 9:45 A.M. and between 5:40 and 5:45 P.M.

Information on the Kelly family also began coming in and
it was learned that Kathryn's mother, Ora, had recently mar-

ried a man named R. G. Shannon who lived on a ranch near the same town mentioned in the airplane report—Paradise, Texas.

Early on the morning of August 10, Special Agent Edward Dowd took Jones's map and drove to the 500-acre Shannon ranch. Posing as an investigator for a commercial organization, he passed the time of day at Boss Shannon's house, then drove the short distance to his son Armon's home, a sagging, weather-beaten shack facing south. There was a well at the northeast corner. So far everything fitted. Dowd asked for a drink of water—it had a strong mineral taste. He noticed three hogs, two pigs, and four cows. Jones's map was coming to life.

Armon invited the investigator into the house to discuss a farm loan. When Dowd saw that one room contained an old iron bed and a battered baby's high chair he was certain this was the kidnap shack.

Dawn was just breaking two days later when three cars headed up the lonely sand road leading to the Shannon ranch and turned into the small clearing in front of the main house. Gus Jones, Urschel, three federal agents, a deputy sheriff from Oklahoma City, and eight police officers from Fort Worth and Dallas, including Detectives Swinney and Weatherford, piled out and began to deploy. Jones started around the corner of the house, for he had noticed a man sleeping on an improvised bed in the back yard. Suddenly, a bald, hawk-nosed old man stepped out the front door. Urschel, armed with a sawed-off shotgun, guessed this was "Boss."

Jones, his machine gun ready, hurried toward the sleeping man and circled the bed cautiously. Beside it were a fully loaded automatic rifle and a .45 automatic pistol. In it lay the man he had been searching for in connection with the Kansas City massacre, Harvey Bailey—who had as much to do with the massacre as he had with the kidnaping. The bank robber awoke, slowly opening his eyes.

"Get up, Harvey." Bailey didn't make a move. "If a shot is fired, I'll riddle you."

"I'm here alone. You have me," said Bailey, blinking thick, long eyelashes. Without moving his hands, he cautiously crossed his feet. "Well, after all, a fellow has to sleep some-time."

He was searched and of the $1,200 found on him $700 was in ransom money. Three women were inside the house: Kathryn's mother and two fifteen-year-old girls—one Shannon's daughter by a former marriage, the other Kathryn's daughter by her first marriage. The northeast room was filled with expensive luggage, tailored men's suits, and numerous gowns, some bearing French labels. There was no doubt that this was the room of Kathryn and Machine Gun Kelly.

The two men were chained to a post and the women left under guard while the main force converged on the nearby kidnap shack where young Armon was busy with his chores in the barn and his girl-wife, Oleta, was making breakfast.

Urschel eagerly entered the squalid shack, excitedly pointing out to Jones everything he had mentioned in their long interview. Then he positively identified Armon as Potatoes.

Later, near the main house, when Ora Shannon saw Armon talking with an agent she shouted, "Armon, keep your goddamn mouth shut; don't tell them a damned thing!" It was too late. Armon had already confessed everything.

That same day, by a coincidence that would be suspect in a novel, Bates—posing as George L. Davis—was arrested by Denver police on suspicion of passing stolen Express Company checks. He was understandably nervous—with Urschel money still in his pockets. Realizing he had to get out of jail before a check of the numbers was made, he smuggled a letter to his wife through a released prisoner.

Mrs. Bates knew about the "promise" made to Kathryn Kelly by the detectives in Fort Worth in case her husband or Kelly got in trouble outside of Texas and wired Weatherford and Swinney:

GEORGE L. DAVIS HELD IN DENVER WANTED IN BLUE RIDGE, TEXAS, BANK ROBBERY. WILL WAIVE EXTRADITION. COME AT ONCE. ADVISE COMING BY AIRPLANE.

GEORGE L. DAVIS

The detectives turned the wire over to the FBI and in a few hours Hoover's agents found $660 in Urschel money on the dejected Bates.

The Kellys were in Des Moines when they read about the arrest of the Shannons. Kathryn burst into tears, cursing Hoover. All at once her anger lashed out at George too. It was his fault, she screamed, that her mother was now in danger of being sentenced to life imprisonment. Kelly tried to weather the storm with bootleg gin but her attacks and recriminations continued. Finally, half drunk, he said he would agree to surrender himself if the government freed Kathryn's mother and stepfather.

On August 18 Kathryn wrote the following letter to Joseph B. Keenan, Assistant Attorney General of the United States, the man assigned to prosecute the case:

> The entire Urschel family and friends, and all of you will be exterminated soon. There is no way I can prevent it. I will gladly put George Kelly on the spot for you if you will save my mother, who is innocent of any wrong doing. If you do not comply with this request, there is no way in which I can prevent the most awful tragedy. If you refuse my offer I shall commit some minor offense and be placed in jail so that you will know that I have no connection with the terrible slaughter that will take place in Oklahoma City within the next few days.

4

No bank robber had ever looked more like a bank president than Harvey Bailey. In addition to his appearance, he also had the reputation—like Pierpont's lieutenant, Makley—of being able to talk himself out of almost any situation. As soon as he was arrested for complicity in the Urschel kidnaping and placed in a cell on the tenth floor of the modern

Dallas County jail, the local newspaper assured its readers that even the ingenious Bailey could not possibly get out:

SEVEN BARRED DOORS OR GRILLS
FACE GANGSTERS IF THEY TRY
TO SPRING BAILEY FROM JAIL

The paper went on to say that the few who had escaped before the present system was put into effect had done so "through trickery" and officers were "keeping a close watch on Bailey to avoid any such turn of events."

It took Bailey only about two weeks to convince one of his jailers, Deputy Sheriff Thomas L. Manion, to smuggle in saws. Bailey, assuring the jailer he was innocent of any kidnaping charges, also promised to split the take of his next few bank robberies if he got free.

Early in the morning of September 4, Labor Day, Bailey—occasionally spelled by his jailer—had almost sawed through three bars. Then Manion brought in a Stillson wrench and a few minutes after 7:00 A.M. Bailey squeezed his big frame through the narrow opening.

Armed with a gun provided by Manion, Bailey took keys from another jailer, walked down to the sixth floor, overpowered a guard and the elevator operator, locked up two jailers, and rode the elevator to the main floor. Here he surprised Nick Tresp, a deputy sheriff. At 7:10 A.M. the two men walked out of the jail to the garage across the street, where Bailey took the first car he saw.

Posses were formed in nearby cities, where roadblocks were set up, and that afternoon, after a hectic chase, Bailey was trapped in Ardmore, Oklahoma. When police handcuffed him to his companion, Tresp indignantly protested, "I'm a jailer."

Bailey was driven back to Dallas, again put in a solitary cell. His only remark as he reflectively puffed on a cigarette was, "Well, I got out, didn't I?"

That same day an itinerant worker named Arnold, his wife, and twelve-year-old daughter Geraldine were trying to hitchhike near Hillsboro, Texas. Finally, a Ford pickup truck stopped and the driver, an attractive, red-haired woman, said, "Can I give you a lift?"

It was Kathryn Kelly in a red wig. She wanted to use the family, particularly the child, as a cover. She treated them to meals all day and put them up at a cabin that night. Next morning she bought clothes for Geraldine and her mother, then said, "I can fix it so you can make some money. Can I trust you?"

After these refugees of the Depression gave eager assurances, she said, "I'm Kathryn Kelly," and handed Arnold $50. He was to go to Fort Worth, contact her attorney, and find out why the trade—mother for husband—hadn't been made.

Arnold did as instructed. Upon his return Kathryn persuaded him to go to Oklahoma City and learn the details of the coming trial of Bates, Bailey, and the Shannons. Arnold found out what he could, then met Kathryn and his family in San Antonio. Kathryn now asked the Arnolds if she could take Geraldine on "a little trip of 250 miles." When the parents consented, Kathryn and the child left in the pickup. Accompanied by Machine Gun, whose hair had been dyed lemon-yellow, they ultimately arrived in Chicago. The Kellys at last had a perfect camouflage, a child.

In Oklahoma City the trial was just getting under way in a courtroom high in the tower of the federal building. On its second day, September 19, Urschel got an air mail letter from Chicago which was signed by George Kelly.

Ignorant Charles:

Just a few lines to let you know that I am getting my plans made to destroy your so-called mansion, and you and your family immediately after this trial. And young fellow, I guess you've begun to realize your serious mistake. Are you ignorant enough to think the Government can guard you forever. I gave you credit for more sense than that, and figured you thought too much of your family to jeopardize them as you have, but if you don't look out for them, why should we. I dislike hurting the innocent, but I told you exactly what would happen and you can bet $200,000 more everything I said will be true. You are living on borrowed time now. You know that the Shannon family are victims of circumstances the same as you was. You don't seem to mind prosecuting the innocent, neither will I have conscious qualms over brutally murdering your family. The Shannons have put the heat on, but I don't desire to see them prosecuted as they are innocent and I have a much better method of settling with them. As far as the guilty being punished you would probably have lived the rest of your life in peace had you tried only the guilty, but if the Shannons are convicted look out, and God help you for he is the only one that will be able to do you any good. In the event of my arrest I've already formed an outfit to take care of and destroy you and yours the same as if I was there. I am spending your money to have you and your family killed—nice—eh? You are bucking people who have cash—planes, bombs and unlimited connection both here and abroad. I have friends in Oklahoma City that know every move and every plan you make, and you are still too dumb to figure out the finger man there.

If my brain was no larger than yours, the Government would have had me long ago, as it is I am drinking good beer and will yet see you and your family like I should have left you at first—stone dead.

I don't worry about Bates and Bailey. They will be out for the ceremonies—your slaughter.

Now say—it is up to you; if the Shannons are convicted, you can get another rich wife in hell, because that will be the only place you can use one.

Adios, smart one.

Your worst enemy,
GEO. R. KELLY

I will put my fingerprints below so you can't say some crank wrote this.

[Fingerprints were inserted here]

Give Keenan my regards and tell him maybe he would like to meet the owner of the above.
See you in hell.

FBI agents checked the fingerprints and found they were Kelly's. The federal building became an armed camp and admittance to the spectators' section was by card only. That morning, while the dynamic young prosecutor was questioning a witness, a low-flying plane swept over the building. Everyone in the courtroom tensed, thinking of the already publicized bomb threat.

In Chicago the man who signed the bloodthirsty letter to Urschel was losing his nerve and begged Kathryn to leave their apartment. He was sure the FBI had traced their car. Kathryn hid her frightened husband in a movie theater while she rented another place but in a few days it became evident even to Kathryn that Chicago was too dangerous, so the Kellys drove, with Geraldine, to Memphis, where they hid in the home of J. C. Tichenor.

Soon their money began to run low. Since most of their share of the ransom had been buried weeks earlier in Texas on the ranch of a relative of Kathryn's, Kelly now persuaded a Memphis attorney, a brother-in-law by a previous marriage, to dig it up. Little Geraldine would go along as a cover.

When the lawyer and child arrived at the ranch Kathryn's relative, Cassey Coleman, was so frightened he pretended he didn't understand what the lawyer was talking about.

The lawyer wired the Kellys:

DEAL FELL THROUGH. TRIED TO GET LATER APPOINTMENT BUT PROSPECT WAS AFRAID. IMPOSSIBLE TO CHANGE HIS MIND. DON'T WANT TO BRING HOME A SAD TALE. . . .

He asked the Kellys to send him instructions by Western Union, then wired the Arnolds in Oklahoma City, advising them that Geraldine would arrive at 10:00 P.M. When the girl stepped off the train Hoover's agents, who had already apprehended her parents and intercepted the lawyer's telegram, were waiting. Geraldine, eager to co-operate with the FBI, told about the farm in Texas and the house in Memphis.

The next morning, September 26, at daybreak, FBI agents and local officers surrounded the Tichenor bungalow. Three men burst in the front door. Machine Gun Kelly, his yellow hair tousled, came from the bedroom where Kathryn was sleeping. Nearby was a Colt .45.

When told to put up his hands he made the split-second decision not to go for his gun and said, "Don't shoot, G-men!" It was the first time the agents had heard their new underworld nickname.

Word of the capture of the Kellys was wired to Agent Jones in Oklahoma City. He arrived at the Coleman ranch at midnight and within an hour, aided by the light of a pale red moon, had dug up a two-gallon Thermos jug and a molasses can. Inside was $73,250 in twenty-dollar bills.

Even as the Kellys were taken to Oklahoma City for trial, Kathryn was protesting her innocence. She wept, she stormed, and then called her sheepish husband a hoodlum who "had brought this disgrace upon my family."

Later she would write:

> There is no bitterness or animosity in my heart toward anyone but the perpetrators of the terrible crime who dragged an honored, honest, respected family down into the depths of blackest despair. My mother ever has been a good, Christian, law-abiding citizen, and my love and marriage to a gangster plunged my family into bitter tragedy through their innocent, hospitable trust and faith in my husband.

If there had been an Oscar for criminals in 1933, Kathryn Kelly—whose "honored, honest, respected family" included a bootlegger, a still operator, a suspected counterfeiter, a car thief, a prostitute, and the proprietor of a hideout for criminals—would have won it easily.

CHAPTER 6

Trapped

1

FOUR DAYS AFTER URSCHEL WAS RELEASED, JOHN DILLINGER, wearing a sailor straw hat, walked into the First National Bank of Montpelier, Indiana. "This is a stick-up," he said, then leaped over the high barrier and began emptying drawers in the cashier's cage.

When Matt Leach learned of the Montpelier leaper he was positive it was Dillinger and intuitively suspected his potential: he might merely be an exhibitionist but Leach thought it more probable such individuality was the mark of a dangerous criminal.

Leach not only had the homes of Dillinger's father and sister, Audrey Hancock, watched but even ordered his first partner in crime, Ed Singleton, arrested and brought in for questioning.

It was almost a month before Leach got his first real clue: the address of an apartment believed to be Dillinger's. On August 14 Leach raided the apartment, arresting three associates of "Desperate Dan." It was typical of Dillinger's luck that he was in Bluffton, Ohio—robbing another bank.

After a week of questioning, Leach finally persuaded one

of the three arrested men to reveal the location of another Dillinger hideout and that evening Leach led a raiding party to the Beverly Apartments in Gary. Once more Dillinger was lucky. An associate was captured but Dillinger himself had stepped out only a moment before. Since the captured man insisted that Dillinger would soon return, Leach ordered three men to stay in the apartment. Only Dillinger would be allowed to go upstairs, said Leach. When they heard a knock one officer would jerk open the door and State Patrolman Art Keller would fire point-blank—to kill.

Leach repeated the unusual orders, then added excitedly, "If I c-c-come up, I'll c-call you first by phone." He turned to Keller, reassuring him no one would be allowed upstairs except Dillinger.

The three men waited in the hot, unlit apartment. Half an hour passed, an hour. By now it was dark. Suddenly there was a knock at the door. As Keller raised his sawed-off shotgun, another officer flung open the door and jumped back. Keller was about to shoot the silhouette in the doorway but hesitated. Dillinger was short and stocky, this man was tall and thin.

"F-for G-god's s-s-sake, don't sh-shoot! It's m-me!" It was only when the door suddenly opened that Leach had remembered his own instructions. Learning that Dillinger had gone to an eating place, he had rushed upstairs thoughtlessly to get his men. By the time Leach reached the restaurant he was again just a moment too late. There was no trace of the elusive Dillinger.

Pinkertons National Detective Agency, hired to solve the Bluffton, Ohio, bank robbery, did have a lead. Through informants they learned that Dillinger had a girl friend in Dayton. They didn't know her address or married name, only that she was the sister of James Jenkins. A letter was sent to the Dayton police:

> . . . Dillinger calls upon this woman regularly and, no doubt, can be apprehended at Dayton, Ohio. He is driving a new Essex Terraplane "S" sedan, black color, and

probably is using Ind. License 418-673, 512-979, 703-736
or 86-927. . . .

The thought is that considering Dillinger is contact-
ing with the woman in Dayton, you could have the police
be on the watch for these license numbers, or probably
they could get some information concerning this woman
and cause the arrest of Dillinger.

That same day Mary Longnaker wrote Dillinger, asking to
see him as soon as possible. She said she'd been sick.

I sure am in a fix. But don't want to tell you about it on
paper. It isn't what you think, because I can just about
guess what you are thinking.

She had recently seen her husband at the Greenville Fair.
He was "awful nice," and apparently wasn't going to contest
the divorce.

If you can come down over Sun. I want to see you so bad.
I have some things I would like to take to Jim, I had my
picture taken they aren't so hot tho. I sure don't take a
good picture.

Dillinger came that Sunday and even drove the new Es-
sex described in the Pinkertons' letter, but he was not caught.
A few days later, on September 2, the Pinkertons again wrote
the Dayton police: they had discovered Mary's last name and
her present address, 324 West 1st Avenue.

When Detectives Russ Pfauhl and Charlie Gross showed
Dillinger's picture to Lucille Stricker, the landlady at the
rooming house, she told them it was a friend of Mary Longnaker's who had a room permanently reserved on the ground
floor. Mrs. Stricker said he wrote Mary quite regularly and
promised to call the detectives as soon as the next letter arrived.

A few days later Mrs. Stricker telephoned—a letter had
come. When the two detectives opened it and read, "I'll be
seeing you soon," they moved into the room opposite the one

reserved for Dillinger. All they had to do now was wait.

But for the moment Dillinger was too busy robbing banks to visit Mary. The prison break was scheduled to take place in about three weeks and he still didn't have enough money. A postponement would mean further risky negotiations—which would increase chances of the plans being discovered.

Just before noon, September 6, Lloyd Rinehart—the assistant manager of the State Bank of Massachusetts Avenue, Indianapolis—was at his desk telephoning when he heard someone say quietly, "This is a stick-up." Since this was a common joke in Depression days, he ignored it until he heard the same voice say with authority, "Get away from that damned telephone." Rinehart turned and saw Dillinger sitting cross-legged up on the seven-foot-high barrier. A straw hat was tilted cockily on his head and he was almost casually pointing an automatic.

Though his two accomplices were extremely nervous—one kept shouting from the getaway car to hurry up and the other spent most of his time trying to keep a handkerchief-mask from slipping off his nose—Dillinger soon collected $24,800 and escaped.

He was amazed when he counted the money. Purely by chance he had hit on the Real Silk Hosiery payroll day and thus committed the second most successful bank robbery in the state. This unexpected piece of luck was doubly fortunate. In one stroke he finally had enough to put the prison break plan into operation; and, since this would involve all his time for the next few weeks, it also prevented him from going to Dayton for the week end—where he would have been captured.

For the past three months Dillinger had been in contact with those on the outside pledged to help Pierpont. His two most important aides were women: Pearl Elliott and Mary Kinder. Pearl was a frowzy, good-natured, middle-aged operator of a combination night club and house of prostitution in Kokomo. Though she had been involved in the bank robbery that sent Pierpont to prison, he had not revealed her name at the trial and now she owed him something.

The other aide, Mary Kinder, was twenty-two. She was slender, red-haired, and an inch under five feet. One of thirteen children, she had helped support the others after her father's death. Her ties with the state prison were diverse. Within its walls she had, in addition to two brothers, a friend she had known for eleven years and an ex-husband. The old friend was Pierpont; the former husband was the son of an Indianapolis police sergeant, who had robbed a grocer. She had agreed to help with the mass break-out, provided her brother, Earl, Pierpont's partner in the Kokomo robbery, was added to the list of escapees.

Dillinger assigned her the job of finding an apartment in Indianapolis where the men could hide immediately after the crash-out. Pearl would act as a general go-between and also pass on money to another confederate whose job was to bribe guards at the prison. Dillinger himself was to get the guns inside the walls. On the night of September 12 he drove to Michigan City and crept up to the wall just behind the athletic field; he then threw three guns, wrapped in cotton and newspapers, over the thirty-foot-high barrier. The gang was supposed to pick them up early the next day before reporting for work.

As was hoped, the guards on morning inspection didn't notice the three packages—but someone else did. Before Pierpont could reach the athletic field, an inmate found the packages and turned them over to Deputy Warden "I, God" Claudy, who never suspected the guns were meant for the Pierpont gang and put another group of desperadoes in solitary. Since time was such a factor, Pierpont couldn't wait for Pearl or Mary Kinder to visit him again and kited a letter out to Dillinger, telling him to hide a new set of guns in a box of supplies that would be delivered to the prison shirt factory.

On September 18 Dillinger visited Mary Kinder at her Indianapolis apartment; he gave her $150 and said the "boys" would arrive on September 27 at the earliest, probably a few days later. He then drove to Chicago, bought four more guns, and turned them over to another conspirator. This man went to a local factory where he bribed an employee to open a box of thread addressed to the prison shirt shop, hide the guns under the thread, reseal the box, and mark it in crayon with an X.

Now for the first time in almost a month Dillinger had time to visit Mary Longnaker and late in the afternoon of September 22 he started for Dayton, unaware that two detectives were waiting for him in the boarding house. He was also unaware that in his absence Mary had met an industrious young man who had already proposed. She was in a dilemma. She wanted to leave Dillinger for a respectable life but was afraid of ruining her brother's chance to escape from prison.

While Dillinger was driving to Dayton, the two detectives in Mary's boarding house decided they were wasting their time. They told Mrs. Stricker to call police headquarters if Dillinger ever returned and then went home.

A little after midnight Sergeant W. J. Aldredge was behind the counter at police headquarters eating lunch when the phone rang.

"He's here," cried a woman.

"Who's here?" asked Aldredge patiently.

"John Dillinger, you dumb flatfoot!"

Within half an hour the captain of the late shift was outlining a plan to capture Dillinger. Pfauhl suggested that since he and Gross knew the house, only they should go in, but the captain insisted that Sergeant Aldredge, a good man with a gun, accompany them. By 1:30 A.M. the big house was surrounded. The two detectives and Aldredge went to the back door where Mrs. Stricker was waiting. Dillinger, she said, was now in Mary's room. While Aldredge stayed on guard at the foot of the stairs, the two detectives silently walked up the heavily carpeted steps, Gross carrying a machine gun, Pfauhl a shotgun. They told Mrs. Stricker to knock on Mary's door.

When it opened, the detectives saw a man in a business suit standing in the middle of the floor holding Kodak pictures.

Gross stepped in, aiming the machine gun at Dillinger while Pfauhl said, "Stick 'em up, John. We're police officers."

As Dillinger slowly raised his hands to his shoulders, the pictures—taken during the recent trip to the Century of Progress—fell. Then his hands dropped slightly.

"Don't, John," said Pfauhl. "I'll kill you."

Dillinger froze. Suddenly Mary moaned and fell, as if in a faint, near his feet, but the two detectives weren't deceived and paid her no attention. "Get on your hands and knees and crawl back where you came from," said Pfauhl. She did so.

At headquarters Pfauhl told Dillinger he could have been killed if he hadn't put his hands up.

"You said you were police but I didn't know," he replied. "I can only tell if they wear uniforms." His sarcasm was meant to hide his deep disgust. His friends were about ready to break out of Michigan City and he was on his way back.

PART THREE

•

CHAPTER 7

"We're Going Home"

1

AT THE DAYTON JAIL INSPECTOR SEYMOUR YENDES, THE LOCAL chief of detectives, was puzzled by Dillinger's composure in the face of almost constant interrogations and his positive identification as a bank robber by several reliable witnesses. Suspecting confederates might attempt to free him, Yendes stationed officers with shotguns throughout the building.

Undoubtedly the man most interested in the prisoner was Matt Leach and the morning after the arrest he drove to the jail with Detective Harvey Hire to consult Dillinger's captors and to confront him personally. Leach was shown a rough drawing found on Dillinger which Russ Pfauhl suggested might be a plan of escape from Michigan City.

Leach's intuition, which had proved so accurate a few days earlier, deserted him. "You've been reading too many books," he said.

Inspector Yendes, somewhat taken aback by Leach's curtness, now showed him another paper found on Dillinger, indicating in tenths of miles the escape route taken after one of his Indiana bank robberies. Though Leach had completely missed the significance of the first drawing, the sight of the getaway chart in Dillinger's own handwriting excited him so much that he grabbed for the paper; stuttering, he said he had to have it. Yendes, startled by Leach's insistence, refused to surrender the document and a bitter argument broke out. Finally Yendes said, "Get the hell out of my office, Leach."

Once in the hallway Leach put hands on hips and threw his head back in an attempt to curb his temper. Just then Yendes called Hire back in the office and told him anything *he* wanted in Dayton was his for the asking.

In the cell with Desperate Dan, Leach did no better in his first meeting with Dillinger. Though he questioned the prisoner at length about the thread mill holdup at Monticello and about several bank robberies, Dillinger never lost his mocking, twisted grin and would only say again and again, "What are you talking about?"

The day after Dillinger's arrest a two-hundred-pound box of thread arrived at the Gordon Shirt Company inside the prison at Michigan City. When storeroom keeper Walter Dietrich, the former disciple of the legendary Baron Lamm, saw an X crayoned on the top he signed for it, saying the box was badly needed in the shop. A moment later he was hiding four guns and ammunition in a shoe box.

There were now nine in on the escape, and several changes had been made in the list. Mary Kinder's brother Earl was in the hospital, dying of tuberculosis. Pierpont had ruled out another name upon learning the man was involved with a "jailhouse girl-boy," because to him this indicated a weakness of character. Three others had been added: a former race track driver, a bank robber, and a murderer.

On September 25 Pierpont, Clark, Makley, and Hamilton conferred during an exercise period. The break was scheduled for the 27th but they were afraid some word of it might reach Claudy and so decided to crash out the next day, the 26th. Pierpont suggested they take the musketeers' pledge: one for all; all for one. Then each man swore he would shoot, or be shot, rather than be captured.

Warden Louis Kunkel—until recently a local lawyer and political leader—had no idea a break was imminent, but recently he had been concerned about conditions in the prison and what they might lead to. Since taking over in June he had been faced with a formidable task. To control more than 2,500 convicts there were only 120 guards and 69 of these were, like himself, inexperienced appointees of the new Democratic administration. He was also worried about the antiquated main gate, and felt that the two turnkeys who manned it would be easy targets for convicts with guns. (Only later would he discover that nothing more than quarter-inch plywood walled a door between the prison library and the trustees' dining room. Any determined prisoner could kick a hole in the plywood and walk down a few hallways through ordinary doors to freedom.)

Unlike Kunkel, "I, God" Claudy, the deputy warden, was aware that a main escape was being plotted inside the walls. According to his informants, however, it wasn't scheduled for at least two days, and until he had some positive proof, he didn't want to alarm the warden needlessly. Claudy was a Republican, and felt that one mistake could mean the end of his job.

September 26 dawned cloudy and chilly.

Not far to the east in South Bend, Harry Leslie, the former governor who had approved Dillinger's transfer to Michigan City to play ball, was telling friends at breakfast that the morale of Indiana prisoners was being shattered by the recent dismissal of veteran guards. "It takes years to become a good prison guard capable of dealing with convicts under all circumstances." He regretted that old guards had been fired because of politics and "replaced with men without qualifications whatsoever," adding, "If this policy is pursued, there's going to be trouble, a big prison break or rioting."

At the prison there seemed little to justify Leslie's fears as the morning passed uneventfully. At 1:00 P.M. long files of gray-clad men shuffled from the cold, forbidding cell blocks and started back to their jobs in the drizzling rain. It was almost 2:00 P.M. when nine inmates from two different shops asked for hospital passes. A few moments later all nine met in the foyer of the main shirt factory, then filed downstairs to a sub-basement storage room.

Here they were joined by a tenth man, the storeroom keeper, Walter Dietrich. An extra man had been added to the list only a few minutes previously—Jim "Oklahoma Jack" Clark, Dietrich's "rap-buddy," the other survivor of Baron Lamm's gang.

Dietrich dug out a brown shoe box, opened it, and handed .45 automatics to Makley, Pierpont, and Hamilton. After the others were given fake guns, recently made, Dietrich climbed the stairs to the second floor, located G. H. Stevens, superintendent of the Gordon Shirt Company, and told him there were a couple of men downstairs who wanted to buy shirts. Stevens, assuming prison officials were the customers, went down to the storeroom without hesitation.

When he stepped inside he heard a voice say, "Turn around, Stevens, we're going home and you're going to lead us out." He turned to see Hamilton aiming a pistol at him. "There won't be any rough stuff if you just come along and mind your own business."

Dietrich had moved on out into the yard in search of Day Captain Albert Evans, a huge man, six feet three and weighing almost three hundred pounds, who had been nicknamed "Big Bertha" and was disliked almost as much as Claudy. Dietrich told Evans the foreman wanted him and Big Bertha lumbered unsuspectingly after the messenger.

As he stepped into the storeroom Pierpont stuck a pistol in his stomach and told him, "We're going home and you're going to do what we tell you. If you try anything," he continued, accenting his words with gun jabs into the captain's belly, "you're dead where you stand. Get it, you big, brave man?"

One of the convicts who felt he had been cruelly punished by Evans wanted to kill him on the spot but Makley said persuasively, "We need 'em. They're going to take us out. Ain't you, fellows?"

The two hostages nodded. Just then a foreman entered. As he was being tied up, five convicts walked down to the storeroom on business and were locked in a heating tunnel.

A pile of shirts was handed to Stevens and he was told to lead the way. Right behind him, their guns hidden by shirts, were Hamilton, Dietrich, and Pierpont. The other convicts picked up a heavy piece of steel shafting, five feet long and four inches in diameter, for use as a battering ram if necessary. Bringing up the rear was Big Bertha. The plan was simple. They would walk across the yard to the Guards' Hall, the building connecting them with the outside world. Once inside, it was only a few steps to the main gate—and freedom.

A few guards standing atop the high gray stone walls saw the little procession heading briskly across the yard in the rain. Since Big Bertha, the day captain, was behind the group, no one was suspicious. One tower guard saw nothing. He was asleep.

"How'm I doing, Walter?" asked Evans. Dietrich, armed only with a fake gun, turned and said quietly, "I'm going to shoot you in the ass at the main gate anyway."

Hamilton beckoned to a friend walking toward them and patted his hip. The inmate, thinking Red wanted only to give him a drink, shook his head and continued toward the shirt factory.

Now they neared Guards' Hall. "No funny stuff," whispered Pierpont. Ranks were closed and guns held in the sides of the two hostages. As Guard Frank Swanson came to the door with his key, one of the escapees stepped out of line and pointed a gun at him. The elderly Swanson, known through-out the cell houses as a man who never abused anyone, opened the gate and the group marched into Guards' Hall. An escapee serving life for murder shoved Swanson into a chair and said, "Sit down, Pop, and you won't get hurt."

By this time the group was approaching the main gate, a cage manned by two turnkeys, with barred doors at either end. The turnkey of the door leading to Guards' Hall saw the shop superintendent and Hamilton, arms loaded with shirts, and, used to such a sight, unsuspectingly unlocked the door. Hamilton kicked it wide open and stepped inside the cage, Pierpont on his heels, and the rest of the convicts rushed in. Ed Shouse, the race driver, hit the other turnkey over the head with a homemade blackjack, grabbed his key, and un-locked the second door, which led to the Administration Building. No one spoke a word as they crowded into the re-ception lobby.

At that moment Warden Kunkel and his secretary were in the suite of business offices just to the left of the lobby. The secretary heard the commotion and cried, "There's trouble!" One of the clerks shouted, "It's a break!" and told Kunkel to hide in a closet. But he said, "I'd rather be shot in the open than caught in a closet."

Two escapees were already scrambling over the counter that separated the chief clerk's office from the lobby. When a third jumped onto the counter, his gun went off, probably by accident, and hit a seventy-two-year-old clerk in the right side.

Howard Crosby, the new chief clerk, had ducked under his desk with a telephone. Quietly he asked operator for 99, the local police station, and though he could see the feet of an escapee only a yard or so away, then whispered, "There's trouble out here at the prison. Send policemen and guns!"

Hamilton had already burst into the next office and was pointing a gun at Kunkel's stomach but didn't realize it was the new official, since those inside prison walls rarely saw the Brass Nuts—the warden.

Pierpont, with another convict, was rounding up the

employees in the chief clerk's office and recognized Russell Blande, the former chief clerk who was staying on to break in Crosby. "We want all the money you've got and the guns," he said.

"I'm no longer chief clerk," explained Blande. "I don't have the combination."

The man who had it, Crosby, was still hiding under his desk.

"Let's get Mutch," said one of the convicts and Lawrence Mutch, Superintendent of Industries, was brought forward. "Where's the combination to the arsenal?" When Mutch said he didn't know, he was hit over the head.

Pierpont now ordered those in the main office to climb over the counter into the lobby. Hearing this, Crosby crawled from under his desk, tapped a startled escapee on the back and asked, "What do you want me to do, climb over too?"

Pierpont vaulted onto the counter. "You do the same," he told Blande's secretary, Clara Lamb.

Guessing they wanted to use her for a shield in the getaway—it was common knowledge she had a car in the parking lot—she said, "I can't."

"Oh, yes, you can." Pierpont waggled his gun.

"I can't and I won't go over that counter," she said determinedly. Pierpont stared at her, then headed toward the front door past the guards; they all had their hands raised stoically, with one exception—he was groveling on the floor, "bawling for mercy."

In the lobby some of the escapees were just staring straight up, as if hypnotized, at the skylight and a few were wandering aimlessly, dazed by freedom. Jenkins, overcome by a desire for revenge, had grabbed one of the turnkeys—he had prevented the mass break in 1930—and was marching him through the lobby. "Come on, buddy, we're going to kill you," he said, then called to Pierpont, "Give me a gun, Pete."

"We're out of here," said Pierpont. "Why kill anyone?"

Back in the prison yard a man was hurrying toward the open gate into Guards' Hall. It was the convict Hamilton had beckoned to—he had finally realized Red hadn't offered him a drink but freedom. Just as he reached the gate, it was slammed in his face. He turned and walked away as innocently as possible.

A moment later the inmates were quick-marched from the shops to their cells. They were puzzled until word was passed of the break, then cell doors rattled and the men cheered. They were in high spirits.

It was raining hard as the ten convicts streamed through the unlocked front door in two groups. Dietrich and three minor members of the gang had captured Charles Neal, a downstate sheriff who had just brought in a prisoner. Neal, a gun in his back, directed them to his car. Dietrich, the last to climb in, turned and thumbed his nose at a tower; then the car sped off down the Dunes Highway toward Chicago.

The other six, including Pierpont and his chief lieutenants, spilled out of the Administration Building; one fired several shots back at the prison either as a warning or as a gesture of defiance. They ran across the grass to the street and up to the Standard Oil gas station at the corner. A prisoner jumped on the running board of a car parked in front. Another accosted the manager with a gun and told him to hand over the car keys before his "damn brains" were blown out.

"Go ahead, buddy," said the manager and ran away with the keys.

The convicts fired twice, and missed. Commandeering another car they headed west a few miles before turning off onto a dirt road. At about 2:30 P.M. they hid in a farmhouse, where Pierpont told the owner and his terrified family, "When you see the prison men tell them that we are not going back."

Out in the barn two of his comrades were guarding the farmer's hired hand, who said that at dusk he had to bring the cows in from the field. The two guards went outside to watch him finish his chores.

The group with Sheriff Neal was now walking in the heavy rain. They had driven their car into a lake, appropriated another, allowed its driver to escape in the woods, and then wrecked it. As they trudged slowly down a muddy road, they had no idea local police were converging from several sides.

By 9:00 P.M. Matt Leach had personally joined the chase and, while he was at a gas station, heard a woman on radio station WIND tell of being questioned by two of the escapees looking for a garage. Her voice was interrupted by the sound of sirens and a fusillade of shots. An announcer described the gun battle so dramatically that many listeners, including Leach, thought it was the real thing.

Leach soon arrived at the scene of the "gun fight," and found instead a radio director and a group of actors. When they admitted the battle had merely been a dramatization with shots supplied by several co-operative officers, Leach stuttered out an order to arrest the director.

In Indianapolis Mary Kinder was reading in the three-room apartment on Daly Street she shared with her mother, stepfather, and sister Margaret. Since Dillinger had said the break wasn't scheduled until the next day at the earliest, she hadn't yet rented a hideout for the escapees.

It was almost midnight when Mary answered a knock at the front door and found Pierpont standing there in his prison uniform, grinning down at her. Mary gasped in consternation. "My God," she said, "you ain't supposed to do it for a while yet!"

After regaining her composure, she asked about her brother and Pierpont explained he was in the hospital. "He was too weak. He couldn't make it." Mary felt like crying. If it hadn't been for Earl, she never would have agreed to get mixed up in the escape.

While Pierpont was telling her that the others were waiting out front in a car, Margaret, as tiny as Mary, came forward and said, "Get them out of here. Take them to that fellow's you were out with tonight."

But Mary's mother said, "You're not going with them!" She was several inches shorter than Mary and was ordinarily unassertive and good-natured. For the first time in her life, she slapped her daughter.

Mary was more surprised than hurt. "Mother," she said, "the boys can't just stay out there in the street." She hurried down the steps with Pierpont and got into the car.

Ralph Saffell, the young man who'd dated Mary earlier that evening, lived in a small rented house on the west side of town. She knocked at his door and he invited her in, but stumbled back in alarm when six uniformed convicts followed her. After hiding their stolen car in the garage and pulling down all the blinds, the escapees relaxed for the first time in years and sat up all night, gossiping and telling stories of their experiences. Mary had known Pierpont since she was eleven, but the others were strangers. Three of them made good impressions on her: Red Hamilton, who seemed good-natured if shy; big Russell Clark with his jokes and easygoing manner; and particularly young Jenkins, who sang several songs and was full of life. The ingenious Makley, however, merely struck her as a rather dull, middle-aged man, and Shouse didn't impress her at all.

The men were in good spirits and the night passed quickly for all but the terrified Saffell. Mary felt sorry for him. He had known her only two weeks and now was host to six escaped convicts. In the morning she said she would go downtown and buy new clothes with the money Dillinger had given her. Pierpont told Saffell to drive, warning him not to try to tip off the police.

While Mary was buying six sets of clothing in different sizes at six different stores, Pearl Elliott, the blowzy madam from Kokomo, called at the Kinder home and asked Margaret if she knew George Washington. This was the gang's password and Margaret told her what had happened. Pearl said she had recently visited Dillinger in the Dayton jail. He had taken money from a secret compartment in his belt—the police had searched but not well enough—and asked her to give it to the boys. Pearl also brought a rather unusual request from Dillinger. Mary Longnaker had apparently fled town after his arrest, and he wanted the gang to locate a half-Indian girl, Evelyn "Billie" Frechette, and have her waiting for him when he was freed.

When the gang had learned the surprising news from Mary Kinder that Dillinger was in jail, there was no question, of course, that they would help him escape. Pierpont said that since Dillinger had kept his word, it was up to them to break him out as soon as possible. The others all agreed.

Soon after dark Harry Copeland, a parolee from Michigan City, who had been told by Dillinger to find a more permanent hideaway, arrived and said he'd located a house in Hamilton, Ohio. Pierpont was delighted, for this would provide a base of operations closer to Dillinger. Copeland said that like Mary he had been caught unprepared by the premature escape— and the Ohio house wouldn't be ready for several days but he had found them another temporary refuge in town.

2

That same day Governor McNutt ordered a probe to be held by the board of trustees amid an atmosphere of charges and countercharges. Some Republicans blamed the whole affair on the sixty-nine new guards but Wayne Coy, McNutt's secretary, declared there was every reason "to suspect that some of the old guards [Republicans who had been dismissed] may be implicated."

Warden Kunkel insisted that "no new guards were involved in the escape"; he was certain that structural defects, the antiquated method of letting inmates in and out of the prison, and the lack of guards were responsible. Former Governor Leslie, a Republican, disagreed, reminding everyone of his ominous prediction at breakfast just four hours before the break.

No matter who was right or wrong, it was generally agreed that more men were needed to catch the escapees, so three companies of National Guard troops began a ground hunt while all available planes from McCool Field made a search from the air.

In Michigan City itself, the town Common Council

called a special meeting and drew up a resolution asking
Governor McNutt to send militia to protect the townspeople.
The resolution—which would have been a slap in the face to
Kunkel, a local man—was voted down as "too dangerous" for
passage.

Perhaps the most frustrated man in Indiana was Matt
Leach, who had just been forced to free the broadcaster
from WIND since there was no law under which he could
legally hold him. Moreover when Leach told reporters that
the Dayton police "prevented us from averting the break," because of their reluctance to surrender letters found on Dillinger, Inspector Yendes had hotly denied he'd kept any
such letters from the Indiana State Police. This gave Leach's
already large circle of critics in Indianapolis the opportunity
of charging that because of the quarrel between the two
lawmen, Dillinger had just been sent to the county jail in
Lima, Ohio, and not returned to Indiana for trial. Actually
Dillinger had confessed to the Bluffton bank robbery and refused extradition, knowing it would be easier for Pierpont
to break him out of an Ohio jail than one selected by Matt
Leach.

Three days after the escape, McNutt ordered Leach to
conduct a separate inquiry. When the Governor was asked
whether the drastic change of guards following the Democratic victory had contributed to the break, he said good-
naturedly, "If you want to fall for a Republican story, that's
your business."

"Why are you appointing a special committee to investigate the case, since the prison board is now doing that?"

McNutt, losing some of his amiability, replied, "For the
protection of the board of prison trustees as well as myself."

Warden Kunkel, disturbed because of a report that Claudy
had told the press that he, Claudy, had prior knowledge of
the break, said, "If I had known of that information, I would
have had the place barricaded." Claudy promptly denied
ever making such a statement but several reporters swore
they had heard him.

Tempers were not improved when a radio and a forty-foot rope ladder were found in the prison shirt factory.

The four convicts with Sheriff Neal had been hiding in a cornfield a few miles north of McCool Field and hadn't eaten for three days. Jim Clark, the former associate of Baron Lamm who had decided to escape only five minutes before the break, had stomach ulcers and was in agony. He told the others he'd stay with the sheriff while they went ahead.

Clark and the sheriff walked into the next town, ate at the latter's expense, then rode a trolley car to Gary. Here Neal was allowed to get off, but Clark warned him he'd be killed if he talked. Dazed from exposure, the intimidated sheriff phoned his wife that he was taking the next bus home but, since Leach had ordered all calls to Neal's home monitored, the sheriff was picked up as he was boarding the bus. Brought before Leach, he said he'd been thrown out of the convicts' car and had spent hours trying to hitchhike.

Clark, arrested a few minutes after stepping off the trolley car in Hammond, was despondent at the thought of returning to Michigan City and said, "I might just as well be dead now because I won't last in that hole." When asked why he tried to escape he would only reply, "I just wanted to be free a few years so I could get proper medical attention."

That night Pierpont and his five companions were informed that their hideout in Hamilton was at last ready. As a precaution, they abandoned their car near Indianapolis and stole another, but this attempt to hide their trail only succeeded in making it more obvious. Leach learned of the theft, and set up such an effective blockade that the escaped men were almost caught by a state policeman in a borrowed armored car. Though they escaped, a door of their auto flew open during a frantic U-turn and young Jenkins fell out.

They sped on, unable to wait, and after stealing another car, eventually reached their Ohio hideout. But nothing was going right for Jenkins. He managed to kidnap a youth driving home from a late date but the next day the captive drove off while Jenkins was peering into the tank to see if there was enough gas.

Later that evening, when Jenkins walked into the hamlet of Beanblossom, Indiana, he was spotted by three farmers with shotguns who were part of the local posse. As they approached him, Jenkins drew his gun, hesitated, then ran up an alley. The farmers fired and the convict fell, badly wounded. A few hours later he died in a doctor's office, his dream of going to South America with John Dillinger ended.

In Hamilton, some 125 miles south of Dillinger's new jail in Lima, Pierpont reluctantly decided that they couldn't help him escape without more money to cover expenses and possible emergencies. Since they had only a few guns, Makley suggested they rob the bank in his little home town, St. Marys, only a few miles below Lima. He said it was a sweet pea—an easy place to rob.

As she had promised, Mary Kinder now rejoined the gang. Pierpont was already in love with her and since, like Dillinger, he had spent too many years in prison to be leisurely in courtship, he asked her without preamble to travel permanently with him. She had known Pierpont many years and liked him; moreover, because of her brothers, she understood what he had gone through in prison—so under the circumstances she consented. It was a relationship similar in some ways to that between Dillinger and Mary Longnaker.

On the morning of October 3, as the gang began loading into two cars at Hamilton for the St. Marys robbery, Harry Copeland claimed he was too sick to go along and Pierpont asked Mary if she would like to drive the second car for an equal share.

She consented. They then drove north to the outskirts of St. Marys, where they stopped near a cornfield. The men piled into one car, leaving Mary at the wheel of another. Time passed slowly as she watched a farmer working in the field.

In town Chief of Police Gilbert Gerstner was checking out a mysterious phone call that Makley, an old schoolmate, was in St. Marys. Gerstner and his two patrolmen, armed with shotguns, made a check of Makley's old haunts, then started back to the station.

At that moment, 2:40 P.M., Makley was entering the bank with Pierpont and Clark while Hamilton and Shouse waited nearby. Outside a poolroom across the street a crowd pressed around a radio that was broadcasting the opening game of the World Series between the Washington Senators and Bill Terry's New York Giants.

Because of their hasty preparations the robbers had no idea the bank had been legally closed by the Treasury Department during the Bank Holiday and would not reopen for several weeks. It was presently engaged solely in the goodwill service of making change for local merchants and it was sheer luck that a fairly large sum of money had just arrived from the mint for use when the bank reopened.

Makley stayed near the door as Pierpont walked up to the teller's window and opened a road map. As the teller started to ask him what he wanted, Pierpont lowered the map to reveal a revolver.

A few minutes later the cashier, serving as federal conservator since the Bank Holiday, walked in the front door. Makley, realizing it was an old school friend, gruffly told him to get to the rear. The cashier, who didn't recognize Makley, did as he was told. After the robbers fled with two sacks of money, the bank employees waited a few minutes, then turned on the alarm; but Chief Gerstner, only a block away, didn't hear it, nor did the large group across the street still gathered around the poolroom radio. They were too absorbed by Carl Hubbell's pitching performance.

By this time Pierpont and Makley had reached Mary Kinder's car and headed south while the others went north. Several hours later Pierpont, who had put Mary in back with the money and guns and taken the wheel, got stuck in a muddy ditch. The men pushed but couldn't extricate the car. Finally a farm woman in an old Ford came by and offered to pull them out with a rope.

Pierpont told Mary to come up front and steer while he

and Makley pushed but she said, "I ain't gonna get out. You know I got a sore foot." Pierpont, puzzled, repeated his request but she insisted stubbornly, "Well, I can't get out and I'm not getting out."

After they were out of the ditch and Pierpont had paid the woman $2, Mary said, "How in hell was I going to get out with all these guns you throwed in the back seat and the money back here?"

When they counted the money in Hamilton they were surprised to find almost $11,000, more than double the amount they thought a bank of that size would have. But the money itself presented a problem—it was too new to spend.

Mary baked the bills in the oven, sprinkled them with water, and rebaked them. They still looked new. She scorched each one with a hot iron, repeated the baking process, and after several days the bills finally looked worn enough to pass.

Though Dillinger had been arrogant with the Dayton police, he showed a different face when he wrote his father from the county jail in Lima.

Dear Dad:

Hope this letter finds you well and not worrying too much about me. Maybe I'll learn someday, Dad that you can't win in this game. I know I have been a big disappointment to you but I guess I did too much time for where I went in a carefree boy I came out bitter toward everything in general. Of course, Dad most of the blame lies with me for my environment was of the best but if I had gotten off more leniently when I made my first mistake this would never have happened. How is Doris and Francis?

I preferred to stand trial here in Lima because there isn't so much prejudice against me here and I am sure I will get a square deal here. Dad, don't believe all that the newspapers say about me for I am not guilty of half the things I'm charged with and I've never hurt anyone. Well,

Dad I guess this is all for this time just wanted you to know
I am well and treated fine.

From Johnnie

This solicitous letter was a perfect example of their new
relationship. Dillinger had often lied to his father but never
before to assuage his worries. The only completely true part of
the letter was the last sentence, his relations with Sheriff Sarber having been pleasant from the first. Sarber and his wife
were considerate—as they were with the other dozen prisoners—and the food was good. In spite of this, time dragged for
Dillinger. He knew Pierpont would eventually free him but
he wished that moment was at hand.

Two days after the St. Marys robbery, Ralph Saffell, the
unwilling young host of the Pierpont gang, was picked up at a
skid row mission in Indianapolis. Mary Kinder had disappeared and he was sure she'd been killed by the gang. Even
though he had been warned by Pierpont not to say anything
and promised $1,000 for his silence, he finally revealed all the
details of the gang's stay in his cottage to Matt Leach.
Leach raided Mary's home but found only her younger
sister, Margaret. Already known as Silent Margaret for her refusal to talk when her husband was convicted for bank robbery, the petite girl answered Leach's questions with nonsensi-
cal pleasantries, so infuriating him that his stuttering words
became almost incomprehensible.

On October 10 Pierpont brought Dillinger's new girl
friend to Ohio. Billie Frechette, in her middle twenties, was
born on an Indian reservation in Wisconsin and was married
to George "Sparks" Frechette, presently serving a fifteen-year
term in Leavenworth for bank robbery. She had raven-black
hair cut in a long bob and usually wore a small, snug-fitting hat
and a Persian lamb coat. Her heavy, dark face was striking but
under the thick make-up were numerous smallpox scars.
It was decided that it was too dangerous to bring Dillin-

ger back to Hamilton, so Pierpont found an apartment in nearby Cincinnati, where he installed the two girls. The following day the men, who had promised Mary there would be no "killing or rough stuff," left for Lima, arriving at dusk. As yet they had no plan and walked past the county jail several times. Impatient as he was to free Dillinger, Pierpont knew they should have more information before making the raid and decided that perhaps they could get Mary inside on some pretext to learn what problems they would have to face. But it was too late in the day to make the necessary arrangements and so they drove twenty miles to the northeast to spend the night at the Pierpont farm in Leipsic.

The next afternoon, October 12, they returned to Lima. It was Columbus Day. About 5:30 P.M. Pierpont and Clark approached Chester Cable, a local attorney, in a cigar store on West High Street and asked if he was a lawyer. The three went up to Cable's office, where Clark proposed that the lawyer get Dillinger's "sister" into the jail. Without realizing it, Cable upset the whole plan by saying he would put the proposition to Sheriff Sarber the next day and let him decide.

Pierpont now knew there was only one thing to do—free Dillinger at once. After he and Clark walked to the big courthouse and told the others what had happened, Makley ordered Shouse, who showed signs of strain, to wait outside the jail as lookout. Copeland would guard the two cars and Hamilton would stand near the Ohio Theater, a few hundred feet away.

Behind the courthouse and connected to it by a passageway was a brick house, the residence of Sheriff Sarber. It was also the county jail. At 6:20 P.M. Pierpont, Makley, and Clark —all armed with pistols—approached it.

The Sarbers had just finished supper—pork chops and mashed potatoes—and were relaxing in the office. Jess Sarber was a heavy, balding, friendly man of forty-seven. Self-educated and well respected, he had entered the race for sheriff when his used-car business was hit by the Depression. He sat down behind his desk with part of that evening's *Lima News*. Across the desk his wife Lucy was working a crossword puzzle. On a davenport sat Deputy Sheriff Wilbur Sharp, his gun and cartridge belt lying on the desk. The sheriff's gun was in the desk drawer.

To Sarber's left was the barred doorway to the cells. The prisoners, some twelve or thirteen, had finished dinner and were sitting around a large table in the day room. Dillinger and four others were playing pinochle.

When the front door opened and Pierpont, Makley, and Clark entered the office, Sarber looked up and asked what they wanted. Pierpont approached the desk. "We're officers from Michigan City," he said, "and want to see John Dillinger."

Mrs. Sarber, glancing up from her puzzle, saw a tall, slender, good-looking young man with piercing light blue eyes.

"Let me see your credentials," said Sarber.

Pierpont calmly pulled out a gun. "Here's our credentials."

"Oh, you can't do that," said Sarber, reaching for the gun in the desk drawer.

Pierpont panicked and impulsively fired twice. One bullet went into Sarber's left side, through the abdomen and into his thigh. He fell to the floor.

"Give us the keys to the cells," said Pierpont but Sarber's answer was to try to rise. Makley stepped forward and hit him over the head with the butt of his gun, accidentally discharging a wild shot. Sarber collapsed, moaning.

"Give us the keys!" Pierpont raised his gun.

"Don't kill him," said Clark, who held a gun on the deputy. Pierpont struck the sheriff another hard blow on the head.

"Don't hurt him any more," begged the horrified Mrs. Sarber and said she would get the keys. While her back was turned, Clark's gun inadvertently went off, nicking one of his own fingers. Now all three men—edgy after so many years in prison—had handled their guns like amateurs.

In the next room, at the sound of the first shots, one of the card players said, "John, your gang is after you." Dillinger made no reply, put one hand on the table, and leaped over it to get his coat and hat.

Pierpont stood in the cell block doorway, two guns in his right hand, one in his left. After firing once into the day room, he shouted at a curious inmate, "Get back, you son of a bitch. We want John. The rest of you can get out when I'm gone."

An elderly couple, Mr. and Mrs. Fay Carter, were at the corner of North and Main on their way to the Moose Temple for dinner when they heard the first two shots. Carter, a friend of Sarber's, started down North Street to investigate.

Shouse, stationed outside because he was supposed to be jittery, calmly walked up to the Carters and said, "Did you hear that noise?" He told them to wait while he went up the steps of the sheriff's house to see what had happened. Shouse walked up to the door of the office, saw Sarber lying on the floor and returned to the Carters. With a smile, he told them there was nothing to worry about: people were moving cabinets inside and several drawers had fallen out.

There was another shot inside. "Oh, my goodness!" said Mrs. Carter.

"Just another drawer," said Shouse with a reassuring grin.

"It must be a Moose," joked Mrs. Carter. Shouse walked with the couple back to the corner, impressing them with his good manners.

After the final shot into the cell block Dillinger came forward and was handed one of Pierpont's three guns. When Dillinger saw Sarber he knelt down to examine the man who had been so considerate to him. Avoiding Mrs. Sarber's eyes, he got up and walked out the door with Clark.

Sarber, who was lying in a pool of blood, raised his head, his face contorted with pain. "Oh, men, why did you do this to me?" He looked at his wife. "Mother, I believe I'm going to have to leave you."

Pierpont told Makley to put Mrs. Sarber in the jail and when she begged them to put Sarber in with her, Makley said, "Why not?" But Pierpont, grabbing her by the arm, forced her into the jail with Sharp, then slammed shut both gates and hurried outside, where he got into a car with Dillinger and Clark.

A few minutes later Deputy Sheriff Don Sarber, the sheriff's son, a recent college graduate, came into the room. His father was on the floor and several people were standing around helplessly. After calling the ambulance, he knelt by his father.

"Turn me over on my side. My . . . back hurts."

The sheriff was taken to Memorial Hospital while Don Sarber helped free his mother and Sharp with acetylene torches. Then young Sarber hurried to the hospital. He asked his dying father if Harry Copeland was one of the assailants. "I don't know," the sheriff said, "they were all big fellows." At 8:05 P.M., little more than an hour and a half after the shooting, Jess Sarber died.

3

That night police cars, sirens screeching, raced up and down the streets of Lima searching for the killers. The American Legion called a special meeting and offered their services. Impromptu, unauthorized posses roamed the city. A member of one of these groups had several drinks, then entered a gas station and, when he refused to leave, was shot in the leg by a lawman. City police, carrying machine guns in the hopes of getting a chance to use them on the killers, fortunately weren't called on to face the desperadoes—the ammunition in the police guns was so old it wouldn't have fired.

Officers from six counties blocked the main roads all over northwestern Ohio. A posse swooped down on the lonely Pierpont farm near Leipsic and found a new eight-cylinder car, full of gas but without license plates, in a barn. In the house the lawmen questioned the indignant Lena Pierpont, her meek husband, and their son, Fred, and his wife. Fred, who claimed Harry had given him the car as a present, was arrested.

It was the logical place to look but it was the wrong direction. The new Cincinnati hideout was some 140 miles south of Lima. Late that night Billie Frechette and Mary Kinder were anxiously waiting there, when the apartment door was pushed open and Dillinger, grinning broadly, came in. He hugged Billie and laughed happily as Pierpont and Clark entered.

Mary said, "It's real nice with Johnnie home and all of us sitting here."

But Pierpont's face was drawn. "We had to beat up the sheriff to get Johnnie out," he said tightly.

Clark didn't believe they had hurt Sarber too badly, but Pierpont said he thought they'd killed him and then turned to Mary and asked if she still wanted to stay with him.

She shrugged her shoulders. "I can't go now. I know too much." Pierpont said they all trusted her and she could go if she wanted. "No," she said, "it wouldn't be right me leaving you boys just because you're in trouble."

Two days after the escape the search had become so intensified in Ohio that the gang decided to split in two groups and meet in Chicago. But that night Dillinger and those in his car made a slight detour and raided a police station in the Indiana town of Auburn, stealing a submachine gun, two steel vests, over a thousand rounds of ammunition, three rifles, and six pistols.

Even more firepower was needed, however, to rob a good-sized bank in the Lamm style and Dillinger said he knew where they could get two more machine guns; a month previously he and Homer Van Meter had heard there was a large arsenal at the Peru, Indiana, police station and had gone to see for themselves, posing as tourists.

At about 10:00 P.M., October 20, three lawmen were sitting in the police station located on the ground floor of Peru's brick City Hall. It was a dull evening. Ambrose Clark, a merchant policeman, was talking to the desk sergeant and a patrolman when Pierpont, holding a machine gun, entered, closely followed by Dillinger with a pistol.

While Pierpont guarded the lawmen, Dillinger broke open the locked glass case and took out a machine gun, several bulletproof vests, and two sawed-off shotguns. After putting them in a blanket, he carried them outside to a parked car, then went back inside, a few minutes later reappearing with a second heavy load.

"My God," said Mary Kinder, one of the four waiting in the car, "what are you going to start—a young army?"

Four days later the announcement that Dillinger's fingerprints had been found in the Peru station rekindled the political battle over the Michigan City escape. When Claudy claimed the guns used by the convicts had been dropped by plane, Leach ridiculed this unlikely theory, claiming the deputy warden knew that they had been smuggled inside the walls in a box of thread. "Claudy was boss there," Leach told reporters. "Where was he when the break was made? He's trying to alibi and make it appear that guns couldn't have been smuggled into the prison. Why, for years it would have been possible to smuggle an elephant into the prison." But those investigating the matter concluded that a shortage of trained personnel and the faulty structure of the prison were most responsible for the escape. Even so "I, God" Claudy and Big Bertha Evans were fired and Lorenz Schmuhl, the night captain, was given the important job of deputy warden.

Not long after this Schmuhl stumbled on what could have been one of the most puzzling aspects of the case. He heard a rumor there was "something" in an old safe in the warden's office. Warden Kunkel didn't have the combination and authorized Schmuhl to get it from his predecessor. When the safe was finally opened, Kunkel and Schmuhl found inside an exact plan of the mass break. This information was never revealed to the public.

Even though almost a month had passed since the prison break, Dillinger's escape from Lima and the two brazen raids on Indiana police stations had aggravated the original public outrage. Several prominent officials stated that the escapees had declared "open warfare" on the law, with the Marion County sheriff even predicting that the Pierpont gang would try to break into the reformatory and prison to enlist an army of desperadoes. In response to public demands the Attorney General put 530 National Guardsmen at the disposal of the state police, while the American Legion and other organizations throughout Indiana formed volunteer posses.

Matt Leach thought such melodramatic measures were of little use in dealing with criminals like Pierpont. He was pondering a far different approach—to destroy the gang from within. Pierpont was an inordinately proud man and if Dillinger were publicly named the gang's leader, anything might happen. A battle for leadership had disrupted more than one gang.

Leach revealed his plan to the local reporters, requesting their help. Most of them, unlike a number of officials, admired him for his bluntness and frankness. He had treated them fairly, even giving them items unfavorable to himself—and they agreed to co-operate.

Leach thanked the newsmen but told them not to expect quick results, adding almost pessimistically, "After a lot of people have been killed and banks robbed, we'll wind it up, and Pierpont will get the works."

CHAPTER 8

The Psychological
Approach

1

EVEN IF LEACH HAD RESERVATIONS ABOUT HIS OWN PLAN, HE could never have predicted what actually happened. When the first newspaper stories naming Dillinger as leader of the gang appeared, Pierpont paid no attention to them. He knew they were false and he was too grateful to Dillinger to be jealous. Dillinger, however, read and reread every story and even saved the clippings; but instead of becoming boastful, his manner and dress grew more conservative.

The gang lived quietly in expensive Chicago apartments, the men drinking only beer and little of that. According to Pierpont's code, a crime not only had to be committed without benefit of drink or drugs but prepared in sobriety. Only the women drank hard liquor, but Billie Frechette had to steal from Mary Kinder because Dillinger refused to buy her whiskey—she was an Indian.

Actually there was no struggle for leadership. While Mary was doing the housework or preparing a meal, the men would sit around the living room or at the dining-room table discussing future plans much like any group of respectable businessmen. Usually Pierpont assembled their various ideas.

Sometimes it would be Makley. But everyone had a chance to voice an opinion, no one overriding a majority.

The day after the raid on the Peru police station, they discussed final plans for their first major robbery: a Greencastle, Indiana, bank. Its interior had been sketched and escape routes laid out by Pierpont, who had once worked in a gravel yard not far away and knew all the back roads. When Makley learned the local merchants had done a brisk weekend business with home-coming alumni of De Pauw University, he suggested the bank should be robbed the next day, Monday, October 23.

At 2:45 P.M. on Monday a large Studebaker parked on the slight hill next to Greencastle's Central National Bank. Dillinger and three others got out and walked to the bank. It was chilly and all wore overcoats. Hamilton stayed outside the door as the tiger—lookout; the other three walked confidently in, knowing that the jug hack—bank guard—had just gone into the basement to stoke the fire. Pierpont headed for one of the cages, ostensibly to change a $20 bill. Then Dillinger pulled out his gun and, still unable to resist the impulse to show off, leaped over a chest-high counter and walked into the teller's cage.

While the bandits inside were systematically cleaning everything out of the vaults and cages, Hamilton was surprised to see an elderly, foreign-born woman calmly walk out of the bank. He told her to get back in until the robbery was over but she had no idea what he was talking about and replied, "I go to Penney's and you go to hell." Ignoring his gun, she stolidly headed up the street.

Five minutes later the robbers walked out of the bank with a reported $74,782.09 in cash and negotiable bonds. Not a shot had been fired.

About the same time a phone began ringing in the International News Service office in Indianapolis. The bureau chief, Jack Cejnar, answered.

"This is King," said a voice. "Central National Bank at Greencastle was just held up."

Cejnar immediately called the bank but the line was busy.

He got a store nearby and a little later an eyewitness was dictating the story of the holdup. Once more INS had scooped the other services on an Indiana bank robbery and once more newsmen wondered how Cejnar had done it. Several years previously he had learned that American Surety carried 98 percent of Indiana's bank robbery insurance. In the small print of a policy he discovered that the insured bank had to flash the news of a holdup to the company in Indianapolis even before it called the local police or sheriff so American Surety could start its own investigation at once. He then persuaded the claim adjuster, a Mr. King, to swap tips on robberies for an almost immediate copy of a professionally prepared news report of the crime.

Within two weeks of Dillinger's release from Lima two police stations had been boldly raided and a bank robbed. The new gang was almost living up to the image created by an hysterical public. Fearing that Dillinger might try to free some of his prisoners, the sheriff of Marion County ordered a gun cage installed in his jail. When the Indiana Commissioner of Public Safety once more requested an increase in his tiny state police force, Governor McNutt promised him the men as soon as enough money could be raised.

The gang was already back in Chicago. Dillinger, always gregarious, told Mary Kinder he was sure she and Billie would get along and suggested the four share a flat. The following morning the two couples drove up to 4310 Clarendon. A bellboy took most of their bags but Pierpont and Dillinger each carried a suitcase containing weapons and ammunition. The manager was delighted to have people who paid in advance.

From the first Mary and Pierpont had little regard for Billie. She spent an hour making up while Mary, who hadn't even had time to comb her hair, prepared breakfast for everyone. Pierpont finally became annoyed and told Mary not to wait on anyone but him. The next morning when Mary didn't lay out breakfast for Dillinger he asked why.

"There's your girl friend," said Mary. Billie protested she knew nothing about cooking.

"Start learning," said Dillinger.

The gang did not hide in their apartments but moved freely around Chicago, correctly surmising that their neighbors wouldn't get suspicious if they acted like ordinary well-to-do citizens. Dillinger fitted into this way of life—almost. Unlike the others he had a wide streak of bravado. Instead of avoiding police, he would seek them out, ask questions, gossip, take their photographs. It pleased him to pose as a friendly out-of-town businessman looking for advice.

In other ways he was conforming to the gang's standards of behavior. When Pierpont and Makley joked about the jump he had made over the railing in Greencastle, he decided never to leap again. He wanted to be considered a professional in every sense.

Now he was forced to find other outlets for his acts of exhibitionism. A week after the Greencastle robbery he telephoned Leach and said, "This is John Dillinger. How are you, you stuttering bastard?"

One evening the gang visited a night club where they met "Terrible Tommy" Touhy, a friend from Michigan City who had been paroled several years previously. The men reminisced about old times at the prison and joked about the firing of their enemies—Big Bertha and "I, God" Claudy.

Touhy told them the law was trying to frame his brother, Roger, for the kidnaping of two men: Jake "The Barber" Factor and William Hamm. His brother, insisted Touhy, was innocent of both charges.

Roger Touhy was a small, boyish-looking man with a shock of dark wavy hair, the son of a policeman. One of six children, he left school after the eighth grade to become a telegrapher, an oil scout, and a union organizer. He enlisted in the Navy during the World War and then, like so many others, drifted into bootlegging. He bought half a dozen tank trucks, painted them to pass for Texas Oil vehicles, and hauled bulk beer of his own manufacture. Touhy's beer was so superior in quality to the Capone brew that his weekly sales rose to

1,000 barrels at $55 each to about two hundred roadhouses, night clubs, and saloons west and northwest of the city. Capone was not at all pleased with such competition and made several attempts to frighten off the young Irishman. When Touhy refused to back off, Capone offered him a large sum to let the Mafia organization operate gambling dens and houses of prostitution in the northwest suburbs. Again Touhy refused and the battle lines between the two gangs were drawn. Since the Capone gang was much larger, the outcome seemed obvious, but in 1931 Chicago elected a new mayor, Anton Cermak, who was determined to wipe out the Mafia. The word was passed down to certain police officers to co-operate with Touhy, by far the lesser of two evils. (Later Touhy claimed that Cermak had personally urged him to wage war in earnest on Capone. When Touhy said he didn't have the strength, Cermak supposedly replied, "You can have the entire police department.")

Though Capone was soon convicted for income tax evasion and sent to Atlanta prison, his mob remained intact. There hadn't been a conviction of an important member in months. The new leaders, realizing that the rival gang was becoming a threat to their crime empire, sent out word that Roger Touhy must somehow be eliminated—if not by force, by frame.

This was the state of Chicago crime and politics when local papers headlined the kidnaping of Factor's nineteen-year-old son. In a few days the youth was back home, unharmed, without a cent of ransom having been paid. It was a curious affair, complicated by the fact that Factor was currently wanted in England for a $7,000,000 swindle.

A few weeks later—eight days after Dillinger and Shaw tried to rob the thread mill—Factor's car was forced to the curb by another. Gunmen allowed his two companions to go free but took Factor. At first some officials thought the abductors might be the College Kidnapers, so-called because their leader, Theodore "Handsome Jack" Klutas, and several of his lieutenants were college graduates. But Great Britain charged it was merely a hoax planned by Factor himself to avoid extradition. Captain Dan Gilbert, a former union official and presently chief investigator for the Cook County prosecutor, told reporters he still believed it was a legitimate kidnaping and suspicion turned to Roger Touhy. He was questioned but freed since Gilbert as yet had no evidence.

Twelve days after Factor's mysterious disappearance, he reappeared on a Chicago street and within minutes was excitedly telling Policeman Bernard Gerard that he had been pushed out of his kidnaper's car. A little later Factor revealed that his wife, without consulting the police, had drawn $70,000 from their bank and, after recording less than 10 percent of the bills, given the money to a friend who had paid off the kidnapers on some lonely road.

By this time talk of Touhy's implication in the affair had died down and he went to northern Wisconsin on a short fishing trip with a friend, Eddie McFadden, an elderly white-haired business agent of the Teamsters Union. They were accompanied by two bodyguards—tall, unsmiling Gus Schafer and Willie Sharkey, short, potbellied, good-natured, and not very bright. On the way home Touhy's car skidded in a fog and knocked over a telephone pole in Elkhorn, Wisconsin. While Touhy was paying $22.50 for the pole, an officer searched the car and found the bodyguards' guns. All four men were jailed.

Before dawn Captain Gilbert and Melvin Purvis, Special Agent in Charge of the Chicago FBI office, accompanied by a corps of newspapermen and photographers, were in Elkhorn. Purvis said there was now evidence that Touhy had not only kidnaped Factor but William Hamm as well.

"What do you mean by ham, Mr. Purvis—a ham sandwich?" joked Touhy. "Or did I kidnap a ham steak?" He told Purvis he hadn't been in Minnesota in two years and that he had an alibi for June 15, the day of Hamm's kidnaping. He also swore he hadn't killed Cock Robin.

Touhy and his companions were taken to Chicago. After a line-up at the police station, the chief of detectives said, "You men are clean so far as we're concerned. Nobody fingered you." Factor, who had been at the line-up, told newsmen

he couldn't have seen any of the kidnapers since he was blindfolded during his capture.

Nevertheless, the four were returned to Elkhorn and
charged with kidnaping Hamm. Since the brewer had been
taken across a state line, it was a federal offense and they
were liable to life sentences under the new Lindbergh law.
"We have an ironclad case," Purvis told newsmen.

The suspects were taken to the county jail in Milwaukee, where they were kept incommunicado, Touhy later
claiming he was questioned night and day, not allowed to
sleep more than half an hour, and beaten. During this time,
he charged, he lost twenty-five pounds, had three vertebrae
in his upper spine fractured and seven teeth knocked out.

On August 12 the four suspects were indicted for the
Hamm kidnaping by a federal grand jury in St. Paul. Ironically, the actual kidnapers, the Barker gang, were also in
St. Paul and, while Touhy was waiting to be tried, robbed
Swift Company messengers of a $30,000 payroll on the steps
of the South St. Paul Post Office. After shooting down a policeman, they escaped to Chicago.

Touhy's prosecutor was Joseph Keenan, the recent victor
in the Urschel trial in Oklahoma City. There, in an unprec-
edented decision that did much to discourage professional
kidnapers, he had not only got life sentences for Bates, Bailey, the Shannons, and the Kellys but severe sentences for the
money changers, Bates's lawyer, and a number of harborers.
It was evident the Department of Justice had declared a war
to the finish on kidnaping. They even brought Factor to
Chicago "to aid the government" in its prosecution of the
four defendants. Though he wasn't allowed to testify, Factor,
who had previously said he couldn't identify his own kidnapers, now told reporters there was no doubt that Touhy and
his men had held him. "I couldn't kill a fly," he said. "But I
could take that guy's [Touhy's] throat and twist it till the
blood came out! And I could drink the blood too—the way
they tortured me."

Keenan made the most of a witness who swore he saw

three of the defendants kidnap Hamm in front of the brewery
and another who testified he saw Touhy in a car near the field
where Hamm was released. On the stand Hamm, of course,
could not identify the prisoners and was publicly criticized for
his refusal to co-operate with the forces of law.

2

In Indianapolis Leach was not at all annoyed by the taunting telephone calls he was getting in increasing numbers from
Dillinger. He felt they were a sign of weakness and in these
brief conversations he would try to draw out his adversary
and trick him into revealing something either by a disparaging
remark or a word of praise.

Amateur psychology was by no means the most important
weapon in Leach's campaign against the gang. By now,
through the co-operation of a private investigator for the
American Surety Company, he had planted a stool pigeon
in Chicago. The informer was a good-looking not very talented criminal named Art who hung around the fringes of the
underworld. He had known Dillinger in prison and recently
had run a few errands for him in Indianapolis. With Art in
Chicago were several of Leach's men, overseeing the operation.

Another stoolie, "Whitey," was also hanging around the
Dillinger gang. Whitey, a dissipated-looking barker at a side
show called The Snake Pit, worked for Lieutenant John Howe,
the head of Chicago's so-called Scotland Yard Squad—an un-
dercover group of about forty crime hunters.

Howe was a big man with a raspy voice, incorruptible,
fearless, and original in his methods. Early in November he
told Whitey he was tired of housing him at the LaSalle Hotel
without any results and when he threatened to throw the
informer back in The Snake Pit, Whitey promised to bring
Dillinger and Pierpont to a parking lot at 220 North State
Street that very night.

An old friend of Howe's, an Indiana police officer, happened to be in town and asked to go along. The two men waited on the corner of Lake and State Streets. At last they saw Whitey walking toward the lot with only one man—Dillinger. Howe grasped his gun. If Dillinger made the slightest move to escape, he would shoot to kill.

Whitey and Dillinger approached but as Howe started to make his move, the Indiana officer convinced him to wait until they could also get Pierpont.

A few days later Whitey told Howe that Dillinger had a definite appointment at a doctor's office. "For Christ's sake, Loot," he said nervously, "take him this time." He was afraid Dillinger was getting suspicious. Leach's men, already working closely with Howe, got a confirmation of this rendezvous from their own informant, Art, and both groups of lawmen agreed it was time to strike, even if Pierpont wasn't present.

The ranking member of Leach's three-man squad, a lieutenant, was put in charge of the combined operation and a final conference was held in the afternoon of November 15 at the Morrison Hotel. Dillinger, according to both informants, would drive a Terraplane with Illinois plates 1-269-037 to the Irving Park Boulevard office of a skin specialist named Dr. Charles Eye at 7:00 that night. When Dillinger walked out of the building after his appointment, Leach's lieutenant would simply kill him with a shotgun—as if it were a gang murder.

At 4:00 P.M. the lieutenant changed his mind and told Sergeant Art Keller, one of Leach's best men, to do the killing. Keller, who had almost shot Leach by mistake in Gary, cut the pocket out of his overcoat so he could conceal the shotgun. Then the lieutenant again wavered—they would revert to a plan originally suggested by Leach: when Dillinger returned to his car and started to drive off, police cars would hem him in and gun him down.

At about 7:00 P.M. a carload of Indiana lawmen met three squads of Chicago detectives several blocks from Dr. Eye's office. It was bitter cold; the coldest November 15 in the city's history. The Indiana lieutenant outlined the plan and assigned each of the three Chicago cars a position. The combined forces now proceeded up Irving Park Boulevard.

In a few minutes Sergeant Keller saw a Terraplane, with Illinois plates 1-269-037, parked on a side street near the doctor's office. Billie Frechette was waiting in the front seat. Three of the police cars, including Keller's, parked on the side street facing the Terraplane. The fourth car, commanded by a Chicago detective, Patrolman Howard Harder, was on the other side of the boulevard headed in the same direction as the Terraplane. To Harder went the key assignment: to close in fast from the rear when Dillinger started driving toward the other police cars, thus catching the gangster in a pocket.

Time passed slowly for the lawmen as they waited in their unheated cars. Finally Harder saw a man come out of the building where Dr. Eye had his office. It was Dillinger.

As he crossed the side street and approached his Terraplane, Dillinger noticed several cars parked up ahead and became suspicious since they were facing the wrong way. But he continued walking in his usual slow shuffle. He casually slid behind the wheel as if suspecting nothing, told Billie to hang on, and suddenly backed into busy Irving Boulevard, narrowly missing the oncoming traffic. He jammed on the brakes and shifted into first.

Harder shouted to his driver to crash into the side of the Terraplane, which was beginning to pick up speed, but the driver, in his haste, killed the motor. Only Keller's driver, John Artery from Howe's office, reacted quickly. Pulling from behind one parked police car, he turned right on the boulevard and chased after the Terraplane.

Dillinger told Billie to hunch down on the floor and a moment later heard the blast of a shotgun. Then a car pulled up on his left and a bullet thudded into the door post only inches from his head. Dillinger shoved the accelerator to the floor, and the Terraplane shot ahead and made a screeching turn to the left.

It was Keller who had used his .38. Now he grabbed the shotgun, leaned out the right window and loosed a blast. A patrolman on his beat, thinking those in the unmarked Indiana

state police car were hoodlums, fired. The bullet hit the windshield, showering Keller with glass.

The two cars, never more than a hundred yards apart,
raced for several miles. Then, as the Terraplane approached a
trolley crossing, it looked as if Dillinger was trapped—two
trolley cars were converging from opposite directions. Instead
of slowing down, the Terraplane leaped forward, just squeezing between the two trolleys.

Artery had to swing around one trolley and lost ground,
but within a mile he made it up. "This time we've got him,"
he shouted. They were on a dead-end street.

The Terraplane, only a hundred feet ahead, abruptly
turned into a court, but Artery was going too fast and speeded
past. By the time he turned around, the other car had disappeared.

"That bird can sure drive," said one of the lawmen.

Dillinger returned directly to his apartment. When he
and the still shaken Billie walked in, he told the rest of
the gang about the ambush. Pierpont guessed Art was the
finger-louse. Another wondered if Chicago gangsters were
trying to get rid of Dillinger because of the publicity he was
giving the underworld. Or could one of the lesser members of
their own gang have betrayed them?

They packed, left the shot-up Terraplane on the street,
and moved to the apartment of Clark and Makley. The next
morning the *Chicago Tribune* headline read:

FIGHT 16 POLICE; ELUDE TRAP
Gun Girl Helps Desperado Flee from 4 Squads
Fire from Porthole in Fugitive Car

Dillinger was called the "desperate leader of a band of
outlaws which has been terrorizing northern and central
Indiana for weeks" and was compared to the James brothers.
The story graphically described how Dillinger held the
wheel with one hand, dropped a window with the other, and
fired back. Equally inaccurate was the description of police
shots bouncing off the "bulletproof" Terraplane and Billie's

leaning out the other window and firing. Even more fanciful was a "concealed porthole" from which a "hidden machine gunner poured a rat-a-tat of bullets upon the Indiana [Keller's] automobile."

Though the inner circle—Dillinger, Pierpont, Makley, Clark, and Hamilton—were still as close as ever, trouble with two peripheral members of the gang seemed imminent. Copeland was drinking heavily and it was becoming increasingly obvious that Shouse—who wore expensive, extremely styled clothes and was considered handsome by many women—was trying to seduce Dillinger's mistress.

On the day after the Dr. Eye ambush the gang settled final details for the robbery of a bank in Racine, Wisconsin, and a date was agreed upon: the following Monday, November 20. During the meeting Dillinger was sarcastic with Shouse and afterwards he pulled Billie into the bedroom, where he began accusing her of deceiving him. He became so violent he finally told her to put on her coat and hat; he was going to give her what she deserved—a one-way ride.

Mary Kinder tried to stop him. "There ain't no sense to it, Johnnie. That girl likes Shouse. So what?" She said it was a girl's right to choose any man she wanted.

Dillinger, too enraged to be reasonable, grabbed Billie and forcibly escorted her out the door. Three hours later they returned arm in arm. He grinned sheepishly at Mary and said, "I didn't have the heart to do it."

That same afternoon Pierpont, Makley, and Mary drove north to Racine. While changing a bill at the American Bank and Trust Company, Mary checked the cages, position of the vaults and personnel. The gang then drove around exploring the best streets for a getaway. Upon their return to Chicago another meeting was held, at which Pierpont suggested they drop Copeland, who was drinking more and more, and choose Shouse as the driver. Dillinger didn't object when the others concurred, but his lack of enthusiasm was pointed.

Shouse was actually planning something potentially much more dangerous than was Copeland's drinking. He wanted to hold up a bank on his own. The next day, while Dillinger and Pierpont were out buying a car, Mary Kinder happened to overhear Shouse trying to convince Hamilton to join him. They would get a third man and do the job by themselves. "You ain't going to do a damn thing," cut in Mary. "There ain't nobody going no place until we all talk it over. This has always been a friendly bunch and you ain't going to take no two or three and go rob a bank."

That evening the gang agreed to get rid of Shouse and when he appeared the following morning, each member threw a roll of bills on the couch. "There's your money," said Dillinger, the self-appointed spokesman. "Now get your ass out." Shouse not only took the money but also Clark's car and headed for California.

On the morning of the proposed Racine robbery, while the gang was eating breakfast in their temporary headquarters in Milwaukee, they saw Dillinger's name in the headlines once more. Copeland, "a Dillinger gangster," had got drunk in a Chicago tavern, started a fight in an alley with a woman he'd picked up, and got himself arrested. Makley expressed everyone's views when he drily said that neither Copeland nor Shouse would ever be missed.

It was a mild 52 degrees at 2:30 that afternoon but a chill breeze blew from Lake Michigan, which lay only a few hundred yards behind the American Bank and Trust Company, a solid stone building. Two city detectives parked their squad car at the side of the bank, let out a representative of a Milwaukee newspaper who wanted to make a deposit, and then strolled over to the Ace Pool Room on the square.

A young, tall, good-looking, well-dressed man with light blue eyes walked into the bank, carrying a roll of paper under his arm. Mrs. Henry Patzke, a bookkeeper, guessed he was a salesman. It was Pierpont and he pasted up a large Red Cross poster over the left-hand window of the bank, almost completely blocking the view of the cages from the street. She thought it rather curious but went back to work.

Three other men now entered. The first was middle-aged,

short, stout, with a red face—Makley; both the second and
third were short and stocky—Dillinger and Hamilton.

The head teller, Harold Graham, who was balancing his
accounts for the day, heard someone say, "Stick 'em up," and
thought it was another comical customer. Without turning he
said, "Go to the next window, please."

Makley repeated his order. Graham turned abruptly and
the startled robber fired a single shot. It went through the teller's right elbow, into his right hip. As Graham fell, he reached
out and pressed an alarm button connected to the police station. But the alarm did not sound inside the bank.

Bank examiners, working in the directors' room, ducked
into a closet.

When Mrs. Patzke heard the shot she looked up and saw
three men trotting down the aisle behind the cages. The nice-
looking man with light blue eyes, Pierpont, shouted, "Everybody flat on their stomachs!"

While employees and customers were dropping to the
floor, Dillinger herded President Grover Weyland, the cashier,
and his assistant back to the main vault. Now just a member of
a well-organized team, Dillinger ordered the president to open
the vault. Weyland—a tall, solidly built, imposing man—said
it was a double combination.

"All right, we'll give you some help then, Mr. President."
Pierpont prodded the cashier with his machine gun. While the
two bankers were opening the vault, the assistant cashier
darted down a stairway and ran to the rear exit in the basement. He looked through the glass door and saw a strange
car parked in the area reserved for bank officials. In it was
Clark. The assistant hid in the boiler room.

The alarm tripped by the wounded teller sent Sergeant
Wilbur Hansen and Patrolman Cyril Boyard heading toward
the bank in a squad car but they felt it was just another false
alarm. Some teller had once more accidentally pushed his button. They would enter and one of the bank officials as usual
would present them with a box of cigars for their trouble.

Boyard saw the squad car of the two detectives parked
alongside the bank and remarked that this time the de-

tectives had won the race to the bank and would get the cigars instead. Boyard walked into the bank first, his gun still in its holster, and heard someone say, "Stick 'em up!" To Boyard it didn't seem real—more like a movie.

Pierpont tried in vain to jerk Boyard's pistol from its brand-new holster with one hand, while holding a gun on him, but the holster, patterned to the pistol, was much too tight. Just then Sergeant Hansen walked in, his machine gun pointed down. Pierpont called, "Get that punk with the machine gun!"

Makley fired. When Boyard saw his partner drop he thought, "It ain't no movie no more." Hansen, hit twice but not seriously, looked up, saw Makley staring at him, and was sure he would be killed.

Makley now grasped the pistol in Boyard's tight holster. It still wouldn't come out, though he tugged violently. He irritably unfastened the buckle and jerked the holster off.

By this time Dillinger had cleaned out the vault and Hamilton had scooped the money from the cages. The smell of gunpowder was strong and the lobby filled with smoke. Several women were screaming hysterically. Dillinger and Pierpont quickly rounded up three girl employees and Weyland as hostages and brought them to the front of the lobby. Here Pierpont decided to take Boyard also and, grabbing the policeman's Sam Browne belt with his left hand, pushed him forward.

At that moment an off-duty policeman in civilian clothes walked in. "Come right in and join us," invited Dillinger. The policeman looked at Boyard and asked, "What the hell's going on?" Boyard shook his head warningly.

The hostages were marched outside, one girl escaping into the large curious crowd which was gathered in front. The rest of the captives were escorted around the corner toward Lake Michigan. Just then Pierpont saw two armed men running across the street. A boy had run into the poolroom and told the two detectives about the robbery. Pierpoint called out to Makley, who turned and loosed a burst with his machine gun as one of the detectives ducked into the Wylie Hat Shop for shelter—right behind a plate glass window. When Makley's bul-

lets shattered the glass, he shouted to his partner, "Get back!"
and the second detective ran into the Venetian Theater, where
he telephoned the police station. In the meantime the first
detective was creeping behind a radiator toward the door. Bullets ricocheted as he dashed to the street.

The group of hostages was hustled to the parking lot behind the bank.

"C'mon, Mr. President," said Pierpont, "you're going with
us. And you with the red dress."

Mrs. Patzke and Weyland stepped on the left running
board of the bandit car, a large black Buick, while Boyard got
on the right running board. Dillinger deftly backed it out of
the parking lot and started toward the lake. Then a police car
appeared from the opposite direction and a lieutenant raised
his machine gun, only to hesitate when Weyland waved frantically.

Dillinger turned right and drove along parallel to Lake
Michigan, with the hostages hanging tightly onto the careen-
ing car. Mrs. Patzke wore only a thin dress, but she didn't feel
the cold. After three blocks Dillinger turned west, then kept
changing routes as Hamilton read off instructions from a
notebook. Once the car skimmed so close to another car that
Mrs. Patzke felt it brush briefly against her.

Dillinger saw the crossing ahead jammed with traffic and
stopped the car. Boyard was ordered to get off. On the other
side Weyland and Mrs. Patzke were being pulled into the car.
The woman was put in the back seat between Hamilton and
Pierpont while Weyland sat on the left-hand jump seat.

Dillinger now drove west, finally turning onto a deserted
dirt road. When a hayrack drawn by a team of horses approached, Dillinger slowed down. As he passed it with care he
waved and called to the driver, "Hi, Joe!"

The excitement had worn off and Mrs. Patzke began to
shiver. Pierpont took off his overcoat, draped it around her
and asked, "Are you comfortable?" She nodded. Weyland was
also cold and wondered if he could cover his head with a
handkerchief. Makley gruffly said he couldn't but Pierpont
handed his own hat to the banker.

Finally Dillinger stopped the car. While Clark changed license plates, Pierpont dumped the money from the white sack into a suitcase, noting that there were many one-dollar bills. "Not as much as I expected," he told the others when Dillinger started the car. Then he tapped Weyland on the back and said in a cold sarcastic voice, "Maybe the folks at home will pay to get you back."

Some twenty minutes later Makley facetiously asked if the hostages were being taken "to the hideout." Dillinger turned his head, grinned, and asked Mrs. Patzke if she could cook.

"After a fashion," she replied.

It was getting colder as the sun lowered and Pierpont asked the two hostages if they were comfortable. Dillinger turned up a lane and stopped the Buick. Now Pierpont told the captives to get out of the car, but when Mrs. Patzke first bent over to tie her silk shoe laces, Makley swore impatiently.

"Cut it out, Mac," said Pierpont, "there's a lady in the car."

Pierpont brought Weyland and the woman to a clump of woods and tied their hands loosely together with new shoe laces. Mrs. Patzke thought they knew too much to be allowed to live but the bank president didn't seem worried and asked banteringly, "Well, how long will we have to stay here? Will ten minutes be enough?"

Pierpont told them to make it twenty. He walked off, then started back, and Mrs. Patzke was sure they were going to be killed. "I'm sorry, mister," he told Weyland. "But I'll have to have my hat." He snatched it from the banker's head.

3

Several days after the Racine holdup, Roger Touhy and his three co-defendants—in spite of positive identifications by several witnesses and a chain of circumstantial evidence—were acquitted by the Hamm kidnap jury. One mordant observer called it the greatest crime of the year. Newspaper editorials excoriated the jury for what seemed a mockery of justice; their

verdict was additional proof of Attorney General Cummings'
charge that St. Paul was "a poison spot of crime."

When an angry crowd at the courthouse and jail threatened to take the law in its own hands, the four acquitted
men thought they were going to be lynched despite their innocence. They were not lynched. Neither were they freed.
They were held to face trial in Chicago for the Factor kidnaping. But one might as well have been found guilty by the jury:
Willie Sharkey, Touhy's not-so-bright bodyguard, hanged himself in the St. Paul jail. The others were returned to Illinois to
be tried by the state, not the federal government, since Factor
had not been taken over a state line.

Touhy's lawyer told him he was sure charges would be
dropped; the U. S. Supreme Court had recently ordered Factor
extradited to England to face trial for swindling. But the
energetic Illinois State's Attorney hurried to Washington, where
he convinced President Roosevelt that Factor should be held
in America to help convict a vicious gang of kidnapers. The
President told Secretary of State Cordell Hull to inform the
British Embassy that Factor's extradition would have to be
postponed.

Crime was only one of Roosevelt's many problems that
December. The summer's honeymoon between big business
and the New Deal was over. The NRA (National Recovery
Administration), welcomed so joyously, was proving ponderous
in action and, among other things, was called the National
Run Around.

A secondary business slump was in the making and the
great dust storms in the Midwest continued, threatening to
lay waste to the great plains. The old fear of mass unemploy-
ment reappeared.

The national gloom was momentarily lifted on December
5 when the Twenty-first Amendment was finally ratified. Prohibition, one of the hottest topics of debate since the war, was
dead and mobs thronged taverns, restaurants, and hotels to
drink legal liquor. Much of it, far inferior to the bootleg variety,
was merely raw alcohol tinted and flavored and many Americans woke up the next day with thumping headaches.

. . .

Dillinger was causing another kind of headache. Of the ten most wanted criminals listed with photographs in the Chicago Police Department Bulletins issued in early December, eight were members of the Dillinger gang. Even Mary Kinder and Pearl Elliott, looking chubby and jovial in a cheap fur coat, appeared on the list.

In Indianapolis Matt Leach had a definite lead—a tip that Harry Pierpont's mother and brother would be driving through Terre Haute in a new Auburn. Leach passed on the information to the local chief of police and sheriff, but warned them not to arrest the pair. If shadowed, they might lead directly to the gang.

Nevertheless Pierpont's mother was arrested with her son Fred. When Leach learned what had happened, he and Harvey Hire started for Terre Haute. As they sped along the National Highway, Leach was slowed down by a car going in the same direction. Unable to pass on the left because of oncoming traffic, he swerved his big open Studebaker to the right onto the shoulder, then back to the highway as though it was a most natural maneuver. It was, thought Hire, typical of the impatient Leach, who would even occasionally leave a car parked with one wheel climbing over the sidewalk.

As Leach approached Mrs. Pierpont's cell, she began berating him, assuming he had caused her arrest. He listened silently while she swore at him, then told the chief of police with stuttering restraint that he might as well free the pair.

But her rage was nothing compared to Harry Pierpont's when he learned of the arrest. He drove to Indianapolis and as Leach walked out of his office, accompanied by Harvey Hire, Pierpont drew a bead on the man he thought had grossly insulted his mother. But when Hire stepped unknowingly in the line of fire, Pierpont lowered the gun.

In Chicago Lieutenant Howe of the Scotland Yard Squad was following another lead to the gang. On December 14, the day after Lena Pierpont's arrest, he got a tip that an Auburn belonging to the Dillinger mob was being repaired at a Broadway garage and passed on the information to city detectives.

When John Hamilton and his new girl friend, Elaine Dent, walked into the garage that afternoon, Sergeant William Shanley was waiting. But Hamilton fired first, wounding Shanley mortally, and escaped.

The woman was caught. At the detective bureau she wept theatrically, claiming she had been the innocent victim of deceit. "He was good to me, bought me this coat and the car. He certainly deceived me, as I thought he was a rich man's son." At any rate, she went on, he acted like a gentleman. "Why I never heard him say 'damn.' And clean! He'd take two baths a day."

Shanley, once a winner of a *Chicago Tribune* hero award, died in Edgewater Hospital, the thirteenth city policeman killed that year in line of duty.

Two days after his death Captain John Stege was ordered to set up a special squad of forty picked men. Stege's sole job was to get Dillinger and he told his men "to shoot to kill—shoot first." Their headquarters at 2259 South Damen Avenue was stocked with machine guns, rifles, tear gas guns, bulletproof vests, and almost completely useless forty-pound curved steel shields.

The Dillinger Squad, on duty twenty-four hours a day, was divided into two watches. Sergeant Frank Reynolds, who commanded the night watch, was a husky Irishman with a round face and cold blue eyes. He had a disdain of danger and an outspoken hatred of all hoodlums, and his real exploits surpassed the legendary deeds of most famous Western lawmen. He had already killed twelve dangerous criminals in face-to-face duels and was eager to meet the thirteenth.

Hamilton's narrow escape touched off an epidemic of hair dyeing among the gang. Pierpont, Clark, and Hamilton became dark brunet. Only Dillinger, always a little different, dyed his hair red. He had already started growing a mustache to hide a scar he had acquired which looked like a harelip.

They also agreed to separate for the time being. Dillinger and Billie Frechette went to Wisconsin; Pierpont, Mary Kinder, and a young man the gang had recently met in an underworld tavern, George Nelson, started a leisurely tour to the south. But by the time they reached Tennessee, Nelson—nicknamed "Baby Face" but never in his presence—had become so obnoxious that the trip was curtailed.

When they returned things were worse than ever. Every lawman in the city apparently was looking for Dillinger, so the entire gang now headed for a longer holiday in Florida.

Just before he and Billie left for Daytona Beach on December 20, Dillinger again telephoned Leach and asked how the search for the gang was progressing. He also called his new antagonist, Sergeant Reynolds. "You'd better watch your ass," he said. "We'll take you." Reynolds offered to meet him anywhere, any time, alone. Dillinger laughed and hung up.

Later that morning another lawman died indirectly because of Dillinger. Following a tip by an informer that the gang would congregate at 11:00 A.M. in Paris, Illinois, a squad of Leach's men formed an ambush outside a hotel. It was not a wholly unfounded rumor. Ed Shouse, who had tried to steal Dillinger's girl, was caught with two women. In the confusion, an Indiana officer was accidentally shot and killed by his superior, Lieutenant Charles Butler.

One of the girls confessed she had met Shouse in California three weeks previously and been his special girl friend since. That night at Leach's headquarters in the State House she told reporters, "You bet I like Eddie. He's a swell guy. It's a shame it had to end this way. But anyway I had three weeks. Well, life is like that."

The other woman was not so philosophical. "I'd like to get out of here," she said flatly.

"Try and do it, dearie," said her friend.

In the next room reporters were talking to Butler, who was near collapse. "Give me all the blame," he said. "I'm the man who killed Eugene Teague." He broke into sobs, burying his head on Matt Leach's desk. "My God, he was my friend—and I killed him."

Shouse, eager to talk to police and reporters, told a highly colored story of how the Dillinger gang, constantly on the alert, slept in their bulletproof vests. Every night they would hold a drill in preparation for a police attack. They were a "kill-crazy" mob, he warned. "Every man knows just what to do when the police come to the door. They'll shoot it out to the last bullet."

4

Two days after Dillinger left town, the Dillinger Squad was still looking for him in Chicago. Late that afternoon an anonymous informant called Captain Stege's headquarters and said the gang was to have a meet—rendezvous—at an apartment on Farwell Avenue with a man named "Mule."

Stege notified Sergeant Reynolds to prepare his night watch for action. The raiders congregated near a modern brick apartment house on the north side at about 9:00 P.M. and Stege—a quiet, self-effacing man who could be tough when necessary—spoke briefly. He said that men in an apartment on the second floor were probably the Dillinger crowd. They had to be taken.

After the building was surrounded, Reynolds and two other sergeants entered the front door. While one rang the downstairs bell and announced, through the communicator, that he was the Mule, Reynolds crept up the stairs. He knocked on the door of the suspected apartment. Someone inside said, "Okay, it's the Mule."

The door opened. Reynolds burst in, saw a man sitting on a settee and fired once. The man shot twice with a Luger. Reynolds ducked. The man rose, tried to get behind the settee but Reynolds put three more bullets in him.

A second man, sitting in a chair next to the settee, rose and began firing. Reynolds hit him with his fifth and sixth shots. The other sergeants entered and wounded a third gangster. As this man wriggled across the floor, Reynolds dropped his empty gun, pulled a Super .38 from his jacket pocket and shot him in the head.

The room was full of smoke and still ringing from the shots when Stege entered, surveyed the three bodies, and asked Reynolds if he recognized Dillinger. The sergeant got a towel and wiped the blood from the face of the first corpse. "Those are Jews," he said.

A little later the elderly deputy chief of detectives examined the bodies. Looking up from the third man, he said without hesitation, "This man's Dillinger. The other two look like Jack Hamilton and Harry Pierpont." Reynolds still disagreed.

For three hours it was believed the Dillinger mob had been wiped out. Then fingerprints revealed the dead men were wanted criminals named Katzewitz, Tattlebaum, and Ginsburg.

The triple killing was headline news in Chicago but Indianapolis reporters were more interested in a local story. That morning Jack Cejnar, whose secret arrangement with an insurance claim adjuster had given him so many exclusives on bank robberies, decided to send Matt Leach a Christmas present, a dime book published in 1862 entitled *How to Be a Detective*. After Mrs. Cejnar wrapped the book in white tissue and pasted on festive holiday seals, Cejnar told his State House reporter to lay it at Leach's door.

But Leach was in no mood for jokes. Stuttering with anger, he accused a local reporter, "Red" Gallagher. When Gallagher denied sending it, one of the news services circulated a story that the practical joker was none other than John Dillinger. It was the beginning of another Dillinger myth that still persists.

5

Dillinger and Billie Frechette arrived at Daytona Beach two days before Christmas and drove directly to a large two-story beach house previously rented from a Chicago agency for $100 a month. Clark and Makley were already there with their girl friends. Hamilton was alone.

On Christmas Eve Dillinger and Billie Frechette began arguing again about Shouse. The jealous Dillinger claimed she still cared for the ex-race driver, then illogically accused her of having a new lover. The argument continued Christmas morning and Dillinger blacked both her eyes.

At that moment Pierpont and Mary Kinder, who had stopped off several days in Indianapolis to visit her family, arrived with Silent Margaret and another girl. Billie was lying on the bed, face bruised, eyes swollen.

Dillinger shouted with rage, "Get back to Wisconsin where you belong!" As she limped to the dresser and began packing, Pierpont and Makley took Dillinger aside, advising him not to put her out. She might talk. But Dillinger wouldn't listen. He threw down $1,000 in big bills and told her she could take his new Ford.

After Billie left, everyone exchanged Christmas presents and Clark's companion, Opal Long—a big, red-headed, good-natured girl nicknamed "Mack Truck"—insisted on cooking the entire Christmas dinner. Late that afternoon when Mary and Silent Margaret looked out the window and saw the water had come up almost to the porch, they shouted, "Flood!" The others explained it was only the tide.

They celebrated New Year's Eve at the beach house, the men as usual drinking beer, the girls whiskey. When Dillinger heard the explosions of firecrackers along the beach at midnight, he decided to join the celebrants and took a submachine gun to the porch overlooking the ocean.

Margaret said she wanted to shoot and Dillinger handed over the gun. As he was instructing her on its use, she impatiently pressed the trigger. To her surprise the barrel jerked up toward Dillinger, spitting out four or five rounds.

He fell back, powder burns on his shirt, frightened but not angry. "Goddamn it, Margaret," he said. "What're you trying to do, kill me?"

A few hours later they were listening to the radio in the living room when a newscaster announced that John Dillinger and his mob had just struck again. They had raided the Beverly Gardens, a roadhouse near Chicago, slugged the doorman and ruthlessly shot two policemen in a gun battle.

Pierpont and Hamilton listened to the broadcast with mounting irritation, but Dillinger merely shrugged. "Now they'll blame everything on me," he said.

PART FOUR

•

CHAPTER 9

Kidnaped

1

WHILE DILLINGER WAS CELEBRATING THE NEW YEAR IN FLOR-
ida, Captain Dan Gilbert of the State's Attorney's office in
Chicago was reaching the end of his search for Handsome
Jack Klutas, the leader of the College Kidnapers, whose profits
in the past few years were estimated at close to $500,000.
Klutas, a graduate of the University of Illinois, confined kidnaping to underworld characters who could not only afford
to pay but rarely complained to the police.

The key lead in the case had come to Gilbert from the
underworld, which had been trying to settle with Klutas. The

Mafia, often a target of the kidnapers, persuaded Julius "Babe" Jones, a member of the gang, to try and arrange a truce. Jones spoke to Klutas, who said he would consider the proposition, but the moment Jones left, Klutas ordered his execution. First Jones's car was stolen. The following day he received a phone call, presumably from the Joliet police; his car had been found and should be picked up in a local garage. But Jones was suspicious and, disguising himself as a woman, he drove past the garage. Across the street two members of the collegiate gang were waiting in a car.

Jones, caught between two mobs, told Captain Gilbert everything he knew about Klutas and in a few days the latter's two chief lieutenants were captured. Then word came from the informant that Klutas himself could be trapped at a bungalow in Bellwood. Extreme caution should be taken; Dillinger was rumored to have joined forces with the College Kidnapers and might possibly be at the same address.

Early in the afternoon of January 6, 1934, Gilbert's chief aid and two squads of detectives surrounded the brick bungalow. When they broke in the front door they surprised a man shaving in the bathroom and another dressing in the bedroom. The man dressing was wanted for a $50,000 gem robbery. The shaver was Walter Dietrich, the protégé of Baron Lamm—one of the ten convicts Dillinger had helped break out of prison.

"I'm glad the Big Guy wasn't here," said the gem thief, "or he'd have made us grab a chopper and shoot it out with you. He says he'll never be taken."

The Big Guy was Klutas and he would be back later in the afternoon.

For almost four hours Sergeant Joe Healy and three others waited inside the bungalow. Finally a car pulled up to the curb and a big, good-looking man stepped out, walked up the steps to the front door of the bungalow, and rang the bell. It was Klutas. As the door was flung open, Healy said, "Hands up. Police officers." Klutas reached for a gun under his overcoat but Healy was quicker. He fired a machine-gun burst into the kidnaper-murderer's chest and the big man tumbled backwards, fell off the porch and rolled to the sidewalk. He was dead. It was the end of the College Kidnapers.

Another group of kidnapers, the Barkers, was still at large, but the character of the gang was changing and Ma Barker was losing control. From the early Central Park days in Tulsa, she had preached that the successful thief stayed away from liquor and women and in the beginning had no trouble controlling her boys, but when Fred Goetz joined the gang—bringing his attractive wife, Irene—the others began to see what they were missing. First, Freddie, Ma's youngest and dearest son, took Paula Harmon as his mistress. Paula, nicknamed "Fat-Witted," was probably the only graduate of an exclusive southern girls' school who was successively a comptometrist and madam of a whorehouse. Not long after this, Volney Davis resumed an old romance with Edna Murray, notorious first as The Kissing Bandit—she kissed her victims after robbing them —and then as "Rabbits" for her three escapes from jail and prison. The latest to deviate from Ma's dictum about women, and probably the one that cut deepest because of their particularly close relationship, was the dour-faced, sour-tempered Alvin Karpis. He was now living with an attractive eighteen-year-old girl, one of three sisters married to criminals.

Ma's control was further weakened by the addition of a number of new members, all mature. They included a former bootlegger who looked like a meek bank clerk, and his ladybird—mistress—a shoplifter and radio singer; a boyhood friend of the old Central Park gang and his girl, a part Cherokee; and a former speakeasy owner with Mafia connections, noted chiefly in the underworld for his wit and humor.

After killing the policeman in the holdup of the Swift messenger in St. Paul, the gang fled to Chicago. Here, using armor-plated cars equipped with smoke-screen devices, they held up two mail messengers of the Federal Reserve Bank. As they were escaping with several bags of almost worthless registered mail, they killed another policeman.

By this time the gang was in desperate need of money—the Hamm ransom had yet to be passed—and when Harry Sawyer, who had sponsored this kidnaping, phoned that he had found a bank that was "a real soft touch," they hurried back to their favorite city.

When the Barker gang—now a cumbersome outfit of thirteen, including the women—arrived in St. Paul, Ma was not with them. Feeling hurt because of their increasing independence, she had pettishly quit them and returned to her Chicago apartment. The Barker brothers and Karpis reported at the farm near St. Paul where Sawyer lived in quiet respectability with his wife and their adopted six-year-old daughter. Sawyer told them he had changed his mind about robbing the local Commercial State Bank. Perhaps the ease with which they had recently taken $100,000 from the Hamm family inspired him—he was a greedy if nervous and vacillating man. In any case he assured them they could get much more money by kidnaping the bank's president, Edward Bremer, whose father was part owner of the Jacob Schmidt Brewing Company and a personal friend of President Roosevelt and Governor Olson.

Karpis objected. They needed cash immediately. What good was more ransom money that would take months to convert? Dock Barker agreed. It was no time for another kidnaping. Look what had just happened to the Urschel kidnapers.

Like so many weak men, Sawyer stubbornly insisted on having his own way. He refused to listen to their objections, insisting his plan was foolproof. If they were afraid to do it, he'd find another gang.

Freddie Barker asked for a delay—so they could consult Ma in Chicago. Sawyer, despite his other limitations, was shrewd and said it was very peculiar that grown men couldn't make a simple decision without "running to Mother." He insisted they declare themselves in or out of the project immediately. Stung by his sarcasm, they all agreed—if reluctantly.

This scheme, conceived so arrogantly and joined so grudgingly, seemed destined for early disaster. On the eve of the kidnaping, Freddie Barker was driving down an alley when he noticed a car containing three uniformed men close behind.

Assuming they were police, Barker abruptly stopped the car and fired.

Two of the pursuers were wounded, one seriously. They were not police but employees of the Northwest Airways Company, living in the neighborhood, on the prowl for a Peeping Tom.

The next morning Sawyer called an emergency meeting. The man who had been so cocksure about his plans was completely shaken. His informant at police headquarters had told him one of the wounded men was near death and every known criminal was being rounded up for questioning, every underworld haunt searched. Sawyer insisted the kidnaping be postponed until the hubbub died down.

Three days later, a little after 8:30 on the morning of January 17, Edward George Bremer dropped off his eight-year-old daughter, Betty, at her private school, then, as usual, drove toward town. He got only as far as the stop sign at the next corner.

Suddenly the right-hand door of his car opened and he saw an arm and a gun. "Don't move, or I'll kill you," said a gruff voice. Bremer put the gear into first but a car suddenly blocked his way. The banker tried to escape out his door but got no farther than one foot on the running board when he felt a sharp blow on his head.

While one of the kidnapers drove Bremer's car, another slipped taped goggles over his eyes. Ten minutes later he was transferred to another car, where the goggles were lifted slightly and he was handed a fountain pen.

In a whisper Dock Barker told him he'd been kidnaped. He was to sign several notes. When Barker asked whom he wanted as contact man, Bremer suggested Walter Magee, a close friend and a prominent contractor. His watch and chain were taken for identification purposes and the kidnap car headed east.

Back in St. Paul Walter Magee was called to the phone in his office at about 10:40 A.M.

"We have your friend Bremer," said Goetz. Magee would find an explanatory note outside his office.

Magee hurried to the side door. On the floor was a note addressed to "Chas. McGee":

You are hereby declared in on a very desperate undertaking. Don't try to cross us. Your future and B's are the important issue. Follow these instructions to the letter. Police have never helped in such a spot, and wont this time either. You better take care of the payoff first and let them do the detecting later. Because the police usually butt in your friend isnt none to comfortable now so dont delay the payment. We demand $200,000. Payment must be made in 5 and 10 dollar bills—no new money—no consecutive numbers—large variety of issues. Place the money in two large suit box cartons big enough to hold the full amount and tie with heavy cord. No contact will be made until you notify us that you are ready to pay as we direct. You place an ad in the Minneapolis Tribune as soon as you have the money ready. Under personal colum (We are ready Alice). You will then receive your final instructions. Be prepared to leave at a minutes notice to make the payoff. Dont attempt to stall or outsmart us. Dont try to bargain. Dont plead poverty we know how much they have in their banks. Dont try to communecate with us we'll do the directing. Threats arent necessary— you just do your part—we guarantee to do ours.

Mr. Chas McGee
I have named you as payoff man. You are responsable for my safety. I am responsable for the full amount of the money.

                    (Signed) E.G. Bremer
                    Deal only when signature is used.

That afternoon local police found Bremer's abandoned Lincoln and, because of numerous blood stains inside, it was feared the banker was already dead.

· · ·

Late the same night the kidnap car reached Bensenville and turned into an alley. Bremer, in spite of his overcoat, was numb from cold. His head throbbed and his left leg—the one he had stuck out the door—ached painfully. When the car stopped he heard two dogs barking. He was led into a house only blocks from the place Hamm had been held. While his head was being washed with hot water he asked if the cuts were bad. "Could have been worse," whispered Dock Barker, then added, "If you hadn't put up a fuss, you wouldn't have got them."

The following morning Goetz and Fred Barker searched the personals column of the *Minneapolis Tribune* and finally found what they were looking for:

We are ready. Alice

A few minutes later a message from Sawyer told them to report to the farm at once. The jittery Sawyer said the town was "crawling with G-men" and they should send all the women to Chicago.

That afternoon a courier from Bensenville brought Goetz three notes that Bremer had written. By now Sawyer had become panicked by a report from his police spy that Walter Magee was under heavy surveillance and he insisted that the notes be left at the home of Dr. Nippert, another friend of Bremer's. He also insisted that delivery of the notes be held up at least a day until "things cooled off."

Though the gang was annoyed by Sawyer's constant nervous meddling in the mechanics of the operation, they consented.

Of course, it was impossible to keep official news of the kidnaping from the public any longer and Police Chief Thomas Dahill told reporters he had not received notification of the crime from the Bremer family but was investigating. The Associated Press announced that one of Hoover's key agents in the Urschel case was flying immediately to St. Paul.

That night Adolph Bremer, the sixty-five-year-old, white-haired father of the victim, finally made a statement to the press. "I am sorry the impression has been spread that information has been given to the police. Whatever information has been passed out has been given against my will and has created, through the newspapers, a wrong impression. . . . We want to get Eddie back home safe."

Three days after the kidnaping, at about 6:00 A.M., Dr. H. T. Nippert, who lived only a few blocks from the intersection where Bremer had been seized, was wakened by a loud crash. Thinking the wind had blown over something or that someone had dropped a dish, he went back to sleep. A few hours later his telephone rang. "Go to the vestibule," said a voice. "See what you can find."

The doctor found the glass in the front door broken. Fragments of a bottle were scattered on the vestibule floor. There was also a folder addressed to him. Inside were two envelopes and a note in Bremer's handwriting asking the doctor to deliver them to his father's house.

One contained a letter to Bremer's wife asking her not to worry. "I'm treated nice & the only thing I have to ask is to keep the police out of this so that I am returned to you all safely."

The second envelope, addressed to Magee, contained a note from Bremer begging him to "work on this all alone—no police." There was also a typewritten letter to Magee:

You must be proud of yourself by now. If Bremer dont get back his family has you to thank. Youve made it almost impossible but were going to give one more chance—the last. First of all all coppers must be pulled off. Second the dough must be ready. Third we must have a new signal. When you are ready to meet our terms place a N.R.A. sticker in the center of each of your office windows. Well know if the coppers are pulled or not. Remain at your office daily from noon until 8:00 P.M. Have the dough ready and where you can get it within thirty minutes. You will be instructed how to deliver it. The money must not be hot as it will be examined before Bremer is released. If Dahill is so hot to meet us you can send him out with the dough. Well try to be ready for any trickery if atempted. This is positively our LAST atempt. DONT duck it.

Later that day Fred Barker drove past Magee's office and when he saw half of a blue eagle NRA sticker pasted on the window, he correctly surmised this meant only half the ransom would be paid. After the frustrations of the last few days, it was all he needed to make him decide to kill Bremer and he drove at reckless speed over the icy roads to Bensenville. Fortunately Dock was on hand to calm him down; he managed to reassure Fred that everything would work out if they were patient, and sent him back to St. Paul.

The next suspenseful hours dragged painfully for the Bremer family. Though local newspapers had guessed that the bottle thrown through Nippert's door had contained messages from the gang, the report was denied by the doctor and Chief of Police Dahill. Bremer's brother, Adolph, Jr., said, "That's all hooey." Mrs. Bremer reportedly was "prostrated with grief," and the victim's father in "a serious nervous condition." The family received hundreds of telegrams and letters, one small girl even sending a dollar bill from her savings to help pay the ransom.

Finally on Monday morning, five days after the kidnaping, another note was found at the office of a St. Paul coal company official and delivered to Adolph Bremer's imposing home, a large stone house across from the brewery.

If you can wait O.K. with us. You people shot a lot of curves trying to get somebody killed then the copper's will be heroes but Eddie will be the marteer. The copper's think that great but Eddie dont. Were done taking the draws and you can go————now. From now on you make the contact. Better not try it till you pull off every copper, newspaper, and radio station. From now on you get the silent treatment until you reach us someway yourself. Better not wait too long.

This threatening but illogical note was proof that Sawyer's nervousness was now affecting the gang. How was the Bremer family supposed to contact the kidnapers?

All the perplexed family could do was plead with the police and newspapers to let them carry on negotiations without interference or publicity and hope this showed the gang their good intentions. For three days nothing happened. On the fourth—the evening of January 25—a Hill Brothers coffee can was left on the front porch of a man who had no connection with the Bremers. Inside was a letter demanding that the $200,000 be delivered that night. Enclosed was a baggage check for a handbag at a locker in the Jefferson Lines bus station. The bag, which would contain further instructions, should not be opened before 8:20 P.M.

Magee went to the waiting room of the bus depot and, at the designated time, claimed a black zipper bag. Inside were a pillow and a note instructing Magee to assume the name of John B. Brakeeham and leave on the 8:40 P.M. bus for Des Moines.

Everything worked perfectly—until Magee arrived in Des Moines. Then the Sawyer-inspired epidemic of jitters broke out again. The man detailed to pick up the $200,000 lost his nerve for no reason at all and fled without the money.

When Sawyer learned of this last mishap, he declared the whole project had been "queered." Acting as though he had been against it from the start, he pointed out that negotiations were becoming increasingly dangerous every day. Why not call the whole thing off?

Most of those in Bensenville felt the same way but Dock Barker and Karpis never wavered. In fact the events of the past nine days seemed to have affected them hardly at all. Little Dock occasionally relieved the tension by giving imitations of a Mexican and Karpis was busy constructing an ingenious time bomb for a future project. A bank president would be stopped on his way to work, the time bomb padlocked to his body; he would be instructed to get the money out of the bank and return; if he delayed, even a few minutes, he would be blown up.

By now a strange relationship had sprung up between Dock and Bremer. Several days previously Dock had said he was worried that Bremer's eyes might be seriously injured by continued darkness and offered to take off the blindfold once a day if the prisoner would promise to face the wall. Bremer agreed.

One evening Dock came into the prison bedroom and asked Bremer in the whisper he always used to disguise his voice if he would like to join him in a drink. Bremer took the glass and said, "Well, pardner, here's to you."

"This thing is stretching out a helluva lot longer than we expected," said Dock. "It won't be too long before you crack up." Then, he said regretfully, Bremer would have to be chained to the bed. Another time Dock asked if it would relieve Bremer's mind if he gave his word to return the banker home safe and sound.

"I'll take your word," said Bremer. "Let's shake on it."

"We'll just say we did," said Dock warily. "I don't want you to feel my hands."

When Karpis learned of the failure to pick up the ransom in Des Moines, he and Goetz visited Ma Barker in her Chicago apartment. In the past two years—during which all except Dock had "deserted" her—she had aged ten years. Though her gray hair was perfectly groomed, her cheeks were loose and saggy and her neck was wattled like a turkey's. Only her eyes were the same—brown, brilliant, and vindictive. She told them that if they had listened to Mother in the first place, they wouldn't be in such a mess. She never had liked Harry Sawyer. He was a weakling and his wife, like most wives, couldn't be trusted. The two men listened patiently to her nagging and agreed that everything had gone sour in St. Paul. Then Karpis said that the three of them would have to work out the plan for the pay-off. It was Ma's happiest moment in two years.

The next day, January 27, Karpis arrived in St. Paul with

a shrewd plan. He said that ten days had already been wasted and that both Ma and Goetz had agreed he was to take full charge from now on, with absolutely no interference from Sawyer. Negotiations for the pay-off, he said, would start in a week.

CHAPTER 10

"Reach for the Moon!"

1

THE RUMORS THAT DILLINGER WAS CONNECTED WITH THE COL-lege Kidnapers did have some basis in fact; he had given Dietrich the gun found at the Bellwood cottage. Whether because of this somewhat tenuous tie or the general dictum of criminals to keep moving, the gang decided to leave Florida, scatter, and meet in Tucson, Arizona, in several weeks.

By now Dillinger was sorry he'd acted so impetuously with Billie Frechette—he needed a woman. He told the others he was going to Wisconsin and try to persuade Billie to accompany him to Tucson; since he would have to drive through Chicago, he offered to cash some of the stolen bonds hidden there in a safety deposit box. Hamilton decided to go along.

As Dillinger was about to drive off, Silent Margaret gave him a cigarette. When it exploded he laughed as loud as the rest and said, "I'll get you for that, Margo."

About the first thing Dillinger did upon arrival in Chicago was again to telephone Sergeant Frank Reynolds, chief of the night detail of the Dillinger Squad, and say he was coming to his home to kill him. The sergeant, who had never

reported any of the previous calls, replied that he could take
two like Dillinger without any help and urged him to hurry.
Though Reynolds waited hopefully, the visitor never arrived.

Dillinger and Hamilton found it impossible to cash the
bonds and decided to get money a different way—rob a
bank. Actually both had plenty of money for the Tucson trip
but Dillinger, who had been inactive almost two months, was
restless.

Hamilton was easily persuaded. On the surface he was
level-headed, steady, but even as a boy he had never been
able to resist a dare, once climbing a 175-foot factory chimney
on a dime bet. Another time he had steered his sled so close
to a passing freight train that two fingers on his right hand
had been sliced off.

The venture agreed upon so recklessly was planned with
even less thought: they decided merely to get a driver and do
the job alone without bothering to leave guards outside the
bank or to keep open an avenue of escape. Dillinger, who
was secretly starting to believe his newspaper publicity,
cockily said that they didn't need outside protection—not if
they wore bulletproof vests. Besides, why share the loot?

On January 15 the two headstrong robbers and their
driver headed for East Chicago, Indiana, a suburb of Chicago
on Lake Michigan. The First National Bank in East Chicago
had marble floors and walls; its high arched ceiling was pierced
with a skylight. At about 2:45 P.M., just before closing time,
Dillinger casually entered with a trombone case. He opened it
like a salesman about to display his samples, drew out a submachine gun, and approached the desk of Cashier James A.
Dalton. "This is a holdup," he said and then turned toward
Walter Spencer, a vice-president, who was talking by phone to
Joseph Walkowiak, an official of a branch bank.

"Hang up that phone, Mr. President," said Dillinger.

Spencer whispered, "It's a holdup, Joe," and hung up. Then
he pressed the bank alarm buzzer.

Dillinger, raising his voice slightly, announced he was
robbing the bank. It was like the carefree days before he
joined Pierpont, and the wonder is that he didn't impetuously

leap over the barrier. When a customer, who had just cashed a check, started backing away without his money Dillinger said airily, "You go ahead and pick it up. We don't want your money. Just the bank's."

Dillinger told the customers he knew the alarm had been turned in and there might be shooting. He herded them into a corner for their own protection, then called confidently to Hamilton, who was waiting in the lobby, "Come in and get it and take all they've got."

While Hamilton was scooping money into a Federal Reserve sack, Dillinger noticed a policeman at the front door. "There's a cop outside," he called. But he was still not at all worried. "Don't hurry. Get all that dough."

There were four policemen outside—three in plain-clothes. They had answered the alarm set off by Vice-President Spencer but thought it was just another false alarm. Patrolman Hobart Wilgus, the one in uniform, entered the bank alone. It was cold and his overcoat was buttoned over his gun. Dillinger stepped forward, pointed his machine gun and said almost casually, "You're just the person I'm looking for. Where's your gun?" When Wilgus pointed, Dillinger said, "Leave it there and get over with the rest of the people."

Looking outside, Dillinger got a glimpse of the plain-clothes men with guns and for the first time the folly of the operation must have struck him. There was nothing to do but grab a few hostages for protection. He imperturbably motioned to Spencer. "Come on out here with me, Mr. President." When Spencer asked if he could get his coat, Dillinger said he wouldn't need it. "You're not going very far." Using the policeman and vice-president as shields, the two robbers walked out of the bank.

Patrolman William Patrick O'Malley, who was standing in the entrance of Newberry's next door, shouted, "Wilgus! Wilgus!" The police hostage jumped aside, giving O'Malley a clear shot at Dillinger. Several bullets glanced off his bullet-proof vest. Dillinger pushed his other hostage to one side and fired at O'Malley, hitting him in the leg. O'Malley fired again, the bullets once more glancing off the vest. Dillinger fired a low burst and as O'Malley fell, a bullet tore through his heart. The other policemen, joined by a passing officer, were shooting at Hamilton, who was carrying the money sack. Hamilton was not as lucky as Dillinger; a bullet ripped through a weak spot in his vest and he fell. Instead of going on, Dillinger returned and helped Hamilton to his feet with one hand, while picking up the money with the other. As he started toward the car, which was parked in the middle of Chicago Avenue, his back was completely unprotected, but in spite of a flurry of shots, his luck held. He was not hit.

The car shot across the tracks of the Chicago South Shore and South Bend Railroad—the power had been cut by the bandits so a train wouldn't interrupt their getaway—and kept heading east. Late that afternoon the robbers returned to Chicago by a roundabout route with $20,376 in cash. After the money was equally divided, Dillinger took the badly wounded Hamilton to an underworld doctor. Then he anxiously scanned the papers—Officer O'Malley was dead.

He had killed his first man.

2

Tucson—then a city of about 30,000, not far from the Mexican border and nestled in a desert plain surrounded by a ring of rugged, bald mountains—still had one foot in its colorful pioneer past. Iron hitching posts dotted Congress Street. It was a friendly, free-and-easy western town with three well-run parlors—houses of prostitution—operating openly.

Tucson was growing with phenomenal speed because of its climate, yet it too had been hard hit by the Depression, and tourists were made to feel especially welcome. Apparently the Dillinger gang could not have picked a better hideout.

Makley, Clark, and Clark's girl, Opal Long—the big, good-natured redhead nicknamed "Mack Truck"—arrived first and were now registered at the Congress, a three-story hotel. They spent the days sightseeing, the evenings at night clubs. Just before 7:00 A.M., January 23, an overflow of oil from the hotel furnace burst into flame, and the blaze spread rapidly since there were no fire stops in the walls.

After Engineer William Benedict was relieved from hose duty, he stepped outside the building for a breath of fresh air with another fireman just in time to see Makley and Clark, trousers over their pajamas, trying to extend a ladder up to the third floor. Benedict asked what the devil they thought they were doing.

When Makley said they wanted to save their luggage, Benedict and the other fireman went up the stairs to Room 329 and kicked in the locked door. While his companion was gathering clothing from the closet, Benedict carried a heavy fabric box about two feet long to the window. Makley saw Benedict apparently about to drop the box and shouted in consternation, "Don't throw it!" It contained several machine guns.

After the two firemen turned over the box and clothing, Makley gave Benedict $2, a liberal tip in 1934. The next morning Benedict saw a picture of the Dillinger gang in a copy of *True Detective Magazine* and noticed that Clark resembled one of the two generous strangers at the fire. He telephoned the sheriff's office and asked if there were any fliers on the gang. There were. When Benedict saw pictures of Makley and Clark, he excitedly identified them as the men he had seen at the Congress.

But the fire which had called attention to them also forced them to move to a new and unknown location, a comfortable one-story house a few blocks from the University of Arizona. The owner, Mrs. Hattie Strauss, was impressed by Mr. Davies (Makley). He was well-dressed and talked with the smooth assurance of a successful businessman. But something about him looked familiar and she said, "I think I've seen you before, or I've seen your picture." Makley smiled and denied he'd ever been in the news or in Tucson.

That same afternoon Dillinger and Billie Frechette drove into town and registered at a motor court as Mr. and Mrs. Frank Sullivan. With them was a Boston bull puppy. A few

hours later, purely by chance, Pierpont, wearing rimless glasses
with plain lenses as a disguise, and Mary Kinder drove into the
same tourist camp and were given the adjoining cabin. They
had spent the past week in Albuquerque, New Mexico, visiting
with his parents.

"Isn't that Johnnie's car?" Mary asked, pointing to a parked
Hudson. Pierpont said it couldn't be.

While they were driving aimlessly around town after un-
packing, Pierpont ran through a boulevard stop sign. When he
noticed that a police car was parked nearby, Pierpont drove
boldly up to the patrol car and told the two policemen inside
he was afraid another car was following him.

Motorcycle Patrolmen Earl Nolan and Milo "Swede"
Walker reassured the timid tourist that he was perfectly safe in
Tucson. Pierpont chatted a few minutes about the fine climate,
told them he was thinking of buying some properties and then
said, truthfully, that he was staying at the cabins on South
Sixth Avenue. Walker, guessing Pierpont was a college professor, advised him to go to the police station if he had any
more trouble. Pierpont thanked him and said, "I certainly feel
better knowing no one is following me."

After returning to the cabin Mary heard a dog barking
next door. She looked out and saw Dillinger and Billie Frechette. Pierpont refused to believe it could be Dillinger, but a
moment later there was a knock at the door.

"I recognized your Buick, Pete," said Dillinger. He explained that everyone was meeting the next morning on the
main highway near the Veterans Hospital.

The gang met as planned, January 25, some two miles out
of Tucson. Mary asserted she didn't want to stay in Arizona.
She didn't know why; it was just a hunch.

The men said it was perfectly safe. They would rent different houses, live quietly, and act like ordinary tourists. Makley, Clark, and Opal returned to the Strauss home, where they
had lunch with May Miller, a local night-club singer Makley
had been dating. About 1:30 P.M. "Mr. Davies" asked if Miss

Miller would drive downtown with him to get a radio he'd left at a store to be repaired. As Makley was helping her into his Studebaker, three policemen were watching from a parked car. They had learned the address from the drayman who had hauled the gangsters' luggage from the scene of the hotel fire to the Strauss home.

The police followed the Studebaker to the business section. When Makley parked and walked into the Grabe Electric Company, they followed him inside. Bruce Hannah, the manager, felt it didn't look good for so many policemen to walk into such a small store and facetiously asked if they were looking for a gang of crooks. The officers walked up to Makley and quietly arrested him. Makley, claiming indignantly that he was J. C. Davies, asked to be taken back to the Strauss home where he had left his identification papers. Instead the police took him to the city jail.

Now Sergeant Frank Eyman and three men—all in civilian clothes—were sent to the Strauss place in an unmarked car. Eyman had angular features and was noted for his fast draw and lack of fear. His plan was simple. Sergeant Chet Sherman would put on a Western Union cap and deliver a fake message while Eyman and another man were breaking in the back door. The fourth man, Dallas Ford, would wait across the street and back up Sherman.

Sherman, small enough to pass for a messenger boy, turned in the front walk. Clark saw him and, though he was not suspicious, took the bottle of Schlitz Repeal Special beer he was drinking into the bedroom while Opal answered the bell.

Sherman said he had a letter for Mr. Long and when Opal reached for it, insisted upon delivering it personally. When Clark came forward, Sherman drew his gun but the big gangster seized it, yanking the small man inside. Clark wrestled Sherman toward the bedroom just as Dallas Ford started running up the front steps. Opal saw him and tried to shut the door. It slammed on Ford's hand, breaking a finger, but he charged into the house.

Clark had Sherman on the bed and was trying to grab his gun with both hands when Ford ran into the bedroom and hit the gangster a glancing blow over the head with his gun butt. Clark reached under the pillow for his own gun but it wasn't there. Opal had put it under the mattress as a precaution.

By this time Eyman and his partner had broken in the rear door. Eyman tried to club Clark with his gun but missed entirely and hit Sherman. A less determined man would have been discouraged; instead Sherman finally yanked the gun away from Clark's tenacious grip and slugged him. Clark crumbled.

Up to this point the Tucson police had acted efficiently and with foresight. Now they made their first mistake. If men had been left at the Strauss home, they could have made another quick arrest. About an hour later Pierpont and Mary Kinder parked out front. He walked unsuspectingly up to the house but when he saw blood on the porch, returned to the car, and drove to their cabin. While Mary packed, Pierpont telephoned a local lawyer and told him to represent a Mr. Davies and Mr. Long who probably had just been picked up by the police.

Pierpont himself was just then being discussed at police headquarters. An alert neighbor reported he had seen a stranger walk up to the porch of the Strauss place, then abruptly hurry back to his car. When Patrolman Nolan heard the description of the man he suddenly remembered the pleasant chat he and his partner had had the previous night with the timid tourist. He even recalled that Pierpont had told him he was staying at the cabins on South Sixth.

As Nolan and Sergeant Eyman neared the tourist camp they passed Pierpont and Mary Kinder going in the other direction, but Nolan recognized the Buick and the police car made a U turn and gave chase.

After several blocks the police driver caught up to the Buick and sounded his horn. The Buick pulled over. Eyman got out, wondering if he could persuade what might be a desperate gangster to drive voluntarily to the station. "How do you do?" he said affably, then asked to see Pierpont's license.

The bespectacled gangster had a gun in his left hand but

he was fooled by Eyman's manner and decided to bluff it out. He hid the gun and showed his license, which, naturally, was in another name.

Eyman apologetically pointed out that Pierpont didn't have a visitor's inspection sticker, suggesting he get one at the station, otherwise he'd be stopped by every traffic officer in town. "I'll even ride down with you," he said, getting into the back seat. It was filled with luggage and he had to sit on a suitcase containing a machine gun, several revolvers, a bullet-proof vest, and ammunition.

Pierpont drove off, adjusting the rear-view mirror so he could see the sergeant. Eyman held out a pack of cigarettes. Pierpont refused. Eyman praised the local climate, explaining he had come there for his wife's health. He took a hurried glance behind but the police car was not in sight so he cautiously drew out his gun, hiding it behind the back of the front seat. It was hard to believe the driver could be dangerous. He had mild blue eyes and spoke softly in a diffident manner.

Still unworried, Pierpont drove to the front of the building that housed the police station. The three walked downstairs to the station and along the corridor to Chief Gus Wollard's office. Now Pierpont saw the luggage of Makley and Clark and realized he'd been led into a trap. He whirled and grabbed for the gun under his left arm.

Eyman drew faster. "Drop it."

Pierpont obeyed, but his right hand went for a second gun stuck in his belt. Eyman rammed his gun in Pierpont's ribs while another officer grasped the gangster's arms. Pierpont's rimless glasses had fallen off and his blue eyes no longer looked mild. He shouted and swore angrily, then suddenly stuck a piece of paper in his mouth.

The lawmen tried to keep him from swallowing it but he fought wildly. An iron claw was put on his arm and tightened. Finally the pain was too much and he spat out the paper. It was blurred but Eyman managed to read: 1304 East 5th, the address of the house rented that day by Dillinger. Now Eyman saw Pierpont had another piece of paper in his hand. Again the iron come-alongs were used and Pierpont gave up an Indiana driver's license made out to John Donovan, one of Dillinger's aliases.

While Eyman was investigating the house on 5th, plain-clothes man James Herron—a short, stocky Irishman from Boston who had come to Tucson for his health—suggested that the Strauss home should also be staked out—watched. Chief Wollard agreed and told him to pick the men he wanted. Herron chose two motorcycle officers, one of whom was Swede Walker, the man who had thought Pierpont talked like a college professor.

It was dusk when the three arrived at the house. They parked in front and went around to the broken back door. Once inside they realized their car might scare off the prey. While Herron was parking it across the street in a driveway, Dillinger and Billie Frechette drove by, made a U turn, and stopped in front of the house.

They had just returned from a sightseeing trip and, of course, had no idea their companions were now in jail. Consequently, Dillinger was not at all suspicious when he saw the house was dark. He told Billie he'd see if it was the right address and walked toward the porch. Hearing footsteps, he turned and saw a short, stocky man. In the dim light he thought it was Makley, but it was Herron coming up behind him.

Just as Herron drew his .38, Walker kicked open the screen door and shouted, "Stick 'em up!"

Dillinger slowly put up his hands and was marched off the porch to the sidewalk. Walker ordered Billie out of the car, told her to cross her fingers and put them on top her head. She did, although Dillinger objected angrily to such treatment of a lady. Now Walker held his shotgun on Dillinger while Herron searched him. The gangster's hands, only shoulder high, began to drop slowly.

Walker pulled the hammer back on his gun. "Reach for the moon!" he said. "Or I'll cut you in two." Dillinger obeyed.

In a space of five hours, without firing a shot and at the cost of only a broken finger, the police of a relatively small

John Dillinger as a child—lonely and sulky; and as a high school student (*below*) headstrong and rebellious.

Homer Van Meter

John Hamilton

Associates of Dillinger during his nine years behind bars. Van
Meter was one of his closest friends at both reformatory and
prison. Hamilton, Clark and Makley were leading members of
the gang Dillinger helped escape from Indiana State Prison after
his own parole. As reward he was allowed to join their ranks.

Russell Clark

Charles Måkley

Harry "Pete" Pierpont, brains of the gang and the convict Dillinger most respected. Labeled a red shirt—incorrigible—by the guards, he plotted ingenious bank robberies from his cell.

"I babied them boys." Mary Kinder, sister of two inmates, helped Dillinger break out Pierpont and nine others from prison; then joined the new gang as Pierpont's girl.

The Kansas City Massacre. On June 17, 1933, "Pretty Boy" Floyd and two confederates attacked lawmen with machine guns outside the railroad station in an attempt to free captured bank robber, Frank "Jelly" Nash. Four lawmen were murdered—and Nash was killed by mistake.

Charles Arthur Floyd

Frank Nash

Hitherto unpublished pictures of Dillinger and his girl, Mary Longnaker, at Chicago's "Century of Progress" soon after his parole.

It amused Dillinger to take snapshots of policemen.

Captain Matt Leach, head of the Indiana State Police. The first lawman on Dillinger's trail and often the recipient of taunting phone calls from his prey. Dillinger became an obsession that ended only with Leach's death.

Narcissists of crime: Bonnie Parker and Clyde Barrow. Their multiple murders and robberies terrorized the Midwest and Southwest. This is one of the many snapshots left after they fled their Joplin, Missouri, apartment.

In a rare action shot, the mortally wounded Buck Barrow (kneeling in his underwear) and his wife, Blanche, are photographed being captured at the fair grounds near Dexter, Iowa. His brother, Clyde, and Bonnie Parker have just escaped.

(*Below*) George "Machine Gun" Kelly and his wife, Kathryn, discuss tactics at their trial for the kidnaping of Charles Urschel.

Dock Barker   Ma Barker   Alvin Karpis

The principal members of the Barker mob—kidnapers of William
Hamm, Jr., a wealthy brewer, and Edward Bremer, a banker.

Roger Touhy (*right*)—recently acquitted of the Hamm kidnaping
—on trial for the kidnaping of Jake "The Barber" Factor. Facing
him is the lawyer Touhy tried in vain to fire, William Scott Stewart.

At Crown Point County Jail, Dillinger impudently leans on Prosecutor Robert Estill—who hopes to send him to the electric chair—and touches off an explosive political scandal. The woman is Dillinger's jailer, Sheriff Lillian Holley.

(*Below*) A few days later in court: the different faces of John Dillinger.

Reunion at Mooresville. At the height of the nationwide search for Dillinger, he and his part-Indian girl friend, Billie Frechette, visit his father (*bottom, left*). Dillinger proudly exhibits a wooden gun, claiming he used it to escape from Crown Point.

Melvin Purvis, the diminutive agent-in-charge of the Chicago FBI office (shown with Attorney General Homer Cummings) joined the Dillinger chase after Crown Point.

J. Edgar Hoover (*left*) directed the FBI's battle against the Midwest crime wave of 1933–34.

U.P.I.

Louis Piquett, Dillinger's lawyer, in a typical courtroom pose. On behalf of his client, he also bribed a judge and arranged for plastic surgery.

(*Below*) An important member of the gang Dillinger formed after his Crown Point escape—"Baby Face" Nelson, killer of three G-men.

LIONEL BENFER, *Milwaukee Sentinel*

After the Battle of Little Bohemia. Sitting in the truck is one of the dogs that barked as FBI agents converged on the Dillinger gang. Van Meter fired from open second-story window.

Dillinger with Emil Wanatka, proprietor of the lodge.

Mrs. Wanatka, whose message in a cigarette pack brought Purvis to Little Bohemia, with the two watchdogs.

Polly Hamilton

Anna Sage

Polly Hamilton, Dillinger's last girl, saw approaching FBI men and warned him—too late. This picture was found in his watch. Anna Sage, the Woman in Red, walked on the other side of Dillinger. Her phone call to the FBI set the trap.

On the sweltering night of July 22, 1934, Dillinger left the Biograph Theater and turned to his left. He was killed by FBI agents, commanded by Samuel Cowley (*inset*), as he ran for the alley.

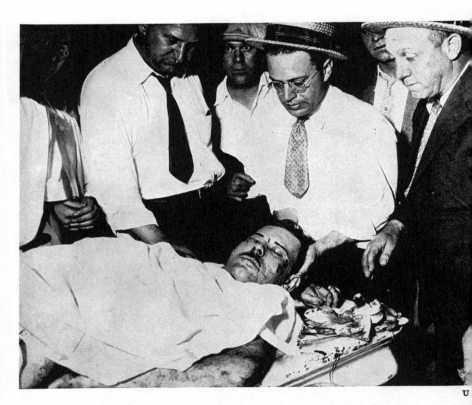

The End of John Dillinger. Dr. Charles D. Parker (with straw hat), identified in newspaper pictures as the coroner, takes charge of the body at Cook County Morgue. Dr. Parker was actually a reporter for the *Chicago Tribune*.

city had done what the combined forces of several states, including that of America's second largest metropolis, had tried
so long and unsuccessfully to do. The Tucson police, of course,
had one great ally—the gang's own false sense of security.

At the station Sergeant Mark Robbins had just made positive identification of Makley, Clark, and Pierpont from their
fingerprints but Dillinger still insisted his name was Frank
Sullivan. William R. Mathews, editor and publisher of the *Arizona Daily Star*, followed Dillinger, who looked to him like an
overworked bookkeeper, into the identification room.

Sergeant Robbins, who was examining a sheaf of pictures,
suddenly held up one. "Look what we have here!" he said. He
examined Dillinger's left wrist. There was a scar. He found
another under Dillinger's mustache. "This man is John Dillinger," he said unequivocally.

The editor went to the door, opened it. Standing outside was one of his reporters, Dave Brinegar. "They've got
John Dillinger," whispered Mathews.

Since the jail at the police station was too small, the gangsters and their women were taken under heavy guard to the
nearby Pima County jail located in the County Courthouse, a
beautiful building of Spanish design with a multicolored ce-
ramic dome. Numerous deputies in high-heeled boots and som-
breros, six-shooters banging against their hips, were already
guarding the building with shotguns. Excitement built as
curious citizens gathered. Truth and fiction began to inter-
twine and rumors spread. One story said that $23,816 had
been found on the gangsters. That was true. Another story
said that more than $30,000 in rewards would be given the
captors. This seemed entirely possible but, in fact, was far
from the truth. The total rewards on all four men amounted to
only a few hundred dollars.

3

The captures had been relatively quiet. The real battle was yet
to come—and it would be fought between lawmen. As soon

as Matt Leach heard the news he requested custody of all
four men. So did Ohio, insisting they had a stronger case because of the murder of Sheriff Sarber. After Clarence Houston,
the Pima County Attorney, made several phone calls, he told
newsmen, "The Indiana authorities agreed with me that Ohio
was the place for Dillinger and his mob."

By this time Leach and five aids were en route to Tucson
by train with the Indiana reward money of $325: $100 each
for the escaped convicts and $25 for Dillinger as a parole vio-
lator. When he heard the report of Houston's statement, Leach
refused to believe it. "They've been my babies for so many
months that I've figuratively eaten and slept with them," he
said. "And fight or no fight I'll bring 'em back."

On the morning after the capture the prisoners and their
women were arraigned.

"Stand up," the justice of the peace told Dillinger, but he
merely slumped farther into his seat and said, "I ain't Dillinger."

The large arsenal of the gangsters was displayed and
Sergeant Robbins testified as to the number of fugitive war-
rants for the prisoners.

Pierpont interrupted. "Just because a fellow has money
does that make him a fugitive from justice?"

County Attorney Houston now asked the court to hold
the gangsters without bail, but their attorney, John L. Van
Buskirk, cited the Arizona constitution's clause on reasonable
bail. The justice of peace, after a glance at the machine guns,
said the gangsters were certainly entitled to reasonable bail:
$100,000 apiece. When bail for Mary Kinder and the other two
women was then set at $5,000 each, Pierpont again spoke up.
"I don't care what you do to me but that little woman had
nothing to do with it."

After the gangsters were taken back to the jail, Jack
Weadock of the *Star* went up to Makley's cell, reminding him
they had been friends years ago in St. Marys, Ohio. Makley
had once shoed horses in his father's blacksmith shop.

"So you're George's kid," said Makley. He was in a good
mood and told Weadock he had bumped into a mutual friend

while robbing the St. Marys bank. Pierpont, he said, was the dangerous one in the gang. "If anything happens here you watch out for Pete. He's a wild man." Dillinger, while nowhere near as tough, he confided, was a man they all trusted. He talked nostalgically of his family. "They were honest at least, even if never rich," he said, but their way of living was not for him. "Look at my dad, he worked like the devil all his life and what did he get out of it? I've lived as long in forty minutes at times as my dad did in forty years."

Swede Walker also visited the prisoners. Clark pointed to his bandaged head and said he was going to buy a football helmet when he was freed. "Every time we get in trouble I get hit over the head."

Dillinger, who had been receiving more attention than all the others combined since he was thought to be the leader, seemed to be enjoying the situation and was expansive. "We're exactly like you cops," he told Walker. "You have a profession—we have a profession. Only difference is you're on the right side of the law, we're on the wrong."

Hundreds of newsmen and photographers were pouring in from all over the country. Overnight Dillinger's fame, which had been confined until now to the Chicago area, was nationwide. Ironically it was his capture, not his crimes, which brought this sudden notoriety. Already Dillinger had become a national household word. The name, almost universally mispronounced with a soft "g," had a bold ring and stuck in the mind. Perhaps it reminded people of derringer and derring-do.

That afternoon B. B. Moeur, the Governor of Arizona, visited the jail. Pierpont stepped out of his cell, smiled affably, and said, "Well, Governor, I'm sorry to see you here."

Dillinger, who had lost his taste for publicity, refused to come out of his cell and would just glare at the Governor. He seemed worried only about the fate of his Boston bull puppy. When he heard that Mike McGuire, a hanger-on who lived at the jail, wanted the dog, he asked the jailer to grant the request. "He likes dogs," he said, "and I know he will treat the pup well."

Makley, on the contrary, was happy to chat with Governor Moeur and they discussed the weather, the Old Pueblo, mutual friends in Phoenix and Indianapolis. "When I get out of here," he said, "I'll be hotter than ever," then added as if to bolster his own confidence, "I've gotten out before."

Some of the lawmen thought it possible the Dillinger gang had kidnaped Bremer and brought him to Tucson and that John Hamilton, the only uncaptured member of the mob, was probably still holding him. This assumption led to a rumor that Hamilton was making plans to break out the gang and the sheriff borrowed a squad of Border Patrol guards as a precaution. Hundreds of civilian volunteers also answered the call for assistance, flocking to the courthouse armed with rifles, pistols, and shotguns.

That same day, Fireman Benedict received a telegram which marked the beginning of a bitter struggle for the rewards. *True Detective Magazine* offered him $100 if news reports of his identification of Makley and Clark were correct.

But when Benedict asked the police to confirm the story, they refused, insisting that the tip leading to the arrests had come from two traveling salesmen. One officer followed him to the door and said the police had hired an attorney to fight for any rewards.

Benedict now went to the sheriff's office and asked if his information had been passed on to the police. A member of the sheriff's staff would only say, "I can't tell you."

If the fight for the rewards had only begun, at least it was in the open, and the struggle for custody of the prisoners seemed to be settled later that day when Ohio offered to let Indiana take Dillinger if it could have the other three men for Sarber's murder. Indiana accepted.

But this jurisdictional peace was short-lived. Wisconsin now announced it too would fight for the gangsters. Its officials felt that their celebrated lightning justice, wherein a criminal could be tried, sentenced, and locked up in the state prison on the same day, was far superior to the systems in Indiana and Ohio, where lawyers could often delay the issue for months. Wisconsin claimed corruption had no chance in its courts and that there would be no spectacular escapes from the Waupun prison.

A new race for possession of the gangsters was on. By the next day, January 27, both Matt Leach and officers from Wisconsin were en route to Tucson determined to bring them back. And whether Leach liked it or not, he was getting reinforcements from Indiana: the Lake County Prosecuting Attorney and the State's Attorney General were on their way by air.

No matter what state got them, Arizona officials wanted the rewards before granting extradition. And one of the local candidates for the money expressed a widely felt opinion when he said, "Give them to the state that will pay us the most."

The only ones apparently unaffected by the controversy were the prisoners themselves. When Sergeants Eyman and Sherman came to the county jail to chat with the men they had helped capture, the atmosphere was almost jovial.

Pierpont said he thought they were two of the smartest officers he had ever seen and denied he had ever called Tucson a hick town or its officers hick cops. He didn't even seem to hold anything against the Tucson lawmen. "I think Frank Eyman was a swell fellow not to shoot me. . . . There are two kinds of officers—rats and gentlemen. You fellows are gentlemen and the Indiana and Ohio cops are rats."

Dillinger would only say he thought they were lucky. "Where you were smart was getting one of us at a time."

"If all this had happened in Ohio, we'd be laying on a slab," Pierpont called out from his cell. "They'd have murdered us."

By now Tucson was crowded with reporters, photographers, and tourists who wanted to see the gunmen. There was a flurry of excitement when more money was found hidden in the gangsters' belts, but that news was no longer as important as the question of who would get it. And who would get their cars and clothes . . . and the rewards?

The following day, Sunday, the struggle for jurisdiction began in earnest. Robert Estill, the Prosecuting Attorney from

Indiana, who wanted to send Dillinger to the electric chair for the murder of the East Chicago policeman, arrived in the city on the early air mail plane to assist Leach. He was a solemn-looking man with glasses and usually spoke in a deceptively soft manner, but in the courtroom he was energetic, aggressive, relentless. To him the New Deal was a religion and he had already made important enemies because of a four-month investigation of the excess profits of Northern Indiana Public Utilities. Insiders said his findings would cost Public Utilities more than a billion dollars in reduced rates.

Estill had turned his energies to the eradication of crime in a county notorious for its corruption, and sending Dillinger to the chair had become part of his crusade. It would also be a long step toward the governorship. McNutt, who was already being considered for the Presidency of the United States, supported Estill and knew that Dillinger's conviction would help both political careers.

Estill brought with him Hobart Wilgus, the patrolman used as a hostage by Dillinger at East Chicago, and when they arrived at the jail Dillinger began nervously pacing his cell like an animal. Wilgus said there was no doubt. This was the man he had seen shoot down Patrolman Pat O'Malley.

Later that same morning Matt Leach and his aids finally arrived by train from Indianapolis. He was so eager to see the gang, he hardly took time to wash up from the arduous two-day train trip before heading for the county jail. Dillinger's phone calls to Leach had indicated he was obsessed by his pursuer—who, apparently, was just as obsessed by his quarry. He walked up to the first cell. "Well, we meet again, John," he said, putting an arm through the bars. Reluctantly Dillinger shook hands.

Leach advised him to waive extradition but Dillinger only smiled; he was in no hurry to return to Indiana. "I haven't a thing to do when I get there."

Leach now stepped over to the cell holding Makley and Pierpont. For a moment Pierpont was silent, then he suddenly shouted, "You dirty son of a bitch, there's only one thing I regret—I came to Indianapolis to kill you and had the gun on

you and then didn't do it! You put my mother in jail at Terre
Haute, you bastard! . . . I'll never forget that. I'll kill you yet,
you dirty rat!"

He shook the bars, screaming obscenities, and Sheriff
John Belton told him to calm down; hadn't he been treated
well in Tucson? "I've nothing against you or any police but
that—that—" Pierpont glared at Leach until the lawman
quietly withdrew.

"There's a man who really loves his mother," Leach
thoughtfully remarked to a reporter. He went on to say that
Arizona didn't realize what dangerous, vicious criminals it
had caught and commended the local police highly for the arrests. Asked if he believed the gang had kidnaped Bremer,
he laughed. "They never played the snatch game."

That afternoon Dillinger was again in a belligerent mood,
refusing to talk to reporters. He answered all their questions
by shaking a tin cup containing a few coins. Only Tubby
Toms of the *Indianapolis News* got a cordial reception. Dillinger seemed to relax in his presence and even smiled. After
answering several questions Dillinger handed the newsman a
rabbit's foot, a present for being considerate to his family. He
didn't need it, he said, adding wryly, "My luck's beginning to
run out."

Tubby noted the foot was relatively fresh.

Dillinger grinned, and said he'd killed the rabbit at
Mooresville about two weeks previously. "I shot him out of
season. I guess I'm just a born criminal."

Later that day the battle of the states was joined when
the three-man contingent from Wisconsin, headed by District
Attorney John Brown, arrived and began a conference with
the outlaws' lawyer, Van Buskirk. They argued that a waiver
to Wisconsin where there was no death penalty would be to
the prisoners' advantage.

Van Buskirk saw the obvious merit of this proposal and
advised his clients to accept. To his surprise they refused to
sign the waiver until they were assured that Mary Kinder, their
"bird dog" at the Racine bank, would not be involved.

When the Wisconsin District Attorney heard of the gang's

unexpected reluctance he lost none of his confidence. "The mob that hung together in Lima," he told reporters, "will not split here."

He was right. Early that evening the gang decided to accept extradition to Madison and the only question was whether the Arizona officials would comply. Dillinger told a reporter that he could personally help the local lawmen make up their minds and promised to boost the Wisconsin reward to top whatever Ohio and Indiana offered.

When Prosecutor Estill heard about this, he phoned the local County Attorney, Clarence Houston, who not only sympathized with the Indiana-Ohio claims but had been impressed by Estill himself. Estill wanted all four prisoners taken to Indiana at once. It was a drastic proposal but if they didn't act right away, Wisconsin might get them. The Governor would only have to sign extradition papers for Dillinger since the other three were escapees from the Indiana State Prison. Dillinger, of course, would stay in Indiana and be tried for the O'Malley killing while the other three would be transferred immediately to Ohio, as previously agreed, for trial at Lima.

Houston now phoned B. B. Moeur. The Arizona Governor agreed to go along with the new proposal but even with this assurance Estill was worried. He knew the gangsters' lawyer was trying to get a writ of habeas corpus. In this event the four men would have to appear at once before a local judge to determine if they had been imprisoned lawfully. This might give Wisconsin time to press its case and win.

Estill suggested they sneak all the gangsters out of town by plane before Van Buskirk could get a writ but Houston said it would only be possible to slip out one. He would hire local aviators to fly Dillinger and Estill out of Tucson the next afternoon. Leach could bring the other prisoners by train.

Unknown to the two conspirators, something new was being added to the routine of the Pima County jail. That night Sheriff Belton unexpectedly declared open house and invited the crowds milling around the building to "come in and see Dillinger and the boys." Though his undersheriff warned that this would only increase the danger of a jail break, 415 visitors viewed the gangsters in the next few hours.

The following morning, while the first of 1,100 spectators were gaping at the prisoners, Estill and Houston were completing the plan to remove Dillinger at four that afternoon. At about 3:00 P.M. the Attorney General of Indiana, Philip Lutz, Jr., returned to Tucson after a morning conference with Governor Moeur in Phoenix and was buttonholed by *Star* reporter Fred Finney, who asked if there was anything new. Lutz, an admirer of the *Star* editorials, revealed Estill's plan. Finney thanked him and started hunting for J. Robert Burns, the paper's part-time photographer.

At about that moment a flight of eighteen U. S. Navy bombers was roaring over the courthouse and one of the guards remarked, "Here comes the rest of the gangsters."

It was only now that the local police learned of the plan to take Dillinger to Indiana. They converged on Houston at the county jail, demanding that the gangsters be sent to the state promising the largest rewards, Wisconsin.

While they were arguing, on the floor above, Sheriff Belton was telling Dillinger that he was about to be returned to his home state.

"They're not taking you to Indiana," called Pierpont from his cell. "They're putting you on the spot, boy!"

Dillinger, wild-eyed, retreated to the back of his cell. "You're shanghaiing me!"

The sheriff and his assistant pushed him against the back of the cell and, though he fought bitterly, his arms were brought behind him and fastened with handcuffs.

"I won't forget it," said Dillinger as he was pulled out of the cell. "I'll come back here and get the whole damn bunch of you."

He was hurried down the back stairs to a waiting car. Everything was done so quickly the crowd around the courthouse didn't realize what was actually happening. On the trip to the airfield Estill noticed that every time the car lurched, the handcuffs cut Dillinger's wrists and he turned white. Soon he was bathed in nervous sweat. Estill wished people who had read glorified reports of the desperado could see him now. At the airfield about a hundred people who had come to watch the Navy planes land saw, to their surprise, a shackled man led, protesting, to a Bellanca monoplane.

J. Robert Burns was excitedly taking picture after picture as Dillinger began another wild struggle to get free, cursing and spitting. In a nearby hangar Finney was phoning a play-by-play description to his paper. He said Dillinger was fighting like a mad animal.

Dillinger turned and shouted, "A nice frame-up you boys pulled on me!" He was pushed into the plane and one leg hand-cuffed to a post behind the pilot's seat. "Hell," he said sarcastically, "I don't jump out of these things."

Finney and Burns were already racing back to Tucson with their big story. Burns alerted the engraver and hurried into the darkroom, while Finney began typing. A few minutes later the photographer came out, his face crestfallen. In the excitement he had forgotten to pull the protective plate from the film pack after it was inserted in the camera. He had only blank pictures.

At the courthouse other reporters, still unaware of the flight, were pounding out a romantic story. The afternoon papers reported a marriage license had been issued to Mary Kinder and Harry Pierpont. According to an interview in the local *Citizen*, Mary said, "I presume no one understands us but I love Harry Pierpont. He has always been gentle and kind to me. . . . I realize that after we arrive in Indiana we may never meet again, for the law intends, if possible, to 'burn' him on a murder charge. That's why I want to marry him and when the vows are taken by us we will be united forever—in spirit at least. If the worst comes, I shall love him more even in death than life."

It was Pierpont alone who had requested the license. When Mary was asked to sign it, her reply—far from the reported flowery dialogue—was a curt, "Hell, no!" Then she told the priest Pierpont had sent that she couldn't get married because her divorced husband was still living. Besides she was not in love with Pierpont; they were only good friends.

Later that afternoon a mentally retarded prisoner who enjoyed the freedom of the courtyard came under her window. For the past few days he had been carrying messages to and from Pierpont. "Bird, bird," he kept repeating. She finally understood he meant a plane and asked whom they were going to take.

"One John. Already gone." She asked what had happened to Harry Pierpont. "He still here. He and Makley and Clark go to Ohio."

She was silent a moment, then said in a low voice, "Oh, my God."

Fifty minutes after leaving Tucson the plane carrying Dillinger landed at Douglas, Arizona, in a pasture known as International Airport. He was taken to the city jail, where he was stripped. About 10:30 P.M. he was given different clothing and driven back to the airport.

Forty-five minutes later a regularly scheduled American Airways plane was about to take off when Dillinger and his escort climbed aboard. There were only two other passengers and one of these, after a scared look at Dillinger, hastily left the plane.

On the tedious flight to El Paso Dillinger was in a talkative mood. "You did quite a job on my friend 'Fur' Sammons," he told Estill.

Estill had prosecuted Sammons on the habitual criminal act and succeeded in sending the gangster away for life. "We do our best," he said.

In a two-hour conversation Dillinger admitted robbing the Greencastle and East Chicago banks. He even confessed killing O'Malley, then said he would deny it, of course, on the stand. "It was self-defense. He was going to stop us. He shot first."

It was snowing in El Paso. Estill noticed Dillinger shiver in his shirt sleeves and put his extra jacket over the gangster's shoulders as they were alighting from the plane. Dillinger looked back at the prosecutor, puzzled.

. . .

In Tucson, the gang's lawyer, still unaware his most famous client was no longer in town, had just convinced a judge to sign an order for a writ of habeas corpus on behalf of the four outlaws. A hearing was set for the following morning. When Van Buskirk learned what had happened he was as indignant as the local police, who were still attacking County Attorney Houston for his part in the removal of Dillinger. Mark Robbins, the police identification officer, apparently expressed the views of his comrades when he said, "I can't understand Clarence Houston's idea that the police department, the fellows who risked their lives to go out and get those fellows, should have no voice of any kind in the disposition of the men."

They became even more enraged when Matt Leach told them he was authorized to give them only $300 in rewards— the $25 for Dillinger as parole violator couldn't be paid since he was being returned to the county, not the Indiana State Prison. Chet Sherman, who had posed as the messenger boy, seized the six-foot Leach by the shoulders and shouted, "You're everything Pierpont said you were. A double-crossing rat!"

Leach walked away without replying.

Just before ten o'clock the next morning the remaining three gangsters were taken to the jammed Superior Court. The involved plot to spirit Dillinger out of Arizona, which had taken such effort and caused so many lost tempers, suddenly proved unnecessary. The judge summarily denied the writ of habeas corpus. Billie Frechette and Opal Long were released but the three men and Mary Kinder were ordered back to Indiana.

Within an hour Harry Pierpont, Charles Makley, Russell Clark, and Mary were put aboard a chartered Pullman entitled "Camp Pike." Now they were in the custody of Matt Leach.

They left behind a debate that has not yet died down in Tucson; and even though Indiana finally had the prisoners, Attorney General Lutz could not control his indignation. He told reporters at the Southern Pacific station that there might have been collusion between the gangsters and the Wisconsin officials. Soon he would telegraph Attorney General Homer Cummings in Washington:

> URGE YOU INVESTIGATE IF ANY COLLUSION EXISTS BE-
> TWEEN GANG AND LOCAL WISCONSIN OFFICERS, WHO BY
> AGREEMENT WITH DILLINGER'S GANG ENTERED INTO CON-
> SPIRACY TO THWART INDIANA AND OHIO CLAIMS FOR EXTRA-
> DITION UNDER CONDITIONS SMELLING OF BRIBERY AND COR-
> RUPTION. LARGE DEPOSITS OF BONDS AS COLLATERAL UNDER
> CONTROL OF LOCAL OFFICERS DID NOT HAVE APPROVAL OF
> GOVERNOR OF WISCONSIN BUT OFFICERS SOUGHT CUSTODY
> THROUGH AGREEMENT OF VOLUNTARY SURRENDER NEGOTI-
> ATED THROUGH TUCSON ATTORNEY FOR GANG.
>
> ONLY THROUGH FIDELITY TO DUTY OF SOME ENFORCE-
> MENT OFFICERS INCLUDING GOVERNOR MOEUR AND COUNTY
> ATTORNEY HOUSTON WAS THE DELIVERY OF THE DILLINGER
> GANG AVERTED. I URGE AN INDEPENDENT FEDERAL INVESTI-
> GATION.

At 6:10 P.M. that day the American Airways plane carrying Dillinger started to land at Chicago's Municipal Airport. Estill generously handed his prisoner $10 for pocket money.

Captain Stege's entire Dillinger Squad and eighty-five other heavily armed policemen from two states were awaiting him. Dillinger's face was pale when Sergeant Frank Reynolds, who had already killed three men just because one of them was thought to be Dillinger, escorted him toward a caravan of cars. "You yellow son of a bitch," Reynolds said, "if anyone tries to stop us, you'll be the first dead man."

Dillinger was shoved into the rear of Reynold's car, shackled to two Indiana officers. Reynolds sat beside the driver and looked back at the prisoner. "Just start something," he said hopefully. Dillinger said nothing to the man he had threatened so often on the phone.

Thirteen cars, accompanied by a dozen motorcyclists, whose sirens shrieked almost continuously, headed toward Indiana, and people lined the streets of every community to watch the procession.

Just before 8:00 P.M. the noisy caravan drove into the seat

of Lake County, the quiet little country town of Crown Point, Indiana. Dillinger was obviously relieved to get away from Reynolds. A reporter, referring to his bare head, asked if he was going collegiate. "Hell, no. Somebody swiped my hat in Tucson just as they did my money."

Dillinger was taken into the sheriff's office, which was jammed with reporters all shouting to get his attention. Treated like a celebrity, he acted like one. His manner was good-natured but a bit condescending as if he were superior to anyone in the room.

A Chicago newsman asked if he really had sent the book, *How to Be a Detective*, to Matt Leach for Christmas. "Well," Dillinger said with a grin, "I was there when it was sent." The crowd laughed and Dillinger grew even cockier.

Judge William Murray, before whom Dillinger would be arraigned, joked about his tumultuous reception at the Chicago airport. Dillinger was not at all impressed by the judge's familiarity. In the past week a governor and a long line of well-known public figures had come to talk with him or ask for his autograph. When someone remarked that today was President Roosevelt's birthday, Dillinger replied, "You can say that I'm for him all the way, and for the NRA—particularly for banks." Again there was appreciative, almost fawning, laughter.

Now a newsreel cameraman began to take movies. On Dillinger's right was Estill, looking exhausted and a bit sheepish. He had tried to leave earlier but Judge Murray had persuaded him to stay for the pictures. On Estill's right was the attractive Lake County sheriff, Mrs. Lillian Holley, mother of twin eighteen-year-old daughters; she was filling out the term of her husband, who was murdered in line of duty.

Photographers started shouting for different poses. G. Reed Thomson, a free lance, called out to Estill, "Bob, put your arm around him."

Estill didn't hear but Dillinger did and he impudently rested his right elbow on Estill's shoulder. The prosecutor put his arm behind the gangster's back. Photographers and newsreel men took pictures as Dillinger grinned sardonically at

Sheriff Holley and then at the man who had vowed to send him to the electric chair.

This tableau would rock Indiana politics, lose one man his chance to be governor, and kill another's hopes for the Presidency.

Another incident that could have had political repercussions took place on the train carrying Dillinger's companions to Indiana. Tubby Toms of the *Indianapolis News* got the story but was afraid to file it. He was sitting with Matt Leach when a senator of a western state introduced himself and invited them to his compartment, where he proudly showed them a gold-plated, loaded .45 pistol. Leach then courteously asked the senator if he'd like to meet the gangsters. A few minutes later the senator was sitting on an aisle seat beside Makley with Pierpont leaning toward him. Wondering what the conversation was about, Toms silently took a seat behind them.

"Senator," he heard Pierpont say, "I'd like to have the use of that gat in your suitcase. You say it's worth a grand. I'll give you two."

Toms reported what he'd heard to Leach, who searched Pierpont but found nothing. The guards were told not to admit the senator again. It wasn't until much later that Toms learned why Pierpont and the senator got along so well. The senator, too, had done time in prison.

Another reporter from Indianapolis, Joe Shepard, interviewed Pierpont several times on the trip. Once Pierpont said, "Those who died deserved to die—and there are plenty more that deserve it and are still alive." Another time, "My conscience doesn't hurt me. I stole from the bankers. They stole from the people. All we did was help raise the insurance rates." And another time, "In the last few years of my life there's never been a day but that some incident hasn't occurred to make me hate the law." Then he noted, almost with pride, "I suppose I'm what you'd call an abnormal mental case, a case for a psychiatrist. Maybe I am. But once I was normal. Place your own construction on what I've said."

CHAPTER 11

Tiger by the Tail

1

WHILE PROSECUTOR ESTILL WAS PREPARING HIS CASE AGAINST Dillinger, the trial of Roger Touhy for the kidnaping of Jake "The Barber" Factor was coming to a close in Chicago. The evidence against him was more convincing than in the Hamm trial. Half a dozen witnesses had positively identified Touhy and his co-defendants as the kidnapers. Factor himself swore that after being held five days he saw Touhy when his blindfold was finally removed so he could write a note. He also said he had been kicked in the stomach and threatened with torture.

The state rested and, though Touhy appeared as cocky and impudent as ever, it seemed likely the verdict would be guilty. When Factor left the courtroom newsmen asked why he had previously claimed not to have recognized Touhy and were told that Captain Gilbert had ordered him to answer that way.

William Scott Stewart, Touhy's lawyer, opened the defense by arguing persuasively that the kidnaping had been faked for two reasons: to prevent Factor's extradition to England and to eliminate Touhy so the Mafia syndicate could control the labor unions. Several witnesses testified that Touhy had been with them during the time of the kidnaping and an eye doctor stated that Factor could not possibly have recognized anyone—not after five full days of being blindfolded.

A character witness, Father Joseph Weber, an aged, alert Catholic priest, said he had visited the Touhy home a week after the kidnaping and was positive Touhy was innocent. Then Policeman Gerard, who saw Factor a few minutes after being released, swore that his shoes were shined, hair combed, and clothes in good shape. He also said a news photographer had pulled out Factor's neatly arranged tie at the police station to make a better kidnap picture.

Touhy was not satisfied with this defense and insisted he tell his story, but Stewart thought this too risky and refused to put him on the stand. When Touhy angrily demanded a hearing from the judge, Stewart threatened to drop the case.

On February 1 the jurors retired and, after a day's deliberation, said they could reach no decision. The judge discharged the hung jury and called for a second trial in eleven days.

Touhy now signed an affidavit requesting a new lawyer. Stewart had no objections and offered his resignation but the judge threatened to jail him unless he continued. Touhy's fate remained in the hands of a man he didn't trust and who didn't want to represent him.

2

By now Bremer's family feared he was dead. Nine days after the fruitless bus trip to Des Moines, his father—not knowing, of course, that Karpis was presently in St. Paul completing plans for the pay-off—made a last desperate attempt to contact the kidnapers. He handed a statement to reporters and said in a broken voice, "Please give this all the prominence you can."

Addressed TO THE PARTIES HOLDING MY SON AND TO EDWARD G. BREMER, it read:

All city, state and federal authorities have consented to allow me in my own way for a limited time to seek the return of my son.

First and last I am only interested in the safe return of Edward, and if the following suggestions are carried out I will have no interest in any activity after my son is returned.

My telephones in home and office have been watched; therefore contact in this way is not desirable. I merely mention this to indicate to you men that I am sincere in my desire and efforts to communicate with you free from any outside interference.

I realize that I cannot publish my choice in making this contact. To convince you that there is no catch in this effort of mine I can see but one way to work out our negotiations. Edward will have to select someone regardless of where he may be located in the United States. Have Edward write this party a letter in his own handwriting referring to this notice in the press so that I will know he has read it. Enclose with Edward's letter your instructions to the party that Edward selects, but be sure to give sufficient time for the instructions to be carried out.

If I have not heard from Edward within three days and three nights, I shall understand that you do not wish to deal with me and I will feel I am released from any obligations as contained in this note.

Nothing happened on Sunday. Then on Monday about 7:30 P.M. the kidnaped man's secretary heard a knock at her back door. A bushy-haired man, Volney Davis, gave her a note which acknowledged the elder Bremer's statement and said that instructions would be sent shortly. The next afternoon Davis handed a note addressed to "Honest Adolf" to a Catholic priest, who promptly delivered it to Mr. Bremer.

It said, ". . . the coppers jimmed the last payoff," and gave instructions for payment of the ransom. That evening at 8:00 Walter Magee was to bring $200,000 in five- and ten-dollar bills to 969 University Avenue, where he would find a parked 1933 Chevrolet coupé with Shell Oil Company signs on each door. Inside would be a note with further instructions. Magee did as instructed and found this note:

Go to Farmington, Minnesota. The Rochester bus will arrive there at 9:15 P.M. and leave at 9:25 P.M. Follow one hundred yards in back of this bus, when it leaves Farmington, until you come to four red lights on the left of the road; then on the first road to the left and proceed at fifteen miles per hour until you see five flashes of lights; then stop and deposit packages of money on right hand side of road. Leave the two notes; get in car and go straight ahead.

Magee drove the Chevrolet to Farmington, then followed the Rochester bus. He passed through Zumbrota. Four or five miles later he saw four red lights on the bank of a hill to the left. He turned off on a gravel road and drove slowly for about half a mile.

A car approached from the rear, its headlights flashing five times. Magee stopped and placed two suit boxes filled with $200,000 on the right-hand side of the road.

In Bensenville Bremer was exhausted and half frozen. His injured left leg ached and he had to be half dragged to the bathroom. In spite of his condition he was memorizing details to pass on to the FBI. Children were playing nearby, apparently in a schoolyard. From an apartment overhead came the sounds of a baby crying; he also heard another, older, child playing on the floor.

He knew there was a stove in the next room for he could hear coal being shoveled from a bin into a scuttle. He could also hear his captors bickering. Two of them were drinking heavily and one even began pacing up and down the alley behind the kidnap house until forcibly dragged inside. Once someone said, "Let's bump him off. It's a bum job and we're not getting anywhere."

To Bremer's relief Dock Barker replied, "No, I gave Ed my word. He took it and it's not going to be broken. I'm running the show."

Early on the morning of February 7 Dock came into Bremer's room and announced that they were taking him home. Again curiously solicitous, he said, "Ed, if you ever get into any other trouble and we're at large, we'll help you, no matter what." He said another gang had offered $50,000 for Bremer now that they were finished with him but had been turned down.

Still blindfolded, Bremer had his heavy beard shaved. Then he was led out of the house and placed in what he guessed was a small coupé. After a short drive he was transferred to the back of a sedan and made to sit on the floor behind the driver.

The ride was tedious and cold. At about 8:00 P.M., as they approached Rochester, Minnesota, Dock Barker told Bremer they were going to set him free. Upon release he would count up to fifteen before removing the blindfold. Barker gave him a few dollars and said to take the 9:40 bus to St. Paul.

The car stopped. Bremer got out and started to count. "We haven't left yet," said someone. "Start again." He heard the car leave and counted to fifteen. When the car suddenly stopped he was sure they were going to shoot him but it started again and left. He removed the blindfold and could barely make out a light. He walked in circles for a while to start circulation since he didn't want anyone to see him stagger. He felt weak. His left leg ached painfully and his eyes were sore. Finally he limped toward the center of town.

At last the FBI could begin a full-scale investigation. The day after Bremer's release agents retraced Magee's route and, on the gravel road near Zumbrota, found four flashlights fitted with red lenses bearing the trademark "Merit Product." They soon learned the flashlights had been bought at the F. and W. Grand Silver Store in St. Paul and when the saleswoman was shown a picture of Alvin Karpis she said it looked like her customer. It was the first break in the case.

The next day, February 9, the FBI distributed a printed list of the serial numbers of the ransom money to all banks in the United States and in several foreign countries. A day later a farmer living near Portage, Wisconsin, found four empty gasoline tins and a funnel. Hoover's investigators, deducing these cans could possibly have been used to refuel the kidnap car, forwarded them to their Technical Laboratory in Washington. The laboratory found a fingerprint of Dock Barker's right index finger and Hoover was convinced that the Barkers were the kidnapers. The search was on.

3

In Chicago the second Touhy trial was nearing its climax. Father Weber had been told by his superiors not to testify this time; he could only send his blessings to Touhy. But something much more damaging to the defendant had come up—new evidence introduced by the state. Two men recently caught robbing a mail truck at Charlotte, North Carolina—Isaac Costner and Basil "The Owl" Banghart—were brought to Chicago. Costner testified they had helped Touhy kidnap Factor. His story was almost the same as Factor's, and the jury was obviously impressed. Again Touhy begged to be put on the stand. Instead, Stewart suggested they call Banghart, who claimed Costner was lying. Touhy reluctantly agreed.

Banghart was not an impressive witness for the defense. When Wilbert Crowley, the energetic prosecutor, proved he hadn't worked for three years Banghart replied he'd had a steady job in 1931. Where? "In the cotton duck mill in the U.S. Penitentiary at Atlanta, Georgia."

A little later Stewart asked what his current occupation was. "I am a fugitive," he said. From where? "From justice."

The dialogue continued like a music-hall routine when Crowley asked if Banghart knew a robber named "Dutch" Schmidt. "You were down in Charlotte with him, weren't you?"

"No."

"What?"

"That has nothing to do with this," said Banghart.

"You mean Charlotte has not?"

"Yes."

The judge now cut in as if on cue, "Are you talking about a girl or a town?"

"Charlotte, South Carolina," said Crowley.

"North Carolina," corrected Stewart.

Banghart swore that he and Costner had been approached by Factor more than a month after the alleged kidnaping. Factor said that some people suspected the kidnaping was a hoax and offered them $50,000 to fake evidence to make it look legitimate.

But the jurors didn't believe a word Banghart said and on February 13 Touhy was sentenced to 99 years in Joliet. Many of the spectators cheered, and as Touhy was being led into the corridor off the bull pen, he vomited.

Fifteen years later Costner would sign an affidavit that he had lied about Touhy and at a habeas corpus proceeding in 1954, Federal Judge John P. Barnes would indignantly declare that Touhy had "incurred the dislike of Captain Gilbert and the enmity of the Capone mob . . ." then accuse Gilbert of suppressing "important evidence" and the state of indulging in "numerous stratagems and artifices . . . consistent only with a design to bring about the conviction of Touhy at any and all costs. . . ." In conclusion Judge Barnes would say, "John Factor was not kidnaped for ransom or otherwise. . . . Roger Touhy did not kidnap John Factor and, in fact, had no part in the alleged kidnaping of John Factor. . . . Perjured testimony was knowingly used by the prosecutor to bring about Touhy's conviction—this being the case, his conviction cannot stand, regardless of the motive."

Touhy was freed but almost immediately was returned to prison when the ruling was appealed on the grounds that he had not exhausted legal avenues in the state courts. Eventually a higher court overruled Judge Barnes' decision on these technical grounds and it was not until 1959—after more than twenty-five years of imprisonment—that Touhy was finally paroled. But he enjoyed only twenty-three days of freedom. On December 16, 1959, he was killed on his sister's front porch by five shotgun blasts in a gang murder reminiscent of the days of Capone.

4

Only a few miles to the southeast, another trial—this one for murder—was being prepared in the sleepy country town of Crown Point, Indiana. At the beginning it was overshadowed by a picture—a picture of a prosecuting attorney with his arm around the man he was trying to send to the electric chair. J. Edgar Hoover said no picture ever made him more angry; Homer Cummings called Estill's conduct disgraceful. Frank J. Loesch, president of the Chicago Crime Commission, was "shocked at seeing newspaper photographs of a prosecutor who is about to prosecute a vicious murderer posing with his arm around the murderer's neck, both of them smiling and exhibiting friendship." To *The New York Times* it appeared to be "a modern version of the return of the Prodigal Son."

Few pointed out that Estill had only been one of many. Since their capture in Tucson the Dillinger gang had been treated with equal familiarity by prominent citizens, including at least one judge, a senator, and a governor. Fortunately for these men—as well as Matt Leach, who had insisted Dillinger shake his hand—no photographer had recorded their actions.

Estill ignored the growing criticism to concentrate on his case against Dillinger. On February 6 the little criminal courtroom at Crown Point was packed with several hundred spectators and almost as many reporters and photographers to hear Dillinger arraigned for trial by Judge William J. Murray.

Everyone had been searched before entering and this encouraged rumors that John Hamilton and several carloads of gangsters were in town, preparing to raid the jail. It was also reported that Sheriff Holley had received several letters threatening to kidnap members of her family if Dillinger were not freed.

"All these rumors, however baseless," said the local paper, the *Lake County Star*, "had the tendency to tighten the guard around the jail until it is now as impregnable as the Rock of Gibraltar or granite quarries of the old world.

"There will be no jail delivery; there will be no kidnaping; there will be no repetition of the Lima, Ohio, jail delivery in which Dillinger was liberated, as long as the 'boys' around the jail can keep their powder dry."

Dillinger, his mustache shaved off, was dressed in a blue shirt with an attached collar flopping in the current college fashion and many women looked at him admiringly. Though the object of scores of cameras, he was as unperturbed as a movie star.

His lawyer filed a motion to set aside the indictment and when it was overruled he asked Judge Murray—a short, heavy, agile man in his sixties—to continue the arraignment until February 9. Estill agreed.

Two days later, in Estill's office, five men positively identified Dillinger as the killer of Officer O'Malley. "There is no doubt about these identifications." Estill told reporters. "They will stand up in any court."

Sergeant Frank Reynolds was present and he wanted one question answered: Where was Hamilton? Dillinger swore he'd been shot four times and dumped in the Calumet River but Reynolds doubted the glib story and told Mrs. Holley that Dillinger merely wanted authorities to abandon the search for his confederate. Then Hamilton would be free to help break him out of Crown Point. Mrs. Holley, heeding this warning, augmented the already strong guard around the county jail with six National Guardsmen.

The next day, February 9, Dillinger was brought from his cell and finally arraigned in the courthouse to another packed audience. He had selected a new fat mouth—lawyer—to represent him. The son of a blacksmith, Louis Piquett was a short, chubby, middle-aged man of vitality and charm. His iron-gray hair stood above the scalp in a formidable three-inch-high pompadour. He had never attended law school but taught himself while waiting on tables and tending bar. After more than a dozen failures he finally passed the Illinois bar exams and went into politics, serving as City Prosecutor for Chicago. When his party went out of power he brought all the tricks he'd learned to the other side of the law. In court his perform- ances in the defense of criminals were always dramatic. Jurors were fascinated by his magnetic personality, melodramatic speeches, and emotional appeals.

A friend once warned him to stop handling hoodlum cli- ents but Piquett—pronounced to rhyme with ticket—just grinned like an aging pixie and said, "They're the only ones who have money these days."

Estill suggested the trial start in ten days.

"That would be legal murder," boomed Piquett, bouncing to his feet. "There's a law against lynching in this state."

"Yes," said Estill somberly, "and there's a law against mur- der, too."

Piquett indignantly flung back his gray mop of hair, shout- ing that he needed at least a hundred and twenty days to get witnesses from Michigan and Florida. Judge Murray com- promised and set the trial for March 12.

But Piquett would not give up. He appealed to the news- papers and to politicians, insisting that it was impossible for him to get his witnesses in time. He kept demanding a continu- ance with the insistence of a terrier worrying a rat and finally convinced Judge Murray of the justice of his claim.

The judge called in Estill and said he had changed his mind. What specifically did Estill have against the continu- ance? Estill pointed out they had tried Fur Sammons within ten days. "This man Dillinger is ten times worse than Fur and I see no reason for any consideration being extended to him."

Murray asked Piquett to explain more explicitly why he needed so much time.

"I've got $40,000 in bonds from the Greencastle robbery," said the chubby lawyer blandly, "and I'm waiting to fence it to get my fees."

In all his years of practicing law Estill had never heard

such a statement in the presence of the court and said he would not agree to the continuance on such ridiculous grounds.

Undismayed, the persistent Piquett now tried a different tack, and Estill soon learned that his opponent had been talking to court and jail officials. Like all prosecuting attorneys Estill felt his main job was to convict, but now he had an additional problem: keeping his prisoner in custody. He was sure Piquett would hesitate at nothing to free his client—including helping him break out of jail.

As in Tucson, Estill decided Dillinger had to be moved, so on the morning of February 12 six police cars from Hammond, Gary, and East Chicago suddenly arrived in Crown Point prepared to transfer the prisoner to Michigan City. Sheriff Holley was summoned to the Criminal Courts building to sign the petition for transfer. Then Estill phoned Judge Murray to be present.

When Murray arrived he urged Mrs. Holley not to sign. Estill was amazed. Why was he advising such action? The judge said that transferring Dillinger from the county jail would be an admission of weakness. This convinced Mrs. Holley. She refused to sign but, as a safety measure, agreed not to let Piquett bring witnesses into the jail to confer with Dillinger.

Now it was Piquett's turn to be indignant. With reporters crowding around, he shook his head accusingly, his hair flopping. "It seems she has taken on herself the duties of the Supreme Court of Indiana," he charged. "As it is now, I have two witnesses here in Chicago from Florida who said they saw Dillinger at Daytona Beach on January 14 at 8:30 P.M. The robbery and killing of the policeman at the bank at East Chicago occurred the next day at about 3:00 P.M. But if my witnesses can't see Dillinger and talk to him—what good are they?"

He waited a few days and when Mrs. Holley was still not impressed by his histrionics, he threatened to ask that the trial be transferred to a less prejudiced location unless his witnesses had free access to Dillinger. To prevent this Estill and Sheriff Holley again conferred with Piquett on Monday, February 26.

After some wrangling an agreement was reached. There would be no request for a change of venue; and Dillinger could see and talk to friends and witnesses. Piquett's maneuvers had balked Estill at every turn but his greatest coup was yet to come. A few minutes later a dark woman, heavily made up, identified only as Mrs. John Dillinger, was actually allowed to speak at length to the bank robber. A jailer who was listening could make little of their strange conversation—they talked mainly in numbers. The mystery woman, of course, was Billie Frechette.

Piquett confidently predicted victory in the coming trial and said he would produce at least ten witnesses to prove that the gang didn't leave Florida until the night of January 14. But he was bluffing. He knew the gang had left a week earlier and that Estill could prove it.

There was only one way to free Dillinger. Sometime in the following week Piquett kept a rendezvous at the grounds of the Century of Progress. There he handed over an envelope containing several thousand dollars—to a prominent Indiana judge. The judge promised to smuggle a gun into the county jail.

On the night of March 2 a low-flying plane made three circles over Crown Point, its pilot gunning the motor each time. Several residents who happened to see it jokingly suggested it might be a signal to the prisoner locked up in the county jail.

Even though Dillinger had already made one escape, those who knew how stout was Lake County's large, three-story brick jail had no fears he could break out. He was securely locked up in the "escape-proof" new section of the jail on the second floor. Between him and freedom were half a dozen barred doors and some fifty guards. In addition to using the regular employees, Mrs. Holley had buttressed the defenses with armed members of the local Farmers' Protective Association and a squad of National Guardsmen. At night floodlights illuminated the area around the big building.

It was a local joke that the great escape artist Houdini couldn't get out of Crown Point now. Dillinger himself seemed resigned. The guards weren't in awe of him—in fact, some even felt sorry for him. He told several of them how he longed to see his family in Mooresville, and this was true, for he often thought of his half brother and sisters. A few days previously he had written his fourteen-year-old half sister, Doris, wondering if his father let the two girls go to the show as often as Dillinger used to take them.

> . . . I would sure like to see all of you kids. Was sorry I didn't get to take you to the world's fair. Maybe, though, you will get a chance to go this summer. The fair will be bigger and better this year.
> I wish you kids could see the country I've been through the last few months. It would sure have been a treat to you.

But that night he had little time to think of his family or even feel sorry for himself. He was planning to escape the next day. He had $14 and a gun. That was all. He didn't even know the complicated layout of the building but he was sure it wouldn't take him long to find out when the time came.

The following morning it was raining. After breakfast Dillinger and the fourteen other prisoners in the felony cell block began exercising in the second-floor corridors of the new part of the jail. Another routine day had started.

A few minutes after 9:00 A.M. Sam Cahoon, an elderly attendant, unlocked the barred door leading into the cell block and let a group of trusties—trusted prisoners—enter for the morning clean-up. Cahoon was a good-natured, well-intentioned man who knew more about his jail than most attendants, having often served time here for drunkenness. Soon he would be characterized by a judge as "good for nothing" and "not a responsible person."

Dillinger casually walked up to the unsuspecting Cahoon, rammed a gun against his stomach, and nodded toward one of the opened cells. "Get in quick or I'll kill you."

Cahoon didn't move but the trusties obeyed the order. "I don't want to kill anyone," said Dillinger quietly. "Now you do as I tell you." He shoved the resisting Cahoon into the cell with the others and, keeping one hand on the gun in his pocket, he began questioning Cahoon.

Once he had a mental picture of the building's layout, Dillinger brought Cahoon to the stairs leading down to the old jail on the first floor. Dillinger cautiously descended a few steps, then looked carefully up the corridor of the old jail. He saw a man. "Call that fellow back here," he said.

Cahoon did, and Deputy Sheriff Ernest Blunk, the fingerprint expert and an appointee of Judge Murray, approached without suspicion. Dillinger jumped from behind Cahoon and pointed his gun at Blunk. He now brought the two hostages back up to the second-floor jail and locked them in with the others.

From Blunk he learned that Warden Lou Baker, the only experienced jailer at Crown Point and the man most likely to prevent the escape, was downstairs in his office. Dillinger led Blunk back down the stairs to the corridor and said, "Call Baker."

"Come on, Lou," shouted Blunk. "Someone back here wants you."

Baker, a slight man, was an inch shorter than Dillinger. Before the Depression he had been a jeweler and his favorite joke was, "I used to sell watches, now I watch cells." When he heard Blunk he was at his desk in the jail office near the front of the building. He walked back to Blunk, who was standing at the foot of the stairs leading up to the new jail. Suddenly Dillinger grabbed him from behind by the collar, poked a gun in his back, and told him to walk upstairs.

Dillinger felt more relieved once the warden was locked up but there were still about thirty other guards in the building, and he now forced Blunk to decoy three of these, one by one, from the outer rooms. Before he could make a break for freedom, however, he first needed more firepower. After some questioning he learned there were machine guns in the warden's office and once more forced Blunk to go downstairs with him. They crept up the corridor of the old jail toward the front of the building and finally came to the receiving room, which was separated from Baker's office by a barred door. Dillinger

stuck his gun through the bars at the turnkey, who unlocked
the door without any argument. Incredibly enough he was a
trusty, in for petty larceny.

As Dillinger stepped in, he saw a National Guardsman
standing just beyond the office and, in a whisper, told the turnkey to face the wall with hands up, then motioned Blunk to
call the soldier.

The unsuspecting Guardsman entered, to find himself facing a gun. Dillinger picked up two machine guns lying on the
window sill. Now he was ready to escape—and freedom lay
only a few feet ahead, out the front door of the big building.

But a dozen guards were stationed there and Dillinger
knew it. He would escape the long way—out the rear.

His luck held and the way was still clear as he marched
Blunk, the turnkey, and the Guardsman back upstairs to the
new jail.

Once there, he gave one of the machine guns to Herbert
Youngblood, a big Negro from Gary awaiting trial for murder,
and asked if anyone else wanted to go with them. Only two
inmates accepted the invitation. Dillinger led the group to the
rear of the building but when they came to the kitchen door,
he ordered Blunk to go in first. Here they surprised three
farmer vigilantes sitting at a table having coffee. Dillinger ordered them to join the party, took two of their raincoats, and
quietly led everyone down the stairs to the jail garage. Youngblood brought up the rear.

At the bottom of the stairs the three vigilantes ducked
into a washroom and were followed by the two would-be escapees. Dillinger didn't care—they were, in effect, locking
themselves up where they could do no mischief. He was too
busy capturing an assorted group in the garage: the jail cook,
kitchen helpers, several trusties, and Warden Baker's mother-
in-law, matron for the women prisoners.

Dillinger ordered the matron into a Buick. When he saw
the keys weren't in the car, he asked Blunk where they were.
The frightened fingerprint man said he thought Warden Baker
had them.

Dillinger was once more only a few feet from freedom but he could think only of the Buick—it seemed such a perfect means of escape. He decided to press his luck and go all the way back to the jail. Leaving Youngblood to guard the hostages, he retraced his steps upstairs and asked the incarcerated warden for the car keys. Baker pretended he didn't know where they were and Dillinger, realizing he had already wasted too much time, hustled back down to the garage. Now all he could do was pull the ignition wires from the police cars and try to find other transportation.

Just above, in the warden's apartment, Mrs. Lou Baker heard a strange rattling noise. She went to the clothes closet, looked through a peek hole, and saw her husband rattling the bars of a cell.

"Irene," he called, "has the car left the garage?" She didn't know what he was talking about. "Call for help. John Dillinger is out."

She picked up the phone connected with the jail switchboard but for some reason there was no answer. Then she remembered her mother, the matron, had just gone down to the garage. She went to the bedroom window overlooking the street behind the jail, saw a mailman and shouted, "My God, John Dillinger is out!"

He looked up in puzzlement.

She ran down into the garage and saw Deputy Blunk with a man holding a machine gun. "John Dillinger is out," she told them. The man with the gun walked toward her. "Oh, no," she said. "You're not Dillinger."

Dillinger took her arm. If he hadn't, she would have fallen.

"Mrs. Baker," said Blunk, "you do as he tells you."

Dillinger led her to the laundry where Youngblood was guarding her mother and the kitchen help as well as several trusties who were debating whether they too should escape. Mrs. Baker ended their parley when she told them the building was surrounded by heavily armed guards.

Dillinger put on one raincoat, handed Youngblood the

other. Then he pushed Blunk out of the side door and followed him to the street. Behind him he left the escape-proof jail and a score of locked-up jailers. He was pleased with himself—even Jesse James had never put on such a one-man exhibition.

There was not a single guard patrolling the rear of the building. Nor, at the moment, were there any on the right side of the jail. Otherwise they would have seen the trio walk behind the Criminal Courts building and into the back door of the Ford Garage.

Blunk and Dillinger approached Ed Saager, a mechanic working on a generator. The sight of a gun was common in Crown Point and even when Dillinger asked which was the fastest car, Saager thought they were a posse.

"The V-8 Ford." It happened to be Mrs. Holley's car.

Dillinger told Saager to get in the car but the mechanic said he was working. "Better do as he asks," said Blunk. Saager, imagining he was being deputized, resentfully got into the back seat.

"Get in and drive, Blunk," said Dillinger, climbing in front. Youngblood silently got in the back seat with Saager.

Robert Volk, a mailman, had just parked his truck inside the garage. Recognizing Dillinger, he ducked behind the truck as the Ford started moving. A salesman came out of the showroom.

"Keep still," warned Volk. "It's Dillinger." The salesman froze. After the car lunged out of the garage and speeded north on Main Street, Volk picked up a phone and called the Gary police. Their reaction angered him: they said only that they would check into the matter. He ran to the first floor of the Criminal Courts building.

"Dillinger's escaped!" he said.

The armed guard said he was nuts and shooed him away. Volk ran across the alley to the jail and pressed a bell. There was no answer. Finally one of Estill's deputies looked out a third-story window of the courthouse and asked what was going on.

"Dillinger's escaped!"

.   .   .

At Dillinger's direction, Blunk drove through a red light in the middle of the business district but there were no police on hand to notice. Once out of town, Dillinger turned, grinned at Saager, and briefly showed a pistol. "It's a wooden gun. That's what got me out." Saager at last realized this was Dillinger, not a lawman. The gun looked real enough to him.

Dillinger nudged Blunk. "You wouldn't think a guy could make a break with a pea shooter like this, would you?" He laughed and put the gun—a real one—in his pocket.

They continued on a zigzag course into Illinois, stopping only once—to unscrew a red police light from the front of the car and put chains on the two rear tires so they could navigate the back roads turned muddy from the rain.

As they drove on, Dillinger sang, "I'm heading for the last roundup." Youngblood didn't join in; so far he hadn't said a word. When Dillinger noticed there were no telephone poles and therefore no way to report their position, he told Blunk to stop. He handed Saager $4, shook hands with the two hostages, and said apologetically, "I'd give you guys more but that's all I can spare."

He directed Youngblood to hide between the seats— together they could be too easily identified. Then he grinned at the hostages standing on the road and said, "I'll remember you at Christmas." As the car churned off through the mud at a conservative speed, chains clonking, he waved.

When Prosecutor Robert Estill drove up to the Criminal Courts building not long after the escape, a deputy sheriff shouted to him, "Dillinger got away!" He found Mrs. Holley in tears. No one apparently was in charge and guards stood outside talking to spectators. Estill immediately filed charges against Blunk and Cahoon, ordered them arrested. He wouldn't know for some time that an hour after the escape only three phone calls had been placed from the jail—to local police stations. Apparently it never occurred to anyone to inform the state police.

.   .   .

In Chicago Captain Stege, who had just disbanded the Dillinger Squad, had to alert it again to be on the watch for a Ford V-8, license number 679,929. "What's the use of arresting Dillinger if we can't keep him in jail," he told a reporter. "I'm sending squads all over the city to nab him if he tries to cross the Indiana border. But even if we do get him, it will probably be the same thing over again. I'm disgusted."

When Dillinger drove into Chicago that afternoon no one stopped Mrs. Holley's Ford. It seemed only a fitting climax to the day's mistakes that the wrong license number had been passed on to Stege by an excited Crown Point official.

The first thing Dillinger did in Chicago was to phone Piquett and tell him to be at a designated location on Belmont Avenue at 4:00 P.M. He wanted money.

Piquett found Dillinger lolling in the driver's seat of the car. Youngblood was still crouched in the rear.

That night newspapers all over the country ran headline stories of the wooden gun escape. A nation, fascinated by Dillinger's impudence when he was brought back from Tucson, was now outwardly appalled. Secretly, however, many were titillated by this dramatic and unexpected turn of events; it was a welcome relief from the realities of the Depression.

When an *Indianapolis Times* reporter told the news to the elder Dillinger tears rolled down his cheeks and he said hoarsely, "And he got away!" He alternated between smiles and tears. Finally the man, who had once thought his son was hopeless, said with a touch of pride, "Well, he was pretty tricky. He's no fool."

The day's events certainly had proved that John Dillinger was far from a fool. Yet he had committed one small mistake: driven a stolen car across a state line. He had stolen other autos before he joined Pierpont and nothing had ever happened but now he had violated this federal statute in a sheriff's car and with the eyes of the world on him. This was all the FBI needed. Now they could join the hunt.

PART FIVE

•

CHAPTER 12

"Gimme the Big Bills!"

1

By Sunday morning, March 4, there was no doubt at all that Dillinger was America's Public Enemy Number 1. People imagined they saw him everywhere. Reports came from dozens of towns and cities in ten states, some as far east as Pennsylvania.

If the rest of the United States was fascinated and even entertained by the escape, the citizens of Dillinger's home state certainly were not. They had been humiliated and demanded an immediate investigation. The hunt for scapegoats began. A former judge of Circuit Court said Dillinger could not have escaped without help outside the jail. "In my opinion the entire prison organization at Crown Point needs a cleaning out." A Criminal Court judge suspected that "corruption and cowardice" played a major part in the affair. A former U. S. District Attorney said, "John Dillinger's escape is one of those things which should never have happened. It is disgusting."

The Republicans, of course, blamed Governor McNutt. Hadn't he paroled Dillinger in the first place? McNutt in turn ordered Attorney General Lutz to conduct a thorough investigation. "The nation is horrified and shocked at the escape of this notorious bank robber," said Lutz, "and I am surprised that Lake County officials let him get away."

Those Wisconsin authorities, recently accused by Lutz of conspiring with Dillinger in Tucson "under conditions smelling of bribery and corruption," could not hide their delight at the Indiana Attorney General's embarrassment. One said, "In view of what happened [at Crown Point], I wonder on whose side the bad odor lies."

In Chicago Captain Stege of the Dillinger Squad said, "How in the name of common sense could a prisoner go through six barred doors to freedom? . . . But I told them it would happen. I pleaded with Governor McNutt's secretary to put him in the penitentiary.

"Now bright and early Monday Dillinger will rob a bank to get funds. Then when he gets together with John Hamilton, the two of them will raid a police station some place and get guns and ammunition. Then maybe they'll come back to Chicago for another game of tag."

It was a remarkably accurate guess. At that moment Dillinger was in Chicago trying to form a new gang so he could rob a bank on Monday or Tuesday at the latest—but he was having his troubles. While Pierpont and Makley had carefully picked their gang over the years, he needed money at once and had no time to be selective.

For his first lieutenant he chose Hamilton, who appeared so steady but had shown at East Chicago that he could be as reckless as Dillinger himself. Their selection for chief torpedo was Lester Gillis, the sour-natured young man, better known as Baby Face Nelson, whom Pierpont and Mary Kinder had considered such a poor touring companion on the trip to Tennessee. He was a stocky five foot five and his innocent, boyish face hid a vicious temper. He was the first of Dillinger's associates who enjoyed using a gun. Dillinger, Hamilton, and Pierpont had all killed rather than be captured but Nelson, like the Barrows, was addicted to violence and had only one thing in common with Dillinger. He liked women and was rarely without the company of his pretty wife, Helen—or an attractive substitute.

Baby Face had been brought up in the Chicago packing-house district and graduated from stealing cars for thrills to crime for profit. After serving a term in the St. Charles School for Boys he began to rob banks, was caught and sent to Joliet. While returning to prison from trial, he escaped and fled to California, where he became a bootlegger. But this paid poorly and he had recently returned to his home town.

Dillinger had one more good contact—his old companion at Pendleton and Michigan City, Homer Van Meter, who was then in St. Paul and had been robbing banks in the Northwest for several months. Dillinger, Billie Frechette, Hamilton, and Nelson drove to the Twin Cities on March 4 and within a few hours of their arrival Van Meter introduced them to Eddie Green, an associate of Harry Sawyer and well-known as a jug marker—one who knows which banks to rob. Green already knew the bank they should hit first and it was in Sioux Falls, South Dakota. He also could supply the sixth member of the team—an expert machine gunner named Tommy Carroll.

Dillinger suggested they follow the same procedure as that used at Racine. Hamilton vouched for its efficiency and the others quickly agreed. That is, all but Nelson, who had his own theories of robbing banks—he liked coming through the front door shooting. Van Meter laughed sarcastically and the short, squat Nelson moved toward him. For a moment it appeared as if the gang would disintegrate as fast as it had been organized but Dillinger stepped between the two good-humoredly.

Though the crisis was over, Dillinger was rightly concerned—trouble could break out at any moment between two such temperamental antagonists, but there was nothing he could do about the situation now. He desperately needed cash; not only for himself but for Pierpont, Makley, and Clark, who were waiting in the Lima jail to be tried for the murder of Sheriff Sarber.

The following morning, March 6, the new Dillinger gang drove into Sioux Falls in a new green Packard, and a few minutes before ten parked in front of the imposing Security National Bank and Trust Company.

A pretty bank stenographer jokingly remarked to a clerk, "There's a bunch of holdup men." The clerk was not joking when he replied he didn't like the way they looked and, as they got out of the big car, he put a finger on the burglar alarm button in readiness.

It was a cold, clear day. Hamilton remained near the Packard. Carroll, a happy-go-lucky ex-boxer, stationed himself in front of the bank, a machine gun hidden under his overcoat, while Dillinger led the other three inside. Suddenly Nelson, right behind him, pulled out his machine gun and began shouting in a shrill voice, "This is a holdup. Lay on the floor."

The clerk pushed the button and the burglar alarm on the side of the building clanged. Dillinger paid no attention to the noise and walked into the cage of the head teller, Robert Dargen. Laying his automatic on the counter, he completely ignored Dargen and began to scoop up the bills. Dargen debated about grabbing the gun, decided not to, and a moment later Dillinger asked, "Is that all of it?" It was. Dillinger now escorted the head teller back to the vaults. But Dargen had trouble with the complicated five-way combination of the money vault.

Van Meter ran up, jammed a machine gun into his side and said, "Open it up, you son of a bitch, or I'll cut you in two."

Dargen said he would if Van Meter would take the gun out of his ribs. Dillinger stood by calmly but the tall, skinny bandit talked and threatened constantly, until the door finally swung open. Van Meter eagerly pulled out about $14,000, then ordered Dargen to open the next vault.

The head teller said he didn't have the combination and that it contained only bonds. Van Meter immediately began shouting for the bank's president.

At the police station the desk sergeant got a telephone call about some trouble at the bank but the caller didn't mention that the alarm was ringing and the sergeant, figuring some drunk was bothering the customers, sent a patrolman to quell the disturbance. When this man walked into the bank a few minutes later, he was disarmed and told to lie on the floor with the customers.

Baby Face Nelson was hopping around the lobby like an enraged bantam rooster. He wanted revenge on the one who had set off the alarm. Bounding up to the front of a cage, he stuck his machine gun at the teller and said, "I'm going to kill the man who hit the alarm and I know you did it!"

The teller argued that the alarm button in his cage was up and if he had pushed the alarm, the button would now be down. Dillinger, still behind the cages, called out, "Forget it and get the money."

The next moment Nelson looked through the side window and saw a man in a khaki uniform getting out of a car. It was an off-duty policeman, Hale Keith, drawn by the growing crowd around the bank. The alarm was still ringing as Keith hitched up his belt, a habit of his.

Nelson, thinking Keith was going for a gun, hurdled a waist-high railing, jumped up on a desk, and began firing through the plate-glass window. He saw Keith fall, then hopped off the desk and shouted, "I got one of them!" His face was yellowish, his eyes wild.

Out front, Carroll was standing in the middle of the street. He had already captured and lined up two carloads of police, including the chief, without firing a shot. A fascinated crowd of about a thousand was pressing around the bank, filling the streets.

Melvin Sells, Sheriff of Minnehaha County, was in his office at the courthouse talking to a court reporter when the phone rang and some man asked if they had any guns. Sells, thinking it was a joke, reckoned they had a few.

"Better bring them up to 9th and Main." The informant hung up.

Sells said he thought he was being kidded but he handed the reporter a machine gun and took a rifle. They walked somewhat sheepishly out of the courthouse, half expecting some practical joker to appear.

Several blocks from the bank Sells saw a mob, with hundreds peering down from upper-story windows. It looked like a fight. Then Sells saw Carroll standing in the center of the streetcar tracks, brandishing a machine gun at a line of police officers. The sheriff and reporter headed for the second floor of a hotel, hoping to get a clear shot at the robbers.

By now they had collected over $49,000 and were rounding up some ten employees as hostages. Those who were too slow got a sharp kick from Van Meter, who was still chattering. The hostages were ordered to surround the gangsters. As the group neared the front door, Nelson, who had wanted to enter with guns blazing, decided to exit, at least, on his own terms. Quite unnecessarily he shot the glass out of the front door.

Once outside, still acting as if he were the leader, he selected five girl hostages and told them to mount the running boards of the bandit car. One said she couldn't hold on and was allowed to step off.

As the Packard started south with the four girls and Leo Olson, a teller, riding outside, Patrolman Harley Chrisman, who had just found a rifle in a hardware store, shot a hole in the car's radiator. When the motor sputtered after a block, the Packard stopped and the hostages jumped off the running boards.

"Come on back here," shouted one of the robbers, firing a shot in the air—and everyone hopped back. One girl told Olson she couldn't hang on and he put an arm around her. Somehow the Packard was started again and a few minutes later it turned right, then left. A car containing Sheriff Sells and three other lawmen was now in pursuit but still out of sight, half a mile to the rear.

Olson, who had always imagined a getaway car would careen at top speed, marveled at the Packard's leisurely, careful pace of less than twenty-five miles an hour. The car turned into Dakota Avenue, slowing cautiously to pass a milk wagon drawn by horses. At a dip in the street it again slowed and before long they were on Route 77, the main highway to the south. There were no police yet in view but Dillinger knew they would soon arrive and he told the driver to stop, so that large roofing nails could be scattered on the road.

"The girls are freezing," called out Olson.

"Well, come in the car," said Dillinger. The four shivering girls crammed into the back seat, sitting on the laps of three robbers.

"What about me?" asked Olson. In spite of the cold, his shirt was soaked with perspiration. When Dillinger told him, "You're through," he stepped to the road, thinking he would be shot.

But Dillinger merely told the driver to get moving. After four miles the damaged radiator began to steam violently. The robbers waved down a Dodge and told the owner, a farmer, to get into the fields until they were out of sight. While the four hostage girls waited fearfully on the road, gasoline cans were transferred from the disabled Packard to the Dodge.

Only one car passed. A woman driving south slowed down when she saw the two stalled cars, thinking there had been an accident. She called to the four girls standing on the highway, warning them they'd catch their death of cold without coats. They hadn't even realized they were shivering.

At that moment Sheriff Sells and his three companions, who had been delayed by punctures from the roofing nails, approached. They stopped a hundred yards from the three parked cars but were afraid to fire for fear of hitting the girls on the road and simply watched the robbers scramble into the farmer's Dodge. They saw Nelson make a move to grab a hostage, then saw Dillinger pull him, protesting, into the Dodge.

Now an all-out chase began with several exchanges of fire whenever the police drew within range. It led almost into Iowa but within two hours the pursuers lost the trail. By this time Dillinger was heading back east and before midnight arrived in Minneapolis. The gang went up to Green's apartment to count the money. Nelson, who had been incessantly complaining because Dillinger hadn't stopped to let him get a good shot, began arguing with Van Meter about who had contributed most to the success of the operation. Nelson insisted that he had saved everyone by shooting Keith through the side window while Van Meter claimed credit for getting the head teller to open his vault.

The bickering stopped when Nelson saw Green laying the money on a table in six equal piles. Grabbing his machine gun, he wanted to know who the hell Green thought he was.

"Let Lester count it," said Dillinger diplomatically.

Nelson scooped up the money and piled it on the floor. Like a petulant child who insists on making the rules of every game, he slowly, methodically made six heaps, the others watching in silence.

Once Dillinger had his share—about $7,600 in currency and bonds—he phoned Louis Piquett that he now could help Pierpont and the others pay their attorney and suggested that Mary Kinder, recently freed after being held twenty-eight days in the Indianapolis jail on suspicion of aiding the Michigan City break, be sent at once for the money. She could be trusted.

2

For the first time Dillinger had been the leader in a major robbery but, ironically, the law refused to believe he had even been in Sioux Falls. The few witnesses who said they could identify him were not believed and the possibility was even ridiculed by the man who headed the combined inquiry, the chief of the northwestern bureau of the Burns Detective Agency.

Bancorporation, a holding company for over a hundred banks in the Northwest, didn't agree, their underworld contacts insisting not only that Dillinger was the leader but that the new mob was going to strike another bank in the same area soon. Explicit warnings were sent out to banks in Minnesota, South Dakota, and Iowa.

Bancorporation was correct: Dillinger was planning another robbery. Green and Van Meter were scheduled to leave that night for Mason City, Iowa, where they would room at the local YMCA and spend the day wandering around the neighborhood of the First National Bank.

A few hours before their departure Mary Kinder arrived from Indianapolis, called the phone number Piquett had given her, and Van Meter made arrangements to meet her several hours later on a deserted road. The two had little regard for each other since Mary shared Pierpont's low opinion of the erratic Van Meter. He told her curtly that Dillinger was too tired to come himself but she didn't believe it. And when Van Meter added, "Johnnie doesn't want to see you because he's afraid of women," she believed it even less.

She said she wouldn't leave without seeing Johnnie and Van Meter finally admitted that Dillinger hadn't been identified at Sioux Falls and wanted to stay under cover. He handed her an envelope from Dillinger containing $2,000 in bills, a good part of his cash share of the robbery.

In Lima Pierpont's trial was being conducted in a carnival atmosphere in a crowded courtroom only a few hundred feet from the scene of Sheriff Sarber's murder. The prisoner was in shackles, guarded by machine guns, and the constant target of movie cameras.

Pierpont's attorney, Miss Jessie Levy, had tried to prove he was at his mother's farm at the time of Sarber's murder but this defense was completely exposed by a surprise witness. Shouse, the man kicked out of the gang in Chicago, took the stand and was telling everything he knew.

Lima was almost in a state of siege. The courthouse was heavily barricaded with sandbags and guards patrolled the surrounding streets. It was feared that Dillinger would attack any minute with a new, heavily armed gang and break his friends out of the same jail he had been freed from.

Since the county had neither the money nor personnel to guard its jail, Governor George White had ordered General Harold Bush, an artilleryman, to form a defense with a contingent of National Guardsmen. Bush, nicknamed "Whispering Willie" because of his booming voice, had already set up three .30 caliber machine guns at strategic spots. Seven dummy guns made of wood and a barrier ten feet high between the sheriff's quarters and the courthouse rounded out the defenses.

The climax of the trial came on the morning of March 11 when Pierpont himself was put on the stand by Miss Levy to testify that he was not in Lima on the night of the murder. But his words had little effect in the face of Shouse's factual account. Pierpont seemed to realize that his testimony had not changed anything but he remained calm, almost detached. In an effort to goad him into disclosing his violent nature, Prosecutor Ernest Botkin began taunting him during the cross-examination, claiming that Pierpont, who had been brought to Michigan City from Tucson, had agreed to leave the prison and stand trial only to get out of the hole.

He had touched Pierpont's most vulnerable spot—his pride. The defendant shouted angrily, "I was in the hole twenty-one months one time!" and a moment later leaned toward Botkin and cried out, "An umpire can win any ball game!" He ridiculed Botkin's ability, charging that the prosecutor had built a fake bank robbery case, "brick by brick," against his brother, Fred. "You framed it right here in your own courthouse and you caused his arrest," he shouted.

When Botkin accused Pierpont of engineering bank robberies that had netted $300,000 in the short time since he'd escaped from prison, the bandit grinned and said truthfully, "I wish I had." Then he added, "Well, at least if I did, I'm not like some bank robbers—I didn't get myself elected president of the bank first."

The crowd burst into laughter and the judge ordered the last few lines stricken from the record.

"That's the kind of man you are, isn't it?" prodded Botkin.

"Yes," retorted the prisoner, encouraged by the audience response. "I'm not the kind of man you are—robbing widows and orphans. You'd probably be like me if you had the nerve."

Late that afternoon Jessie Levy delivered her closing argument. After a plea for mercy she said, ". . . and I now leave the fate of Harry Pierpont in your hands and, 'Even though I walk in the valley of the shadow of death, I fear no evil.' I know God is with me, with the defendant, in the hearts of every one of you." For the first time Mrs. Pierpont was sobbing. The defendant and his father sat with heads lowered. "So I hand him over to you, and I pray God in His goodness will show you the way to do the right thing."

In his closing argument Botkin remarked, almost as an aside, that if it hadn't been for a tip from a certain informer, they "probably would not have been able to round up this gang."

Again Pierpont reacted, rising part way from his chair and shouting, "Yes, and if you had never heard of Matt Leach, you wouldn't have heard of me. Matt Leach gave you my address!"

Later when Botkin said Mrs. Pierpont was "partly responsible for her son being in crime" the heavy-set woman who sat beside Pierpont at the defense table outdid him. She leaped to her feet and yelled, "I'm glad you're not the judge!" Across from mother and son, the elder Pierpont sat, frail and subdued.

Botkin demanded the death penalty. "If this evidence doesn't require the chair, I don't know what I'm talking about. . . . It is our duty to uphold the law, impose the proper sentence. Members of the jury, if you'll do this, you will have nothing to fear or regret. The only thing you need to fear is violation of that thing that your conscience tells you to do."

After deliberating only fifty-five minutes the jury returned with a verdict of guilty—and no recommendation for mercy. Pierpont sat quietly with a half smile on his face. Judge Everett said he would pronounce sentence later and asked if the prisoner had anything to say.

"No, not a word."

Photographers swarmed around the defense table but Mrs.

Pierpont held a scarf in front of her son's face. He whispered something and kissed her. Then he was unchained and led through lines of National Guardsmen to the jail. Here Makley called from his cell, "Well, Pete, what was it?"

"Well, what would it be?"

The next day General Bush announced he had just been warned that Dillinger was on his way to Lima. "I'm not going to call out a regiment," he told reporters. "I think we're set."

Chicago police thought the threat serious enough to transfer Pierpont immediately to the state penitentiary. They believed that Dillinger was hiding in Chicago—only two days before there had been a gun battle in Schiller Park.

Just after Makley's trial began that morning, Judge Everett added to the tension in the courtroom by mysteriously declaring, "We have received direct word that Dillinger is on his way here with armed men."

In Columbus Governor White and his daughter were put under heavy guard for fear Dillinger might kidnap them and demand Pierpont's freedom as ransom. This precaution seemed justified when police in northwestern Ohio were alerted that night to watch for an Illinois car containing three heavily armed men, one presumably John Dillinger.

3

At about 7:00 that same evening Harry Fisher—assistant cashier of the First National Bank of Mason City, Iowa, and the man responsible for opening the main vault every morning—was reading the *Globe-Gazette* when his wife came from the kitchen and said someone was looking in the front door.

It was Eddie Green, Dillinger's jug marker. Fisher came to the door and Green asked if this was 1228 North President.

Fisher, a small man of fifty-nine, said 1228 was a few doors up the street.

"Oh." Green looked intently at the key man in Dillinger's

plan. He had to recognize him the next morning. Then he left without saying anything else and walked off in the wrong direction.

March 13 was cold and though the sun occasionally shone through clouds, there were flurries of snow. After lunch Green and Van Meter checked out of the YMCA, a location appealing to the latter's sense of humor, and drove their Buick almost four miles to the southeast of town where they parked in a sand pit just across from a rural school. Soon a large car came from the north; Dillinger, Carroll, Hamilton, and Baby Face Nelson got out and transferred to the Buick. At about 2:00 P.M. they headed toward town.

Mason City was a prosperous community of 25,000, typically Midwestern in appearance and manner, eventually to be immortalized by one of its native sons as the setting of *The Music Man*. In addition to being a center of rich farmlands, it had withstood the Depression better than most Iowa towns because of the local cement plants.

On that day the First National Bank had almost $240,000 in cash within its vaults, an astounding sum in 1934 for such a relatively small city. Eddie Green had done his research well and if this robbery succeeded, the gang would have enough to afford the best equipment, lawyers, judges, politicians, and police spies. With this one robbery they could possibly insure themselves a long and safe career in crime.

But Dillinger had already decided on a far different future. With his share, some $40,000, he would at last be able to do what he and Jenkins had spent so many hours talking about in prison: escape to Mexico or South America to "live like a king."

The officials of the First National, like those of the other banks associated with Bancorporation, had been warned they might be robbed any day, but they weren't particularly concerned. Robbery was like death; it happened to someone else. Besides they felt well protected. Some fifteen feet above the lobby on a balcony attached to the front wall was a seven-foot-high steel cage. Within this shield sat Tom Walters, the bank

guard. Through its bulletproof window he could survey everything below and at the first sign of trouble he was to fire his
gas gun half a dozen times; within minutes the robbers would
be overcome by fumes. That was the plan, and the man upon
whom it depended was experienced and determined.

At 2:20 P.M. Harry Fisher, who had been visited by Eddie
Green the night before, was at his cage waiting on a customer.
He had completely forgotten the odd incident. Suddenly he
heard a wild yelling "like Indians on the warpath." Looking
up, he saw three men, resembling well-dressed salesmen, waving guns. He ducked down.

The gunmen were Green, Hamilton, and Van Meter. The
latter was looking for the bank president, Willis Bagley. When
Van Meter saw Bagley sitting at a desk facing the other direction, he walked briskly up, machine gun at the ready.

At that moment Bagley swung around in his swivel chair.
Seeing the wild look on Van Meter's face, he thought a "crazy
man" was loose and ran toward his private office, a few yards
away.

"Stop," shouted Van Meter. The president ducked into the
little room and started shutting the door but Van Meter
thrust the barrel of his gun forward against the jamb, prevent-
ing the door from closing. For a moment it was a stand-off.
Then Van Meter yanked the gun free. Bagley slammed the
door and locked it. Van Meter fired once through the door,
the bullet grazing Bagley's chest. Frustrated and angry, Van
Meter began rounding up hostages for later use.

In the meantime Hamilton, armed with a pistol, had gone
behind the cages and ordered the employees into the lobby
where Green, waving a machine gun, was shouting, "Everyone
on the floor!"

Margaret Johnson, the switchboard girl, was standing on
the mezzanine balcony at the back of the bank, about to go
downstairs to check some calls when she heard the first yelling.
Almost simultaneously she saw Bagley chased into his office.
She opened up the switchboard so the president would have
an outside line, and then pressed the Western Union button,
hoping it would attract their attention.

At that moment a call came in from the wife of a teller. "You can't talk to him," said Margaret, "the bank is being robbed."

On the balcony across the room Guard Tom Walters had thought the first noise was a customer complaining about a loan. He rose from his chair inside the steel cage, looked through the thick window, and saw Green cradling a machine gun. He picked up his tear-gas gun and fired through a horizontal slit in the cage. The eight-inch-long pellet hit Green in the back and began releasing its 25,000 cubic feet of gas.

Green swore in pain, anger, and surprise.

"Get that son of a bitch with the tear gas," called Hamilton from behind the cages where he was already scooping money into a sack.

Green grabbed a bank director, swung him around as a shield, and fired a burst at the steel cage, several bullets spitting through the gun slit. Walters, nicked in the right ear and chin, ducked down. He tried desperately to pry the swollen, empty shell from the gas gun with his jackknife blade but couldn't budge it. Finally the blade snapped. He reached for gas candles but there were none. The plan for defense had bogged down.

The auditor's assistant, however, was already running back into an office off the mezzanine balcony. He found a gas candle, pulled the fuse, and threw it down to the marble floor. Fumes began shooting out of perforations as the candle rolled across the lobby. An elderly man lying on the floor kicked it away. Another elderly customer kicked it back. It was like a game and a few intrigued spectators on the balcony almost laughed.

Margaret Johnson was also looking down at the coughing, choking customers. She stood half paralyzed, half fascinated.

"I said everybody down," Green yelled, then loosed a burst of shots over her head. She and a bookkeeper started crawling back to the storeroom. En route the middle-aged bookkeeper noticed his companion had lost a shoe and gallantly went back for it. But she hurried to the window overlooking the alley behind the bank, completely unaware she had only one shoe. "Hey, you," she called to a short man wearing a cap and brown overcoat. "Get to work and notify somebody. The bank is being robbed."

Baby Face Nelson looked up, pointed his machine gun at her. "Lady, you're telling me?"

By now Van Meter had rounded up a dozen hostages from the lobby and was conducting them to the sidewalk in front of the bank. Here Dillinger, dressed in gray fedora, gray overcoat, and striped muffler, lined them up as a living shield. This done, he left Van Meter in charge, ducked into the bank building and entered the investment department—opposite the lobby—where Lydia Crosby, a young stenographer, and several others were hiding on the floor. She had hated to drop down; her dress had just been cleaned.

Dillinger ordered them all outside and, when Lydia hung back, tapped her on the arm, telling her to hurry along. As these new hostages went out the revolving door, he said, "Stand close to me." They hesitated and he chided mildly, "Come on, get up around me." They too were lined up on the sidewalk, hands in the air, backs to the bank, but they soon tired and their hands dropped. Dillinger was like a scolding schoolteacher. "Can't you get your hands up any higher than that?" A machine gun was strapped to his right arm; he held an automatic pistol in his left.

A driver, not realizing why the cars ahead of him had stopped, swung his car around the stalled traffic and went past the bank. Dillinger fired into its radiator with his pistol and no other cars tried to run the gauntlet.

A large crowd was gathering across the street. Some of them had no idea the bank was really being robbed. A freelance cameraman had been shooting motion pictures of the business section that morning, and now they thought a film of a robbery was being made. So they eagerly shoved forward to get a better look at the movie stars.

Van Meter was recruiting more human shields from the nearby Nichols and Green Shoe Store. About half a dozen obeyed. The rest retreated to the stock room.

.   .   .

About the time Dillinger entered the bank for hostages, Enoch Norem, city editor of the *Globe-Gazette,* was ordering his reporters to go out immediately and get at least one city brief apiece. He bawled them out for not bringing in enough local items. Reporter Carl Wright was heading up a side street toward the center of town to get his brief when he heard shooting and saw Baby Face Nelson standing on the sidewalk near the rear of the bank. Across the street, in front of the Prescription Shop, was a second machine gunner, Tommy Carroll. Squarely between them, blocking traffic on the side street, was the bandit car.

Nelson saw the reporter and fired a few warning shots. At that moment an auto went past Wright, innocently heading toward the parked bandit vehicle. Nelson fired at the car, which stopped with a scream of brakes and backed up full speed for three blocks, miraculously hitting nothing.

The reporter ducked into a bookstore, telephoned his skeptical city editor, and ran outside again just in time to see R. L. James, the School Board secretary, completely unaware of the danger, casually walking toward Nelson. Baby Face suddenly turned and fired again. James, hit in the leg, slumped to the sidewalk.

Chief of Police E. J. Patton, in civilian clothes as usual, heard the first shots when he was walking toward the courthouse where he'd been subpoenaed for a trial. As he crossed into Central Park and saw the large crowd, he too thought movies were being made.

Then he heard someone say, "They're robbing the bank!" He cut through the park and saw people across the street lined up in front of the bank, hands in air. He ran into the Weir Building, a structure with a vaguely Japanese flavor, one of Frank Lloyd Wright's early designs. The chief climbed to a second-floor office and saw Dillinger walking back and forth behind a line of people, but it was too dangerous to risk a shot. Then he noticed one of his patrolmen dart across the park toward the bank with a sawed-off shotgun.

Dillinger fired his pistol, and the patrolman ducked behind a meteorite, a Civil War monument. He stuck out his gun menacingly but, like his chief, he was afraid to pull the trigger.

"Stand up and shoot it out like a man," called Dillinger from across the street and hit a parked car with a bullet.

He was safe from the police but there was one man who decided to take a chance. John C. Shipley, an elderly police judge, was peering almost straight down at Dillinger from his office on the third floor of the bank building. He disappeared and came back with an ancient pistol. He took careful aim and pulled the stiff trigger. Dillinger clutched his right shoulder, whirled and fired his machine gun up at the window but the judge had disappeared once more.

In spite of the pain, Dillinger calmly told Van Meter to get inside and warn the others that it was time to leave. The skinny bandit ran into the lobby and excitedly shouted out Dillinger's order.

"Give us three more minutes," answered Hamilton. He had collected only $32,000 from the cages. The big money was in the vaults. He pressed a gun in Harry Fisher's back and said, "Now you come on back and open up." The assistant cashier was trying to figure out how he could keep from surrendering the money in the vault. There was a fortune there, over $200,000, and he didn't want to be the one to give it up. Hamilton kicked him in the buttocks. "Hurry up, damn it!"

The great round door of the main vault was open and Fisher stepped inside with Hamilton just behind. The cashier went past the safety boxes to the barred door leading to the money vault. After unlocking this door, he pushed it open and automatically reached for a heavy bag of pennies he used as a door stop. Hamilton beat him to the pennies, then deposited them—a treasure, he thought—into his big sack. Fisher could hardly believe his luck. He stepped inside the vault and released the door. With no bag of pennies to hold it open, it slammed shut and locked. Now there were bars between Hamilton and Fisher.

Fisher went up to the safe where the money was kept. He could simply have pulled open the door but instead, he spun the dial, locking it. "I don't know whether I can see to work this combination," he called out to Hamilton, who was standing impatiently on the other side of the barred door. Tears from the gas were streaming down the faces of both men.

"You'd better open it goddamn quick," warned Hamilton. The cashier fumbled for another minute and finally opened the safe; then he turned, took hold of the barred door and shook it. "Now this door is locked and I can't open it," he said.

Hamilton was so anxious to get the money he forgot Fisher had unlocked it a moment before with the key that was still in his pocket.

"All I can do is shove the money out through the bars," said Fisher. Hamilton told him to do it quickly. Fisher returned with ten bundles of one-dollar bills and slowly shoved each package, one at a time, through the narrow opening of the bars. After he finished he made a second deliberate trip for more ones.

"If you don't hurry up, I'm going to shoot you," said Hamilton.

Outside, the crowd was growing and Dillinger, seeing the situation might soon be out of hand, told Van Meter to order those inside out at once. Van Meter ran in, shouted the message. "Just gimme another minute," pleaded Hamilton. When he saw Fisher getting more ones he said, "Gimme the big bills!" Fisher, pretending he didn't understand, kept handing out packages of one-dollar notes.

Van Meter ran in a third time. "We're going!"

"It's hell to leave all that money back there," complained Hamilton. Of the almost $200,000, Fisher had doled out only $20,000. Hamilton picked up the sack weighted with the heavy bag of pennies and, with his free hand, grabbed Francis De Sart of the Savings Department, the Scoutmaster of Troop 13. "C'mon," said the bandit, "let's go." The two went out the front door.

Lydia Crosby saw Hamilton come out, tears running down his cheeks. Then she heard Dillinger tell the hostages to move around the corner.

The robbers, surrounded by citizens, began turning left down the side street just as Judge Shipley—the self-appointed deputy—again peered out of his third-story window and got off a hasty shot at the last robber to turn the corner. Once more his aim was remarkable. The bullet struck Hamilton's right shoulder.

The first thing Dillinger saw after he rounded the corner was James, the school secretary, bleeding on the sidewalk; he knew Nelson had shot him. "Did you have to do that?" he said, then ordered the hostages to crowd onto the running boards of the Buick. It was Sioux Falls all over again except that this time there were almost three times as many hostages and it was hard to see how they could all get aboard.

Baby Face Nelson jabbed at the assistant cashier, Ralph Wiley, called him a "bald-headed son of a bitch," and told him to climb onto the back bumper and hang onto the back window frame—the glass had been carefully removed. With Wiley were Lydia Crosby, Scoutmaster De Sart, Emmet Ryan—another bank employee—and the white-coated owner of the Mulcahy Prescription Shop.

Women—some were bank employees, some depositors or shoppers—were herded into the back seat of the Buick. Other women and men filled the two running boards. Two men were even perched on the front mudguards. Lydia Crosby counted twenty-one on and in the auto, Wiley twenty-three and De Sart twenty-six. Whatever the figure, it looked like a comedy car in the circus.

When Chief Patton, from his vantage point in the Weir Building, saw the bandits drive away he got a sawed-off shotgun at the police station and set off in pursuit in an unmarked car with two of his officers. By now the free-lance cameraman, H. C. Kunkelman, was finally taking movies of the excited crowd around the bank.

The Buick ponderously proceeded north at less than fifteen miles an hour. De Sart saw some girls he knew coming out of a beauty shop and resisted an impulse to wave at them. The car began to turn west at the Kirk Apartments. Miss Minnie Piehm, an elderly hostage hanging desperately on at the right side, cried hysterically, "Let me out! This is where I live!"

As if it were a bus, the Buick stopped and Miss Piehm got off. Wiley also descended but someone inside shouted sharply, "Get back on, you." He did and the Buick started off again, this time at a more rapid pace—twenty miles an hour.

Chief Patton's car was held up by the traffic. "They turned at the Kirk Apartments," a boy yelled; so the police vehicle also turned and, by the time the Buick swung west onto Highway 18, was only a block behind. "Don't get too close," warned Patton. "They can shoot us. We dassent shoot at them."

A little later a man taking his wife and daughter for a ride turned onto Highway 18 and saw the overloaded Buick ahead. Thinking it was a "merry party" or a wedding shivaree, he became curious and drew closer. A bullet suddenly struck his car and, splitting in three parts, wounded him three times.

Baby Face Nelson had also begun shooting at the police with a high-powered rifle. At the top of the hill near the city limits the Buick stopped. Nelson jumped out and again fired. The police car turned off the highway into a farmer's driveway.

Nelson, holding the rifle under his arm, started to sprinkle tacks on the cement road but did it so excitedly that many bounced under the Buick.

Dillinger leaned out and said in a remarkably calm voice, "You're getting tacks under our own car." Nelson kicked several out of the way and said, "Those cars following! We'll shoot 'em!" Dillinger ordered him to get back in.

The Buick continued almost a mile on the highway, then turned south on a dirt road. About this time it was discovered that one of the hostages, Bill Schmidt, who had been en route to a customer with a paper sack of sandwiches, was still clinging to it. The bandits ate the sandwiches. As they were crossing Highway 106, one of the women inside said she was getting sick.

"For God's sake," said Dillinger, "let her out." They stopped near a farmhouse.

As she stepped to the road, Baby Face shouted, "You phone the law. Tell them if they don't stop following us we're going to kill everyone in this car. That's some law you got!"

Then he jumped out again and spread more tacks on the dirt road.

A woman on the running board said hysterically, "I don't want to die this way." Dillinger told her to get off and the Buick resumed its journey through the open country, carefully avoiding bumps and holes. Soon it turned east, back again south and once more east, never at a speed of over twenty-five miles an hour.

The hostages clinging to the car were suffering from the cold. Sharp flurries of snow spit in their faces and Lydia Crosby was sure her glasses would blow off any moment. She wondered how much longer she could hang onto the rear window frame and considered quitting her job at the bank. It wasn't worth such trouble.

In the last forty-five minutes they had driven almost thirteen miles but were only three miles due south of Mason City. They stopped soon after crossing Highway 65 and Nelson jumped out, ordering everyone to get off and raise their hands so he could search them for weapons. When Emmet Ryan, the paying teller, stared at him, Nelson said, "Don't look at me, you son of a bitch!" Ryan ignored the order and kept staring.

One woman was kept in the car as a hostage and a woman friend insisted on staying with her. Then the Buick headed for the sand pit where the other bandit car was parked. Several minutes later the last two hostages were released and the gang headed toward St. Paul in two cars.

They arrived close to midnight. First-aid bandages had been put on the shoulder wounds of Hamilton and Dillinger but, since there was a strong possibility of infection, Green promised to get a doctor. He went into the Green Lantern Café on Wabasha Street, where he found Pat Reilly—formerly mascot of the St. Paul baseball team and presently a waiter for Harry Sawyer—who agreed to help. Reilly's wife was one of three sisters with similar tastes; the other two were married to Tommy Carroll and Alvin Karpis.

Reilly took Dillinger, Hamilton and Van Meter to the home of his family doctor, N. G. Mortenson, the city's health officer, and told him Dillinger and Hamilton had been wounded in a shooting scrape in Minneapolis. The jittery Mortenson removed the dressings and examined the wounds. "They're not dangerous," he said and hastily reapplied the bandages. He was frightened and, claiming he had no first-aid kit at home, told them to come to his office at eleven the next morning if they wanted further treatment.

As they were leaving, the doctor noticed a machine gun sticking out of Van Meter's overcoat. Now he was sure they were gangsters and started to telephone the police. But he hung up. They might come back and kill him.

CHAPTER 13

"You Should Have Seen Their Faces. Ha! Ha! Ha!"

1

THE CHICAGO BRANCH OF THE FBI WAS ON THE NINETEENTH floor of the Bankers' Building. In the past few months it had become the busiest field office in the Bureau's history; since the Kansas City Massacre, it had also been used as headquarters for the Special Squad set up by J. Edgar Hoover to combat the Midwestern crime wave.

The number of agents assigned to this group varied. They had no private rooms in the limited space, merely the use of a few desks in an open area. Melvin Purvis—the diminutive but dapper Special Agent in Charge of the Chicago office—was the nominal chief of these special crime hunters. In practice, however, Hoover himself directly supervised the activities of the Special Squad, which spread into half a dozen states.

His concentration on Midwestern crime was felt first by the Barkers; and soon after Bremer was released, Ma decided it was too dangerous to congregate in any one place. The gang began to scatter. By the first week in March, Fred Barker and his mistress, Fat-Witted, were in Toledo. Bushy-haired Volney Davis and his girl, Rabbits, went off by themselves to Aurora, Illinois, a pleasant town some forty miles from the Loop, but to their disgust were quickly followed by three gregarious companions.

The rest of the gang stayed in Chicago, adopting various disguises. Some dyed their hair and wore dark glasses; several grew mustaches. Karpis and Freddie Barker felt it was necessary to take more drastic measures; they were too well-known to the FBI. One mid-March evening Karpis—now nicknamed "Old Creepy" because of his expressionless eyes—and Freddie Barker came to the office of Dr. Joseph P. Moran on the ground floor of the Irving Park, a relatively secluded hotel only a few blocks from Dr. Eye's, where Dillinger had almost been trapped.

Moran, who bore a remarkable resemblance to New York's Mayor Jimmy Walker, assured them he could alter their fingerprints and change their faces—for a proper fee. When he began practicing in Illinois he was apparently headed for an honorable, perhaps brilliant, career. But the young doctor started to drink heavily, became a pin artist—abortionist—and was eventually sent to Joliet prison. When he was paroled he was selected as physician for the Chicago Chauffeurs', Teamsters' and Helpers' Union and then set up private practice at the Irving Park Hotel, where he presently led a double life, treating gangster as well as ordinary patients.

Although he was only thirty-nine the night he operated on Karpis and Barker, he was already a physical ruin and his fumbling fingers did little more than butcher his two patients, who were injected with morphine and sent off to recuperate.

Ma Barker tried to nurse them. Though Karpis was stoical, Freddie often screamed from the pain and had to be restrained. In addition to nursing duties, Ma was completing arrangements with a survivor of the "Bugs" Moran mob, a bookie, and an ex-Illinois State Legislator for the passing of the $100,000 Hamm ransom.

These men also agreed to handle the Bremer money when enough time had elapsed. The bulk of the $200,000 from this kidnaping had just been hidden by Fred Goetz in the garage of his wife's uncle. About a week later, on March 20, Goetz was spending the evening at his favorite saloon on Cermak Road in the neighborhood Capone once called home. Near midnight he stepped out of the saloon. Suddenly an automobile drew up to the curb and the barrels of several sawed-off shotguns were shoved through the side windows. There were four explosions. Goetz's head was almost blasted off.

On him were found a $1,000 bill and membership cards made out to J. George Ziegler for the Onwentsia Club, the Chicago Yacht Club, and the Mohawk Country Club of Bensenville. The police had no idea he was Fred Goetz wanted since 1929 for robbery and the St. Valentine's Day Massacre.

The next day fingerprints revealed his identity, but Goetz's murderers would always remain a mystery. There were at least three theories: Goetz had been killed on Ma Barker's orders because he was losing his mind and boasting about the Bremer kidnaping; the syndicate had eliminated him for leaving them; and the anti-syndicate mobsters had done it in revenge for the St. Valentine's Day shooting.

Whether Ma Barker grieved over Goetz or rejoiced, it took her only a few days to persuade his weeping widow to turn over the Bremer money.

2

Six days after the Mason City holdup Dillinger and Billie Frechette moved from Minneapolis to the Lincoln Court Apartments in the exclusive Hill section of St. Paul, only one block from the scene of the Bremer kidnaping. They lived on the third floor as Mr. and Mrs. Carl T. Hellman; next door was a minister and his wife.

In the following week there were so many visitors to Apartment 303 the lady manager became curious. She also wondered why the Hellmans kept their shades lowered from dusk till morning, left the building only by the back stairs, and refused to let the superintendent fix the bathroom sink. Should she report her suspicions to the police?

Even though the gang was idle, it was a rare day when a

story about Dillinger wasn't on the front page. On March 16 Youngblood, the Negro who had escaped from Crown Point with Dillinger, was trapped by three deputy sheriffs in a little tobacco and candy store in Port Huron, Michigan. In the ensuing gun battle one lawman was killed, the other two wounded. Youngblood, dying from six bullet holes, claimed Dillinger had been with him the day before, and he was soon reported crossing the St. Clair River into Canada with two companions. U.S. immigration and customs border patrolmen were alerted.

On the same day in Indiana, Ernest Blunk, the fingerprint expert whom Dillinger had used to round up jailers at Crown Point, was spirited from Lake County by Matt Leach and brought to the Indianapolis city jail for interrogation. Blunk's attorney called it kidnaping and threatened to file an affidavit.

In Lima Makley's trial had taken a dramatic twist— Shouse, for reasons of his own, refusing to testify against him. It didn't matter; on March 17 the jury found Makley guilty of murder and did not recommend mercy. Now it was Clark's turn to be tried.

Two weeks had already passed since the trials had begun and even though no actual attempts had been made to free the defendants, the tension was kept alive by frequent scares. The latest came that day when Prosecutor Botkin claimed Dillinger had recently cashed bonds from several bank robberies and it was naturally assumed he was getting finances for a full-scale attack on Lima. General Bush strengthened the guard around the courthouse, enlisting law-enforcement officers of surrounding counties and members of the American Legion.

Shouse again reversed himself and testified against Clark. On the afternoon of March 24 the case went to the jury and while the jurors were still out, Pierpont and Makley were called into court for sentencing. Pierpont came first, flanked by guards and followed by young Don Sarber, who had replaced his father as sheriff. Pierpont wore an expensive dark gray suit; his freshly cut hair was neatly combed. He smiled as he briskly walked in and sat down with his attorneys.

Makley, also well dressed, entered with a broad, confident grin. When brought before Judge Everett their smiles faded and neither said a word, although Makley was chewing gum energetically. The judge sentenced both to die in the electric chair on Friday, July 13. A few minutes later the Clark jury came in with a verdict of guilty, but mercy was recommended. Clark just stared until Jessie Levy leaned over and said, "Well, that saves you, kid."

Back in the cell block Pierpont momentarily lost his composure. His lips quivered and his hands shook. "This is the first time I've been nervous in a long time," he told the guards. He called to Makley, who was being brought back from the court, "I thought the judge was going to cry when he sentenced me." Then added, "I guess it's that unlucky thirteen." His name had thirteen letters as had Judge Emmett Everett's; he was born on the thirteenth of the month and was scheduled to die on the thirteenth.

Makley, still chewing gum, only said, "We all have to die once."

Jessie Levy told Judge Everett she would appeal the cases of Pierpont and Makley to the Supreme Court on the basis of prejudice, citing the controversial Scottsboro Case in which nine Negroes had been sentenced to die for allegedly attacking a white woman.

"The facts are entirely different," said Everett.

"The only fact different," she replied with a straight face, "is color."

That same day Dillinger's elder sister, Audrey, was reading a letter from him in which he tried to be reassuring. It also bolstered the fiction of the wooden gun and reiterated his desire to be the breadwinner of the family.

Dear Sis,

I thought I would write you a few lines and let you know I am still perculating. Dont worry about me honey, for that wont help any, and besides I am having a lot of fun. I am sending Emmett my wooden gun and I want him to allways keep it. I see that Deputy Blunk says I had a real forty five thats just a lot of hooey to cover up because they dont like to admit that I locked eight deputys and a dozen trustys up with my wooden gun before I got my hands on the two machine guns and you should have seen their faces Ha! Ha! Ha! Pulling that off was worth ten years of my life Ha! Ha! Dont part with my wooden gun for any price For when you feel blue all you will have to do is look at the gun and laugh your blues away Ha! Ha! I will be around to see all of you when the roads are better, it is so hot around Indiana now that I would have trouble getting through so I am sending my wife Billie. She will have a hundred dollars for you and a hundred for Norman. I'll give you enough money for a new car the next time I come around. I told Bud I would get him one and I want to get Dad one. Now honey if any of you need any thing I wont forgive you if you dont let me know. I got shot a week ago but I am all right now just a little sore I bane one tough sweed Ha! Ha! Well honey I guess Ill close for the time give my love to all and I hope I can see you soon. Lots of love from Johnnie

By the end of March Dillinger was reported to have robbed a railroad freight terminal in Detroit and was seen in Los Angeles, Phoenix, Arizona, Grants Pass, Oregon, Dunellen, New Jersey, Sonora, Mexico, and a score of other cities.

He was still in St. Paul recuperating from his shoulder wound, eating well and attending the neighborhood movie theater. He was also experimenting with a new weapon that would give gangsters a great advantage in the crime war—a machine gun made from a pistol, so small it could be concealed under a suit coat. Its inventor, a gunshop proprietor in San Antonio, had sent five to St. Paul through a friend of Tommy Carroll's. More would be available in a few weeks.

Dillinger had no idea that he would be using one of these ingenious guns so soon. The apartment manager had finally reported her suspicions to the local office of the United States Attorney. For several hours on the night of March 30, Good Friday, FBI agents R. L. Nalls and R. C. Coulter watched the Lincoln Court Apartments. The next morning at about 10:10

these two, now joined by a city detective, Henry Cummings, decided to investigate. Coulter and Cummings walked up to apartment 303 and knocked on the door.

Dillinger and Billie Frechette were still in bed, and when the knocking persisted she fastened the latch chain, then opened the door about two inches.

"I'd like to talk to Carl Hellman," said the middle-aged, heavy-set Cummings.

She was confused, momentarily forgetting that Dillinger's name was now Hellman. Finally she said, "I'm Mrs. Hellman," and told them her husband had left but would be back in the afternoon.

Cummings said, "We are police." They wanted to come in and talk. When Billie protested that she wasn't dressed Cummings said they would wait. She closed the door, hurried into the bedroom, and told Dillinger that police were in the hall.

"Keep your shirt on and get dressed," he said brusquely. Then he saw she was petrified and added soothingly, "Never mind, never mind."

About nine minutes later Coulter and Cummings, still waiting to be let in, saw a tall, thin man coming up the stairs toward them. Coulter stepped forward and asked who he was.

"I am a soap salesman," said Homer Van Meter.

"Where are your samples?"

"In my car. Come down there and I'll prove my identity to you." Van Meter started down the stairs followed by the FBI agent. When Coulter reached the first floor Van Meter was waiting with a drawn pistol. "You asked for it," he said, "so I'll give it to you now!"

Coulter darted past Van Meter through the front door, taking him by surprise. Van Meter followed and began shooting but the agent's return fire was so accurate he ducked back into the apartment and ran out the rear door into the alley.

At the first sound of shots Dillinger fired through the door of 303 with the new machine pistol.

"My God," cried Billie. "Don't shoot! Try and get out without shooting!"

Dillinger seized a standard submachine gun, kicked open

the door and swept the hallway with bullets, some ripping into the next apartment, almost hitting the minister and his wife. Cummings, hiding in the front stairway, shot back as Dillinger and Billie ran down the rear stairs.

A College of St. Thomas student saw Billie, carrying a suitcase, run out of the back of the apartment house and down the alley. Dillinger followed unhurriedly, cradling the machine gun and covering their flight. Behind him he left a red trail in the snow. Facing the apartment house, he waited unperturbedly, while she frantically backed a large Hudson out of a garage, and after he got in, it caromed off another garage, then continued unsteadily up the alley.

Less than half an hour later Homer Van Meter burst into Eddie Green's apartment in Minneapolis and while he was boasting how he had forced a truck driver to drive him to safety, Billie knocked at the door.

"Johnnie's shot in the leg," she said. He was outside in the Hudson.

A few miles away, the St. Paul grand jury investigating alleged inefficiency and corruption of the police department was just submitting its three-month findings. This investigation had been prompted by the *Daily News* campaign for a cleaner city and the nationally publicized statement of Attorney General Homer Cummings that St. Paul was a "poison spot of crime."

The report of the grand jury, however, began:

> We believe there is no justification for any charges that an excess of crime exists here—we believe further that a comparison with other large cities will prove that St. Paul cannot be shown in an unfavorable light.
>
> Charges of official incompetence and neglect—these charges have not been sustained by evidence.
>
> Charges of collusion between police and underworld —no evidence of centralized graft has been found.

While it was being read, news of the shooting on Lexington Avenue was passed with delighted satisfaction from reporter to reporter. What they had been trying to point out to their readers for many months was being graphically demonstrated at a most timely moment and that afternoon the *Daily News* headline read:

MACHINE GUNS BLAZE AS JURY
WHITEWASHES POLICE

Eight suspicious characters were arrested by the local police as hundreds of clues and tips poured in but the multiplicity of leads so hopelessly tangled the case that J. Edgar Hoover insisted on taking charge. He was also afraid that Dillinger, like the kidnapers of Hamm and Bremer, might have a paid spy in the police department. The search, begun by Matt Leach and continued by Captain Stege and his Dillinger Squad, had passed into the hands of the man who was becoming America's most celebrated crime fighter.

He had long argued that the mobility of such gangs as the Barkers' and Dillinger's could only be matched by an equally mobile force: the FBI. Hoover sent his assistant, H. H. Clegg, to St. Paul to take personal charge.

FBI agents launched an intensive investigation to locate other Dillinger hideouts and within twenty-four hours found an emergency apartment in St. Paul rented by Eddie Green several weeks previously.

Agents watched it all that night. The next morning, April 3, the apartment was searched by FBI men and local police. Three notebooks listing getaway routes from banks were found as well as assorted ammunition, a piece of dynamite fuse, and the stock of a submachine gun.

At 11:30 A.M. a Negro woman let herself into the apartment. She told the FBI agents her name was Lucy and she'd been hired to clean the place. Her sister, Leonia, had brought her and was parked out in the alleyway.

The two agents now questioned Leonia, who said a Mr. and Mrs. Stephens—Eddie Green and his wife, Bessie—had just stopped at her home on Rondo Street and asked her to get a suitcase, a coat, and laundry they'd left at the apartment.

"Stephens" promised to give her $10 when he picked up the things at Rondo Street later in the day.

Three agents accompanied the two women to a frame house in the Negro section. The agents hid inside. Late that afternoon a Terraplane sedan stopped across the street and Eddie Green got out, leaving Bessie behind. He climbed the steps to the side door and knocked. Leonia handed him a bag, then slammed the door and cried, "That's the man!"

Green, who had started down the stairs, abruptly whirled and reached toward his hip to draw a gun. An agent shouted to surrender but he didn't raise his hands. The agents fired and Green fell, shot through the head. His move to draw had been futile; he had no gun.

Bessie ran from the car toward Green. "Please don't shoot any more," she cried. "We're alone." Weeping, she held her husband's head and tried to bandage it.

3

Bonnie and Clyde Barrow were still enjoying freedom but to young Jones, their companion, freedom was no joy. Since their narrow escape at the fair grounds, this trio had had a dozen other escapes and killed three more men, bringing their total to nine. Unable to endure any more life and love with the Barrows, Jones deserted them and made his way back to Texas. When he was picked up by Houston police four months after the death of Buck Barrow, the young man was not at all dismayed. In a twenty-eight-page confession he revealed a fantastic story of crime and suffering, then begged for a life sentence. Behind bars he would at last be safe from the pair that had kept him in unnatural bondage for months.

With Jones gone, Bonnie and Clyde looked for a new partner. One January morning, accompanied by a criminal who had recently been released from the Eastham Texas State Prison Farm, they hid in a ravine near the brush-covered river bottoms adjacent to the Prison Farm, which was so familiar to Barrow from his own term at the institution. Soon a party of convicts emerged through the fog.

Bonnie and Clyde stood up and attacked with machine guns, mortally wounding a guard. Covered by this withering fusillade, five prisoners dashed toward the ravine. The Barrows led the way through the tangled undergrowth to two cars. Four of the inmates took one car. Raymond Hamilton—serving terms totaling 263 years, their first partner in crime and love—got in the car with the Barrows.

These three later picked up another escapee, young Henry Methvin, and continued to plunder the Southwest, which was now experiencing a crime wave of its own. Pretty Boy Floyd was reportedly responsible for many of the killings and it was reasonable to assume that he, the Barrows, and others were hiding in the Cookson Hills of eastern Oklahoma—the sanctuary of badmen since the days of Jesse James. On the night of February 17, 1,000 lawmen, including four companies of Oklahoma National Guardsmen, began surrounding the wild territory in the drizzling rain. By dawn the great raid was under way, with orders: shoot to kill. Nineteen people were picked up but the Barrows escaped. As for Pretty Boy he had been 1,000 miles away, hiding with Richetti and two girl friends in a house in Buffalo, New York. It had become a prison of their own making since the Kansas City Massacre and they were even afraid to go outside for a newspaper.

Ten days after the disappointing man hunt, the new Barrow gang held up a bank in a small Texas town. Afterward they drove to Terre Haute, Indiana, where they got into a violent argument over the loot when Bonnie accused Raymond Hamilton of wanting too big a share. Hamilton deserted, leaving the Barrows with Methvin, a quiet, reticent country boy with blond hair and clear blue eyes.

Living in a single car day and night, they headed back for Texas. On Easter afternoon, the day after Dillinger's flight from his St. Paul apartment, two Texas Highway patrolmen investigated a car parked on a side road and were coldly murdered by Bonnie and Clyde. The demand for their capture rose and Clyde became Texas' Public Enemy Number 1.

On April 6, five days after the double killing, the Barrows got stuck on a muddy road known as the Lost Trail half a mile west of Commerce, Oklahoma. It was a desolate spot with great chat piles from the lead and zinc mines on both sides of the road. The Barrows tried to stop a local man who drove slowly by but when he saw guns stacked up inside the Ford he speeded into Commerce and reported the incident to Police Chief Percy Boyd and Constable Cal Campbell.

The two lawmen drove out to the Lost Trail. As they approached the parked Ford, it suddenly backed up full speed, wobbled, and ran into a ditch. Boyd and Campbell got out of their car and walked forward. Campbell, a man near sixty with a large western-style mustache, saw Barrow standing next to the Ford with an automatic rifle and drew his pistol. He fired three times. When Clyde and Bonnie replied with automatic rifle fire Police Chief Boyd got off four shots. Then a bullet knocked him down. As he hugged the ground, he could hear Constable Campbell, sprawled out near their car, groaning. Barrow ran down the road and ordered a man in a truck to pull the Ford out of the ditch. The wounded Chief Boyd was put in the back seat with young Methvin and the Ford headed west.

Just before dark they drove into Fort Scott, Kansas, and bought food, which they ate in the woods. They also got a newspaper and learned Constable Campbell had died.

"I'm sorry I killed the old man," said Barrow. "But I had to. He shouldn't have shot at me."

Bonnie assured Boyd he'd be released at the first opportunity, then asserted that a much-publicized picture of her taken with a cigar was only a joke. "Tell the public I don't smoke cigars," she said. "It's the bunk."

4

By this time the special grand jury investigating the Crown Point escape of Dillinger had finally submitted its report. In-

dicting Blunk and Sam Cahoon, the elderly and not always
sober jailer, it charged them with aiding and abetting Dillinger's escape. More important, the jury severely censured the
executive department of Indiana, from Governor McNutt on
down, for failing to transfer Dillinger to the state prison as a
parole violator pending his trial; Judge Murray and Sheriff
Holley were criticized for opposing the transfer. Only two men
were singled out for any praise in the entire affair: a trusty for
spreading the alarm that Dillinger had escaped, and Prosecutor Estill "for his zeal in the prosecution."

Judge Murray attacked Estill for approving the report. "I
don't see why I should take the advice of a prosecutor who
had his picture taken hugging Dillinger," he said. Then he
irately declared that the grand jury itself was not justified "in
mentioning the court or its presiding officer in scandalous or
contemptuous language . . ." and, in a drastic move, ordered
its members to appear in court to answer charges of contempt.

The jury, six shaken merchants and farmers, now faced
jail sentences up to six months. After the jurors apologized at
the hearing, Murray forgave them and said, "The jury is now
dismissed from further service in this court and I am expunging
from the records the report filed by the jury in relation to the
escape from Lake County Jail of John Dillinger."

So ended the long public investigation—with the indictment of only two minor officials.

But it was far from the end of a secret investigation being
held by the Hargrave Secret Service of Chicago—and at the
request of a man now falsely accused of being related to John
Dillinger: Governor McNutt. George Hargrave, son of the
founder of the firm, had just discovered that Piquett had bribed
the Indiana judge to smuggle a real gun into the prison. When
Hargrave finally submitted proof that Piquett had passed a
large sum of money to the judge at the grounds of the World's
Fair, McNutt and Attorney General Lutz quite properly decided to keep the information secret, not wanting Dillinger to
know that certain informants, whom he might still trust, had
talked to the private detective. (By the time Dillinger was

killed, the judge had died and the findings were never made public.)

One of the few Indianans who seemed unaffected by the whole controversy was the man who had started it. Dillinger was too occupied, perhaps obsessed, with something more important—a sentimental journey. When he was first brought back to Indiana from Tucson he had dreaded seeing his father until he learned that Mr. Dillinger had actually boasted to newsmen about his son's "tricky" escape from Crown Point. On the night of April 5, to his father's astonishment, he boldly walked into the farmhouse at Mooresville. He even brought along a companion, Billie Frechette. His father worriedly said that two FBI agents were in the neighborhood and probably watching the farm. Dillinger, guessing as much, had concealed his car on a parallel road a mile behind the farm and simply guided Billie along the familiar gullies which led to the house.

Dillinger and Billie relaxed all the next day but after dark he sneaked back to the hidden car and, accompanied by a male relative, drove to Leipsic, Ohio, to give Pierpont's parents more money for lawyer's fees. But he found the Pierpont farm deserted.

On the way back to Mooresville the relative fell asleep at the wheel and their big Hudson smashed into another car, shearing off its left rear wheel. The Hudson shot through a ditch, plunging almost a hundred yards into the woods. The two Dillingers, unhurt, ran back to the other car, which had careened into a field. Dillinger apologized to the unharmed occupants, then took his machine gun from the Hudson and hid in a haystack, while the relative went for another car.

Several hours later Matt Leach was telling reporters he was sure the wrecked Hudson was the car in which Dillinger had escaped from St. Paul. "Just look at that. There is some more Dillinger luck." It had miraculously missed a dozen trees. "Nobody could have been so fortunate but Dillinger."

About 11:00 that morning Fred Brewer Whiteside, Dillinger's boyhood comrade, was walking toward Maywood, the home of Audrey Hancock, his friend's sister. Fred Whiteside had been working in his garden and was dressed in old clothes. A car passed, then backed up.

"Hi, Schnickelfritz," said Dillinger. He handed Whiteside a $20 bill and told him to get some good shoes. They chatted a moment but when Dillinger noticed a telephone lineman working on a nearby pole he said, "See you again," and drove toward the house of the sister who had been his second mother.

That afternoon, while Billie was buying a new car at a local Ford agency, Dillinger brazenly walked into the office of an Indianapolis newspaper, leisurely read about his exploits in the back issues and ordered copies of these papers sent to another person who would appreciate them—his father.

By the following day a great many people in Mooresville knew Dillinger was at the farm. Friend told friend—but never the FBI agents, who could only get a glimpse of the farm by driving discreetly past as often as possible. Tired and hungry, the two G-men kept at their tedious task while America's most wanted criminal was enjoying a large party in his home. The agents watched as car after car of relatives drove up that Sunday. Close friends in town were also invited. One of them heard Dillinger—whose hair, to everyone's surprise, was now a henna color—say, "Something you don't have to worry about, Dad. I never killed a man and never will. You shoot at a man and cripple him and he might kill you. But if you shoot close and just scare him, he's gone." Dillinger also took great pains to convince everyone that he and Billie were legally married. To him this was almost true; he did want to marry her.

After the chicken dinner dozens of pictures were taken. Dillinger, grinning cockily, even posed several times with the wooden gun he said he'd used at Crown Point.

Late that afternoon Jack Cejnar of INS drove to the farm. As he interviewed the elder Dillinger in the parlor, Billie chain-smoked and occasionally looked furtively out back. Cejnar had no doubt Dillinger was hiding in the barn.

At dusk Dillinger drove to Mary Kinder's new home in Indianapolis and honked his horn until she came out. By coincidence Pierpont's parents arrived at the same moment. When Dillinger gave Mary another $1,000 for Jessie Levy, Mr. Pierpont objected. Why should she get any more money after losing the case? But Dillinger pointed out that perhaps Miss Levy could get a new trial.

Mary went back into the house and, with her coat still on, sank into a chair. A moment later there was a knock at the door. It was a police officer. A cavalcade of police cars jammed the street. Several lawmen searched the house. One tried to get in the locked bathroom, then knocked and said he wanted to come in to see if Dillinger was there. Silent Margaret, who was taking a bath, shouted, "Well, if you want to wash my back, come on in."

Sergeant Claude Kinder, Mary's former father-in-law, who was holding a gun, suddenly swung on her and shouted, "You've ruined my name!"

By now Dillinger had picked up Billie and was en route to Chicago over the back roads he knew so well. Within hours of their arrival, however, agents of Hoover's special Dillinger group learned they were in the city. The following evening, FBI men located Billie and arrested her at a local tavern.

When Dillinger learned of the arrest, he immediately telephoned Piquett, instructing him to defend Billie in case she was tried. It was the first time the lawyer had heard his client's voice waver with emotion. Dillinger was actually shaken and he was willing to spend anything, he said, to keep her free. Then Piquett got a second surprise: Dillinger insisted Billie get a divorce so they could at last be married.

For the next few days Dillinger hid out in Fort Wayne with Homer Van Meter. Both were again running low on money but before they could take another bank they had to replace the bulletproof vests left in the St. Paul apartment. Van Meter, as usual, had the answer; there were several, he said, in the Warsaw, Indiana, police station.

At 1:15 on the morning of April 13, Police Officer Judd Pittenger had just finished patrolling the business section of Warsaw. He was forty-nine years old, talked little, and worked efficiently; in seventeen years on the force he had physically tangled with several armed criminals, once being shot in the neck when he climbed into a hayloft to capture a robber.

As Pittenger stood on the corner near the Candy Kitchen, two men in long raincoats walked up behind him.

One said, "We want your bulletproof vests and we mean business."

When Pittenger turned, Dillinger poked a machine gun into his side and told him to start walking toward the police station. But Pittenger twisted and seized the barrel of Dillinger's gun.

"Don't try to grab it away from me," warned Dillinger.

Pittenger hung onto the gun. "Well, go ahead and shoot it."

As the two men struggled, Van Meter circled behind Pittenger and rammed a gun sharply into his left side. The policeman released the machine-gun barrel.

Van Meter pulled the pistol from Pittenger's Sam Browne belt, and then, needlessly, struck him over the head from behind four times with the gun's barrel.

"Don't hit me any more," said Pittenger.

"Don't hit him," said Dillinger. They went through an alley and continued toward the police station. The first thing that struck Dillinger's eye when he entered the main office of the station was a series of five newspaper pictures of himself posted on the wall. A caption read: "If you see this man, telephone the police at once."

"Where's the key?" asked Van Meter, pointing to the door of the inner office. Pittenger said he didn't know.

While Dillinger was studying his pictures and Van Meter was prying open the door, Pittenger ran out of the room. At a nearby restaurant, he picked up a phone and told central, "Dillinger's in town and got our three vests!"

By midmorning some 5,000 Indiana lawmen were blocking roads and searching the hundreds of empty cottages in the lake district. That day the Associated Press reported Dillinger "seen" two hundred times, sometimes ten places simultaneously in a half-dozen states. Lawmen all over the Midwest were harassed by countless false leads, some deliberately concocted; but far-fetched as some of the clues were, all had to be run down.

In Indianapolis a young man confessed he had lied to the police when he reported Dillinger had given him a lift on the highway and dropped him off at a nearby tourist camp. "I must have been crazy," he finally apologized. "I just wanted some of the publicity."

A nineteen-year-old girl confessed to police and the FBI that she was with Dillinger at the Warsaw raid but eventually broke down to reveal she was on a hitchhiking tour from her home in Michigan and merely wanted her name in the papers.

"Sometime one of those tips is going to be true," said Melvin Purvis. "And then we're going to catch Dillinger. That time is going to be soon. We'll get him."

Civic irresponsibility extended to the press. On April 17 the FBI learned Dillinger was going to get his wounded leg treated by a physician in the Starks Building in Louisville. A squad of Hoover's men, assisted by city detectives, surrounded the building but somehow word of the trap leaked to the *Herald Post* and that afternoon a story on page one was headlined:

> U. S. LAYS DILLINGER TRAP AROUND
> STARKS BUILDING

He failed to appear for his appointment.

5

Late in the afternoon of April 17 two cars drove into the historic border city of Sault Ste. Marie, Michigan. In the first car were John Hamilton and his new girl friend, Patricia Cherrington, a plumpish, flashy but well-educated brunette. Dillinger followed by himself; Billie Frechette was now in St. Paul awaiting trial for harboring him at the Lincoln Court Apartments.

Hamilton led the way up a steep hill not far from the place where he had so long ago lost the two fingers of his right hand in a freak sleighing accident. In a small frame house on top of the hill the three travelers were warmly welcomed by Hamilton's sister, Mrs. Anna Steve.

When brother and sister were alone Hamilton said he didn't think it would be long before they all were captured. But the reunion wasn't gloomy. On the evening of April 18 a boyhood friend of Hamilton's was invited over and they reminisced for hours about the old days in the Soo.

The following morning a salesman came to the office of Sheriff J. Willard Welsh and said he'd heard a story that might or might not be true. A friend had just boasted he'd been at the Steves' the previous night and met John Dillinger, Red Hamilton, and a buxom brunette.

Welsh telephoned the FBI and told Purvis what he had heard. Purvis immediately sent five agents to the airport; they chartered a plane and left at 4:00 P.M. but due to strong head winds it was necessary to land at Green Bay, Wisconsin. Taking off again as soon as the weather permitted they landed at St. Ignace, Michigan, early the following morning and were met there by Sheriff Welsh, who drove them to Sault Ste. Marie.

But Dillinger had already left town with his two companions—a step ahead of his pursuers as always. That night they joined Van Meter, Carroll, Baby Face Nelson, and their women at a restaurant near Chicago and during dinner decided to find a safe place where they could relax for the next few days. Someone said there was a lodge in northern Wisconsin called the Little Bohemia, which would be practically deserted at this time of year. It sounded exactly right to Dillinger and he suggested that they leave early the next morning.

In the meantime the good impression he had made at the recent family reunion had a strange aftermath. A group of Mooresville citizens were already circulating a remarkable petition asking Governor McNutt to pardon Dillinger if he surrendered. It read:

We submit the following several reasons for this unusual petition.

1. We find precedent in the case of Governor Crittenden's pardon of Frank James in the state of Missouri, in

which case James became a useful and respectable citizen of the state until his death.

2. John Dillinger has never manifested a vicious, revengeful or bloodthirsty disposition, there being considerable doubt as to whether he has ever committed a murder.

3. It is our belief that Dillinger fell into the wrong channel of life in his youth, from which escape is almost impossible, and that if given the above opportunity he would gladly avail himself of it and live up to it.

4. This would probably prevent bloodshed in his capture and salvage a being who, no doubt, has considerable worth if his energy were properly directed.

5. In case he should refuse, or violate the above agreement, no self-respecting citizen could honestly entertain any sympathy for him and his punishment would then be the just deserts of his premeditated guilt, and the state of Indiana could be proud of the generous helping hand she had extended to her prodigal son in error and in need.

6. It is our opinion that many of the financial institutions of the state have just as criminally robbed our citizens without any effort being made to punish the perpetrators.

7. While we do not in any case condone crime, we feel that the new deal can manifest itself in no better way than to remove from the execution of the law the vindictive spirit of the barbaric past and let it stand for wholesome protection imbued with the humanity and consideration of a new and better day.

The next day the *Indianapolis Star* revealed in a front-page story that Dillinger had recently spent a week end in Mooresville, surrounded by relatives and friends. The Commissioner of Public Safety was dumbfounded and said, "It's mighty queer that people would tell a newspaper about Dillinger's visit before they told police or other law enforcement agencies."

Other public officials also excoriated the citizens of Mooresville for their "anti-social" attitude. Yet the people who had drawn up the petition had partially, and perhaps accidentally, expressed a point of view that was shared by many penologists. In a few weeks even Governor McNutt's own secretary, Wayne Coy, would say, "There does not seem to me to be any escape from the fact that the State of Indiana made John Dillinger the Public Enemy that he is today. The Indiana constitution provides that our penal code shall be reformative and not vindictive. . . . Instead of reforming the prisoner, the penal institutions provided him with an education in crime."

This charitable feeling was by no means confined to Indiana. No badman since Jesse James had won such widespread sympathy. He robbed banks—not people—and had become to many a sort of Depression Robin Hood. The dash and derring-do of his escape, his impudence to those in authority, and his occasional chivalry during a robbery made them see him as a folk hero.

CHAPTER 14

Death Comes
to Little Bohemia

1

The Little Bohemia Lodge was about thirty yards from the shores of Little Star, one of a series of connected lakes deep in the wild North Woods of upper Wisconsin. At this time of year overnight guests were infrequent—a hunter or a traveling salesman. Occasionally local residents or men from the nearby CCC camp patronized the bar.

The lodge was a two-story log building. Downstairs were a large kitchen, a bar, and a spacious living room that could be cleared for dancing. Upstairs there were ten bedrooms.

It was built in 1931 by Emil Wanatka, who had emigrated from Bohemia as a boy after agents from San Francisco flooded Austria-Hungary with pamphlets inviting immigrants to help rebuild their destroyed city. When young Wanatka arrived in New York after a seventeen-day trip from Bremen in steerage—fare $18.20—he knew one American word: sonofabitch. He was short, stocky, with tremendous energy and a buoyantly outgoing personality. After several years he drifted to Chicago, where he became a bartender at a famous restaurant-saloon. During Prohibition he prospered, bought a half interest in the restaurant and finally owned it outright. He became intimate with politicians and sports figures; gangsters, racketeers, and bootleggers—including every one of the victims of the St. Valentine's Day Massacre—were frequent customers.

He lost most of his money in the early years of the Depression and now owned only the lodge—and it was heavily mortgaged.

Very early in the morning of April 20 the Dillinger gang left Chicago in three cars for the four-hundred-mile trip to Little Bohemia. Dillinger, following Harry Pierpont's precedent, kept them well strung out on the highway with Homer Van Meter in command of the first car. Van Meter was to determine if the lodge was safe, then survey the surrounding area for emergency escape routes. At his side was his companion, Marie Conforti, an attractive girl of twenty-one who looked eighteen and anything but a gangster's moll. She held a Boston bull puppy in her lap. Their driver was Pat Reilly—a meek, good-natured young man who abhorred all violence; it was he who had recently brought Dillinger and Hamilton to his family doctor after they were wounded at Mason City. Though he had hung around gangsters since his days as mascot for the St. Paul baseball team, he had never been more than an errand boy. The coming week end would be the high point of his life.

At about 1:00 P.M. Van Meter's car reached an imposing arched gateway made of cement and rocks with a sign reading: LITTLE BOHEMIA LODGE. It turned left into the narrow driveway, passed through a small pine woods still marked with patches of snow and, after some five hundred yards, came to the lodge. As Reilly backed into the parking area—so he could pull out quickly if necessary—another car was just leaving. Reilly went over and asked which door was the entrance.

The driver was Lloyd La Porte, a guide and Wanatka's brother-in-law. He pointed to the main door and said to ask for Emil. As they drove off, La Porte remarked to his wife, "I'll bet that car is hot," then thought nothing more of it.

While the gangster trio was eating a lunch of pork chops and the puppy was lapping a bowl of milk, Van Meter asked

Wanatka if he could put up ten guests for several days. They were on their way to Duluth. Wanatka said there was plenty of room. After lunch Van Meter walked behind the lodge to a steep bank which ran down to the lake front. In an emergency the gang could escape along the shore, completely protected by the bank.

A few hours later Dillinger and the others arrived. Nelson and his petite wife, Helen, were put in a three-room cabin a few yards from the lodge along with Tommy Carroll and his wife, Jean. Dillinger, Hamilton, and Patricia Cherrington were given rooms on the second floor of the main building.

After dinner Carroll asked Wanatka if he played cards. The proprietor sat at a table in the barroom with the six gangsters, none of whom drank. Carroll and Nelson were the most talkative, joking with the barkeepers, but Dillinger, Hamilton, and Van Meter said little.

Soon Wanatka had everyone's name straight. Nelson was called Jimmy; Van Meter, Wayne; Dillinger was Johnnie. Then he learned something much more important about them. After Dillinger won the first pot and reached for the money, Wanatka saw a .45 in a shoulder strap. Moments later he discovered guns on Nelson and Carroll.

He was alarmed—the man called Johnnie had the Dillinger shuffle, the same mole between his eyes. He excused himself, went to the kitchen, and looked through a recent newspaper until he found a picture of the famous gangster. It looked exactly like his guest. He whispered to his wife, Nan, that he'd seen guns on the men and returned apprehensively to the game.

Mrs. Wanatka, a local girl, was introspective and retiring. Since dinner the new guests had somehow made her nervous and when Wanatka told about the guns she almost panicked, but finally got control of herself and continued gossiping with her sister, Mrs. Henry Voss, who had just dropped in. She didn't want her to become suspicious of the ten strangers.

Finally Mrs. Voss left and Nan Wanatka went upstairs to bed. After some time she convinced herself there was nothing to worry about and fell asleep. Then she was wakened by her husband, who whispered, "Shut up and don't talk but I think the man with the dyed red hair is Dillinger."

Now she couldn't get back to sleep. The two watchdogs kept barking. She heard floors squeak, knobs turn. It was a nightmare.

As soon as they got up next morning Wanatka showed his wife the newspaper picture of Dillinger. She too was sure it was "Johnnie." After the guests breakfasted, Wanatka asked Dillinger to come to the office and, once they were alone, said, "You're John Dillinger."

Dillinger grinned. "You're not afraid, are you?"

"I just don't want no shooting match here. Everything I got to my name is right here. Why don't you do me a favor and you fellows get out?"

Dillinger patted Wanatka's arm. "Emil, I'm hungry. I'm tired. I want to sleep and eat a few days. I want to rest up. I'll pay you well and then we'll all get out." He put his hands on Wanatka's shoulders. "Don't worry about anything."

The proprietor could do nothing but agree. Before lunch he joined Van Meter, Carroll, and Nelson in a shooting match behind the helps' quarters. At a distance of about eighty yards the gangsters weren't very good marksmen and Wanatka had no trouble outshooting them. Then the men began throwing a baseball around. Wanatka's ten-year-old son, Emil, Junior, joined the game but quit when Baby Face intentionally kept throwing the ball so fast the youngster's hands stung.

To the boy Nelson was a mean bully, but others had got a different impression. The two bartenders thought Jimmy was a likeable young fellow; he joked with them and tipped lavishly. To the three girls who worked in the kitchen he was cute; the previous night he had even invited them all to the bar for a friendly drink.

The elder Wanatka saw him as a boastful, dangerous hoodlum. That morning Van Meter had asked for a cabin, saying that the lodge was too public. A moment later Nelson, who had been eavesdropping, cornered Wanatka, said he gave "all the orders," and told the proprietor to pay no attention to anyone else.

That afternoon Dillinger told Pat Reilly to drive to St. Paul and get $2,500 and more ammunition. Patricia Cherrington asked if she could go along to see a doctor.

By now Nan Wanatka was determined to get her son away. Every time a car drove up, Dillinger would ask Wanatka if he knew the occupants. Every time the phone rang, one of the gang would stand by and monitor the conversation. Wanatka agreed with his wife and a perfect excuse was at hand: the son of Nan's other brother, George La Porte, was having a birthday celebration that afternoon. When Wanatka asked if he could drive the boy to the party, Dillinger made no objection and even gave Emil, Junior, a quarter. But he insisted that Homer Van Meter go along to make sure Wanatka didn't "say anything smart to anybody."

By the time Wanatka and his guard returned to Little Bohemia he was beginning to feel more than resentful about being ordered around in his own place. He'd taken enough and decided to inform the police about the gangsters. But he couldn't use the phone or sneak out and tell a neighbor. Finally he sat down and wrote to a friend who was Assistant United States Attorney in Chicago. The problem now was to mail the letter—and as soon as possible.

While he and his wife were eating an early supper in the small dining room, he surreptitiously slipped the letter to her. She went to the kitchen and hid it in her corset. She knew what she had to do—but how? When she returned, Dillinger was chatting with Wanatka and she asked her husband if he minded if she ran over to the birthday party; her whole family was there, she said. Wanatka looked to Dillinger for permission.

"Sure," he said.

Mrs. Wanatka, expecting he would insist that one of the gang go along as guard, waited—but Dillinger only smiled. It was so unexpected she was frightened. She got into the family Chevrolet. Snow was falling lightly in great flakes and it was almost dusk. Suspecting that Dillinger was only testing her, she pulled the choke so the engine would keep dying. Several minutes passed, yet no one came out to stop her.

Hardly able to believe her luck, she drove slowly to the main road, Highway 51, then turned left. After half a mile she saw a car behind her but thought little of it. She passed the house where the party was being held, deciding to mail the letter herself in Mercer; but a minute later when she got to the other side of the village of Manitowish Waters she noticed the car was still following her. She slowed down. When the other driver slowed too, she was suddenly seized with panic.

She had reason to be. It was Baby Face Nelson.

She tried to think of a plan. Her brother, Lloyd La Porte, lived several miles ahead on the other side of a big S curve. She drove slowly until she got to the first turn on the S, then, once out of Nelson's sight, stepped on the accelerator and drove full speed into her brother's driveway, skidding to a stop. As Lloyd La Porte came out the door she called excitedly, "Jump in!"

He did and she quickly backed into the highway. Just as she was again heading toward Mercer, Nelson came around the curve, unaware that she had picked up anyone.

"I'm in trouble," she said.

"Family?"

"No, I wish it were that."

La Porte asked just what was going on at the lodge. He told her about the suspicious way Reilly had parked and facetiously said, "I guess Dillinger is there."

"Dillinger *is* there!" She told him she was trying to mail a letter to the police but she was afraid one of the gang was in the car just behind. She handed him the letter. As they neared Mercer she realized she had to let her brother out secretly and used the same trick: speeded, turned a corner in town, and abruptly stopped. La Porte jumped out and she continued to the general store. If her pursuer asked what she was doing in Mercer, she would say she was buying candy for the party.

While she was at the grocery counter, Nelson appeared and stared at her through the store window. He leaned out the car which he had driven onto the sidewalk and pointed a finger at her warningly. She thought: I'll never see Junior again.

She picked up her purchases and walked out the door, then impulsively ran back inside.

The storekeeper, noticing her strange behavior, asked if he could do anything for her.

After a brief hesitation she said, "No," and started outside again. If they searched her she had nothing to be afraid of. Her story about the candy was logical. She got into the car and started the motor.

At that moment her brother called casually from across the street as if it were the first time he had seen her that evening, "Hey, Nan, give me a ride." La Porte got in and said he'd mailed the letter at the railroad station without being seen by Nelson.

They drove to their brother George's house in Manitowish Waters, where the birthday party was in full swing. Their sister, Mrs. Voss, almost immediately noticed Nan's pale face and her nervous manner. "What's the matter?" she asked, wondering if she'd had a fight with Emil.

Mrs. Wanatka told her sister she'd almost had an accident in the car.

An hour later someone said jokingly, "I hear Dillinger is out at your place, Nan."

She could not hold her secret any longer. Calling her two brothers, sister, and brother-in-law, Henry Voss, into the bedroom, she told them everything. Voss was worried. It was Saturday and the letter wouldn't be delivered until Monday. "You could all be dead by then," he said. He felt the local sheriff's office was inadequately equipped to cope with the Dillinger gang and suggested driving to Rhinelander, some fifty miles to the southeast, where he could safely telephone the FBI in Chicago for immediate help. As a precaution, young Emil would stay at the La Portes'.

Nan agreed to the new plan—if it had her husband's approval. She told Lloyd La Porte to come to the lodge the following morning and she would give him a pack of cigarettes. If Wanatka approved, there would be a note inside reading, "Go ahead, Lloyd."

She went home. To her amazement neither Nelson nor Dillinger questioned her about the unscheduled trip to Mercer. When Wanatka came upstairs about 10:00 P.M. she told him the plan. He agreed.

That night the two watchdogs continued their barking—apparently at nothing. And Mrs. Wanatka stayed awake wondering what was going to happen.

The next morning she wrote the short note and put it in a pack of Marvels. Though she rarely drank, she was so nervous she went to the bar and washed down two aspirins with a shot of whiskey. A few hours later her mother and Lloyd La Porte dropped in as planned. Baby Face and Dillinger hovered in the lounge, near enough to overhear every word.

"Gee," said La Porte casually, "I left my cigarettes home. Have you got any, Nan?"

Her throat was dry and she couldn't say anything; she could only hand him the package of Marvels. He took several, then while talking of inconsequential matters, casually put the pack in his pocket.

Just then Wanatka came in. "Lloyd, you look tired. Go in the bar and get a drink." While handing him the drink, Wanatka whispered, "Go in the men's room and get the cigarettes by the flush box."

La Porte casually walked into the men's room. In the flush box he found a pack of Camels—on it Wanatka had written the license numbers of the three gang cars and the names of the gangsters.

La Porte returned to the kitchen and chatted for some time with Mrs. Wanatka, who was getting more and more nervous. Finally he got up to leave and his sister said, "Lloyd, as long as you have to stop at the Vosses', take this dress material and pattern along."

He picked up the material and walked with his mother out the kitchen door. None of the gangsters paid any attention to them.

An hour and a half later, after a fifty-mile drive over bad roads, La Porte and Voss were in Rhinelander. They headed for the nearest telephone.

. . .

Melvin Purvis was relaxing in his Chicago bachelor apartment, one of the few days in the past year he wasn't on duty. It was Sunday. He was a small man with bright, alert eyes who dressed fashionably and was so fastidious he often changed shirts three times a day. A law graduate of the University of South Carolina, he spoke with such a polite, pleasant drawl, a member of his staff nicknamed him The Southern Gentleman. One might have thought he was a successful young bond salesman perhaps—but certainly not a G-man.

Unlike other agents he was not averse to publicity—he did have a flare for the dramatic—and occasionally violated the Bureau's unwritten law of avoiding the limelight. Nevertheless he was a competent executive, a man of unquestioned courage despite his excitability, and was well liked by those who worked under him.

About one o'clock that afternoon Purvis' house boy said he was wanted on the telephone. It was the U. S. Marshal of Chicago. A Henry Voss of Rhinelander, Wisconsin—a reliable source—claimed he knew where Dillinger was. Purvis called the number given him by the marshal.

"The man you want most is up here," said Voss tensely.

Purvis wanted to know whom he meant. Voss refused to mention names. "You mean Dillinger?" asked Purvis.

Voss at last said that Dillinger and five other men were at the Little Bohemia Lodge. When Purvis learned that the nearest airport was at Rhinelander about 275 air miles from Chicago, he told Voss to wait there for him. "Wear a handkerchief around your neck so I can identify you." Purvis then called his office and ordered two planes chartered. Every available man was to report at once. He also phoned Hoover in Washington, who told him to request the St. Paul office to fly all available men to Rhinelander, only 185 air miles away. Assistant Director Hugh Clegg, who had been sent to St. Paul by Hoover after Dillinger shot his way out of the Lincoln Court Apartments, was still in town and would accompany this group and take charge of the entire operation.

Within minutes the first agents began to report at the

Bankers' Building. Some looked as if they had just been routed
out of bed; some had been working for thirty-six hours without
sleep on other assignments. But it was no novelty for an agent
to tell his wife he'd be home for dinner and not show up for
three weeks. Purvis himself was still tying his necktie when he
reached the office. Within an hour more than fifteen had gathered and were collecting guns, bulletproof vests, and tear gas
equipment. Purvis selected eleven men to go by plane. The
rest would drive.

When the two chartered cabin planes took off—one belonged to film actress Ann Harding—their pilots had only road
maps to guide them. It was an uncomfortable trip—even one
pilot got airsick—but the discomfort hardly mattered to Purvis
and his men; their tedious and dangerous chase seemed to be
approaching its climax. In some three hours they would land
at Rhinelander. An hour and a half later they should be at
Little Bohemia.

But at that moment in Little Bohemia, Dillinger and his
men were already paying their bill. Once more it looked as
if the law would arrive too late. Dillinger told Wanatka he
had changed his mind and was leaving as soon as Pat Reilly
and the girl returned from St. Paul. He wanted an early dinner: steak with garlic.

Nan Wanatka prepared the meal as if in a dream, so nervous she hardly knew what she was doing. She still didn't
know if her brother-in-law, Henry Voss, had been able to
reach the FBI. If the gang left before help arrived, would
Dillinger kill everyone to keep them quiet?

About 4:00 P.M. Dillinger and the rest sat down to dinner.
While they were eating, Mrs. Voss and her daughter drove up
to the kitchen door. Then, in an excited whisper, Mrs. Voss
told her sister that Henry had gone to Rhinelander to phone
the FBI. Help should be on the way by now.

Mrs. Wanatka tried to hush her. Dillinger was eating in
the next room and might hear. "We bought so much meat for
the week end," she said in what she hoped was a casual tone.
"Won't you take some?" She dragged her sister into the re-

frigerator room and said, "They're leaving as soon as Reilly gets back!"

Mrs. Voss said she and her daughter would drive as fast as possible to Rhinelander and pass on the news to Voss. After they left, Mrs. Wanatka went to the bar for more whiskey and aspirin. Since morning she had taken so many drinks she'd lost count, but the liquor appeared to have had little effect. As she was putting the whiskey bottle back on the shelf, she felt a hand on her shoulder.

She turned in fright. "Nan, are you drinking?" Wanatka asked incredulously.

Suddenly Baby Face Nelson, who had approached soundlessly, was standing beside them. Mrs. Wanatka felt a stab of panic but controlled herself. Her husband tried to smile.

Nelson just stared at them. He had been suspicious of Mrs. Wanatka since the trip to Mercer the night before but Dillinger had told him he was imagining things. He started to follow Mrs. Wanatka into the kitchen, but turned and joined his wife at a table.

If he had gone to the kitchen he would have seen, as Nan Wanatka did, a car drive into the parking area. In it were Reilly and Patricia Cherrington. Reilly looked around. The driveway was completely empty because that morning Dillinger had ordered the two cars hidden in the garage—just to be on the cautious side. Reilly became alarmed. Where were Dillinger and the others? Had they been captured? He was tempted to go inside, then felt he might be walking into a trap. So he quickly swung the car around, skidding in the mud, and drove off. As soon as it got dark he would come back to see what had happened.

At that moment Purvis was only an hour's flight from Rhinelander.

When Nan Wanatka saw Reilly look around suspiciously and drive away, she was elated. Perhaps now the FBI might arrive in time. Then she realized this would mean a gun battle. She thanked God that Emil, Junior, was still at her brother's.

The bar was usually well patronized on Sunday afternoons

and today was no exception. A group of men from a nearby town had just come in for drinks. One, a husky tavern owner, noticed Hamilton had no glass and offered to buy him a drink. Hamilton said he was sorry, he didn't drink. "Damn you, you'll drink with me, or I'll pour it down your mouth!" He jerked Hamilton out of his chair, almost jarring the gangster's gun from its holster.

Wanatka interrupted nervously and introduced Hamilton as his "good friend, Miller, from Chicago."

Hamilton turned to Wanatka and said good-naturedly that he'd better drink. "This man is pretty tough." A few minutes later the belligerent tavern owner asked "Miller" if he was going to buy drinks for everybody. Hamilton treated and even bought a pair of tickets for a local baseball game. Then he meekly asked if he could leave.

Dillinger saw none of this. He was upstairs in his room, checking a road map. He was also getting impatient: What had happened to Reilly? It was already a little past 6:00 P.M.

The two planes from Chicago were just approaching the Rhinelander airfield. As Purvis's plane touched down, a wheel brake failed and it ground-looped twice, almost tipping over. The plane from St. Paul had already arrived, and within minutes Assistant Director Clegg was counting his combined forces: seventeen men. Purvis acted as second-in-command.

Clegg, in contrast to Purvis, was stocky and looked as solid as a football guard. One of those whose exceptional ability had caught the eye of Hoover, he had been made Assistant Director after only six years' service. He had already been greeted by a man with a handkerchief stuffed in his collar—Henry Voss. Since his wife was still en route to Rhinelander, Voss had no idea Dillinger's plans were changed, and he told Clegg there was no particular hurry. The gangsters would not leave until the next morning. An agent was instructed to return with Voss to the latter's lodge about a mile and a half below Little Bohemia. Clegg and the others would follow as soon as cars could be rented.

Since Voss had told Clegg that Wanatka would herd all innocent persons into the basement of the lodge at 4:00 A.M., the raid was scheduled for that time. By then the car from St. Paul would have arrived with men to block roads around the lodge.

But before all of the equipment was unloaded from the planes, Voss ran back across the field. He had just met his wife on the highway and learned that Dillinger had changed his plans. He was leaving around supper time.

Clegg was dismayed. He knew he couldn't possibly get to Little Bohemia until 8:00 P.M. even if he left immediately. And as yet he had only Voss's car. It seemed hopeless, but his depression was quickly overcome by a fever for action.

A young man in a Ford coupé, Isidor Tuchalski, agreed to drive Purvis into the Rhinelander business section. On the way Tuchalski proudly said his car was a "special job" capable of 103 miles an hour.

When the agents discovered it would take an hour to round up five autos for hire, they borrowed Tuchalski's Ford and four other cars. Then Clegg gathered his men in the Ford garage and quickly mapped out an attack based on a sketchy diagram of Little Bohemia drawn by Voss. Three agents wearing bulletproof vests would storm the main door of the lodge. A group of five would flank the lodge on the left in a line all the way to the lake and intercept anyone who tried to break through. A similar group would do the same on the right. Thus the gang would be trapped on three sides. The fourth side, the lake, was impassable since there were no boats on it.

The plan was good but it did not take into consideration three key terrain factors, all missing from Voss's map: a ditch on the left of the lodge, a barbed-wire fence on the right, and the steep bank near the lake which could mask an escape along the shore. Nor did it occur to Voss to warn Purvis about Wanatka's two watchdogs.

At about 7:15 P.M. the five cars left Rhinelander. The road was muddy from melting snow and pocked with holes. After thirty miles two dilapidated vehicles broke down and their

eight occupants jumped on the running boards of the other
three cars. It was now biting cold and these men, encumbered
by rifles and shotguns, had a difficult time hanging on.

In the meantime only one thing of note had happened at
Little Bohemia. Nan Wanatka had left. But it had taken three
phone calls from Mrs. Voss to persuade her. Finally Mrs. Voss
had said, "Damn it, Nan. Get in that car and leave." Dillinger,
who was about to go himself, naturally had no objections.

When Mrs. Wanatka reached the end of Little Bohemia's
long driveway, she turned right on Highway 51 and started
south toward her sister's place, Birchwood Lodge. At last she
was safe—but her husband wasn't.

About half an hour later the FBI party stopped in front of
Birchwood Lodge. It was pitch dark. Voss ran in and learned
from Mrs. Wanatka that Dillinger had not yet left Little Bohemia. Clegg knew he had to attack at once. There was no time
to notify the local authorities of what they were going to do.
He gathered his men around and briefly outlined the plan
again in his calm, positive manner. Then he ordered all cigarettes out, and the three FBI cars, lights extinguished, slowly
headed toward the Wanatka lodge.

Pat Reilly, with Patricia Cherrington beside him, was
again approaching the same destination from the opposite direction and was closer to it; but he lost his nerve again, decided to wait a few more minutes, and parked.

Clegg and his men groped their way along the dark, deserted road for another mile and a half before reaching the
entrance to Little Bohemia, where he ordered two of the cars
parked across the driveway in a V-shape.

The agents rubbed their numbed hands and made a final
check of their weapons. Then at a signal they slowly moved
out toward the lodge through the trees. Five fanned to the
left, five to the right. Purvis, Clegg and the others who were to
storm the front of the lodge went straight ahead, their twenty-
four-pound bulletproof vests feeling twice their weight. Purvis
vowed never to use one again.

Now he could see the glow of lights coming from the lodge. The entrance door was brightly lit. Suddenly two dogs began to bark. The startled G-men could have imagined nothing worse. Thinking all hope of surprise was gone, they began running to their positions.

But inside, the noise was hardly noticed. Dillinger, who was playing cards in the bar with several members of the gang, didn't even look up. The dogs had been yelping at the slightest provocation the past two nights and he had become used to them.

The irony was not that the dogs had barked without warning Dillinger but that the last three customers at the bar —a gas salesman from Mercer and two men from the nearby CCC camp—happened to choose that very moment to go home. They paid for their drinks and started for the main entrance.

When the dogs' howling persisted the two bartenders, George Bazso and Frank Traube, said they would find out what was wrong. They stepped onto the kitchen porch just as the three customers went out the main door and headed toward their car parked a few feet away.

When the agents saw the five men emerge almost simultaneously from two adjacent doors of the lodge they were sure the Dillinger gang had been alerted by the dogs. Several of them called out that they were federal officers, but the three men, now in the car, didn't hear. In switching on the ignition, John Hoffman, the salesman, had also turned on the radio, and music blasted so loudly that the agents' repeated demands to halt were inaudible.

The car began to move. Thinking the gang was trying to escape, Purvis and Clegg shouted orders to shoot the tires. Bullets smashed the glass, riddling the car. John Morris, an elderly cook at the CCC camp, stumbled out the right door, sat down and took a drink from a bottle he was clutching. Though wounded four times, he managed to stagger onto the kitchen porch. Hoffman, also wounded, jumped out the other door, crept into the woods and hid. Only the man in the middle, Eugene Boisneau, a young CCC worker, did not move. He was dead.

With the first shot, every member of the gang began moving. Dillinger didn't have to give orders. Each man knew his post.

"Better duck," Dillinger told the three girls, and put out the light.

Almost immediately a machine gun began to chatter from a second-story window—Van Meter. And a few seconds later another from the roof—Carroll. Now a much quicker, nervous series of bursts—almost like the cackling of a loon—could be heard from the cabin a few yards right of the lodge. These bore the unmistakable touch of Baby Face Nelson, who had gone out to pack.

The fusillade from within the lodge lasted only seconds. Then as planned, Dillinger, Hamilton, and Van Meter climbed out a second-story back window onto a porch facing Little Star Lake. They jumped into a pile of snow, crept about twenty-five yards, and slid down a steep bank to the lake's edge. There they turned right and, hidden by the bank, escaped along the shore.

A few moments later Carroll leaped out the same back window, scrambled down the bank and also turned right at the lake's shore. By that time Dillinger was out of sight ahead.

Nelson, intoxicated by battle as always, was the last to leave. He fired a final burst from the cabin at the attacking agents, then trotted through the pine trees to the shore. Unlike the others, he went left in the opposite direction. When the plan was discussed he must have been talking, as usual, instead of listening.

The two FBI groups ordered to flank the lodge to the lake had run into unexpected trouble. In the dark the agents on the left stumbled upon a deep drainage ditch; those on the right were tangled in a barbed-wire fence. By the time any agent reached the lake, all five gangsters had slipped through the trap.

Purvis was still pouring lead into the front of the lodge, unaware that the quarry had vanished, when Pat Reilly finally drove into the Little Bohemia driveway. Several agents ran up to the car and ordered Reilly to get out but he rammed the gear into reverse and backed up full speed.

Agents opened fire, hoping to hit the radiator. The window near Patricia Cherrington disintegrated, showering her with glass fragments. A tire exploded and the car lurched. Reilly desperately maneuvered the wheel, somehow keeping the car from lunging into the ditch. Once on the highway he slammed on the brakes, then jammed his foot on the accelerator. For a brief moment the car was a standing target, then it shot to the north, its flat tire thumping noisily.

Six people were huddled in the cellar—Wanatka, his two bartenders, and the three girls. One of the bartenders, thinking robbers were outside, hid his wallet in the coal bin. The gangsters had given him more than $50 in tips.

On the floor above, Morris, the wounded CCC cook, now staggered into the kitchen, unhooked the telephone receiver and said, "Alvin, we're at Emil's!" He was talking to Alvin Koerner, who ran the local telephone exchange. "Everybody has been knocked out!"

When Wanatka, directly below in the basement, heard Morris he ran upstairs and picked up the dangling receiver. Koerner connected him with an FBI agent, who advised him to turn on the lights and go outside with hands up.

Wanatka returned to the basement and told the others what the agent had said. The three gang girls refused to leave but Wanatka and the two bartenders walked out, hands up, followed a moment later by the wounded CCC cook.

Wanatka said there were three girls in the basement and Clegg, even though he thought Dillinger was still inside, ordered his men to stop firing. They were to give the girls time to come out, then lob tear gas shells into the lodge. For the moment it was ominously quiet.

Nan Wanatka's brother, George La Porte, heard the first shots as he was standing guard with a rifle about a mile away outside a neighbor's house where he had taken Emil, Junior. The firing continued so furiously that he felt sure there would be casualties and, with a friend, he drove, as fast as possible to the nearby CCC camp to get medical aid. At first, the camp doctor refused to believe La Porte's story but finally agreed to bring the CCC ambulance to the lodge.

La Porte followed in his Ford. As he neared Little Bohemia, anxiety over his friends at the lodge was mixed with concern for his own family; the night before he had canceled his life insurance. A quarter of a mile from the lodge entrance a tall, thin man stepped onto the road and tried to flag the car down but La Porte didn't stop.

The hitchhiker was Homer Van Meter. Dillinger and Hamilton came from behind a clump of bushes after La Porte passed. They had to have a car quickly. Across the highway, they saw a truck parked outside a large house.

Inside, Mr. and Mrs. E. J. Mitchell, an elderly couple, were trying to explain the meaning of a word to their hired man, a German flier in the Great War, when they heard a knock at the door. Hamilton asked Mr. Mitchell for a drink of water and then calmly walked across the room and tore out the phone.

Dillinger came in. Seeing the terrified expression on Mrs. Mitchell's face, he said, "You've probably heard stories about me but I'm not as bad as I'm pictured."

"You couldn't be Dillinger?"

He grinned at her. "You couldn't have guessed better." Now he turned to her husband, who was about his own father's age, and said reassuringly, "Never mind, old man, I'd never harm a hair on your head." He told them he only wanted a car. Mitchell said his Model T was on blocks in the garage; the Ford truck was the hired man's. Dillinger told everyone to get outside while they started the truck.

"My wife is just getting over the flu," said Mitchell.

Dillinger got a blanket. "Here you are, mother," he said, draping it over her shoulders.

The truck wouldn't start and Dillinger asked about a Ford coupé parked in front of a nearby cottage. It belonged, explained Mitchell, to a local carpenter.

Dillinger shouted until the carpenter came to the door, then said Mrs. Mitchell was sick. "We want you to go after a doctor."

The carpenter shuffled forward in his bedroom slippers. Still yawning, he was hustled into his car and forced to drive the gangsters over a seldom used country road toward their goal, St. Paul.

A minute later, Tommy Carroll also emerged onto the highway near the Mitchells'. He had been trying to catch up with Dillinger but now realized he had to escape alone. He walked north along the main road, looking for a parked car, but got all the way to Manitowish Waters, a mile above Little Bohemia, without seeing one. Finally as he was leaving the village, he saw a Packard outside the Northern Lights Resort.

He was almost caught by the car's owners as he drove off; then instead of continuing on the highway to Mercer he turned right when he came to a fork in the road and escaped. It would take him several hours to discover he was on a dead-end lumber trail.

The only gangster to go south along the lake's edge was Baby Face Nelson. After about half a mile he left the shore and began stumbling and tearing through the thick underbrush, but he was a city boy with no sense of direction and wandered in circles some forty minutes before running across a resort run by Mr. and Mrs. G. W. Lang, an elderly couple. He ordered them into their car and drove south down Highway 51—straight toward the FBI headquarters at the Voss lodge.

But the headlights went out half a mile from the Vosses'. Nelson noticed a well-lighted house, a hundred yards off to the left, and the Langs said it was the home of Alvin Koerner who ran the telephone exchange. Yes, Koerner had a car. Nelson parked.

The two phone calls from embattled Little Bohemia had made Alvin Koerner so nervous he kept looking out the window at the highway and it was not surprising that he saw Nelson park the unlighted car not far from his house. Appre-

hensive, he went to the switchboard and informed the FBI
men at the Voss place of the incident. As he hung up the phone,
Nelson and the Langs approached his front door.

George La Porte, Mrs. Wanatka's brother, was also heading for Koerner's. After refusing to pick up the hitchhiker, Van
Meter, he had continued on to Little Bohemia, arriving only a
few minutes after Wanatka and his two bartenders had run
out of the lodge in their shirtsleeves. He was now driving them
to Koerner's to get coats. La Porte turned his Ford into the
Koerner driveway and stopped in front of the house. He followed Wanatka and his two employees as they entered the
front door.

Nelson was inside—holding an automatic pistol on the
Koerners and the Langs. One of the bartenders, who had been
impressed by Nelson's generosity, said, "Hello, Jimmy."

"Never mind the bullshit," said Nelson, waggling his gun.
"Just line up against the wall with the rest of them."

Wanatka grabbed Nelson's gun hand. "Put that gun down,
Jimmy," he said. "Those people are friends of mine."

Nelson jerked his hand away, then asked about the car
outside. La Porte said it was his.

Nelson selected two hostages—Wanatka and Koerner.
Mrs. Koerner screamed but Nelson ignored her and told the
two men to get outside.

Koerner climbed into the back seat. The friend who had
accompanied La Porte to the CCC camp was still there. So
was La Porte's rifle.

Nelson sat next to Wanatka in the front seat and kept jab-
bing him with a gun. "Why put the gun in my ribs, Jimmy?"
said Wanatka. "I'm not armed. What are you afraid of?"

Nelson told him to shut up and start the car. Wanatka
stepped on the starter. Nothing happened. "You haven't got
the switch on," said Nelson.

Wanatka turned on the switch. This time the car choked.
Nelson was enraged.

Just then a car turned in from the highway, bathing Nelson and the others with its headlights. In it were two FBI
men and a local constable. It was almost 11:00 P.M.

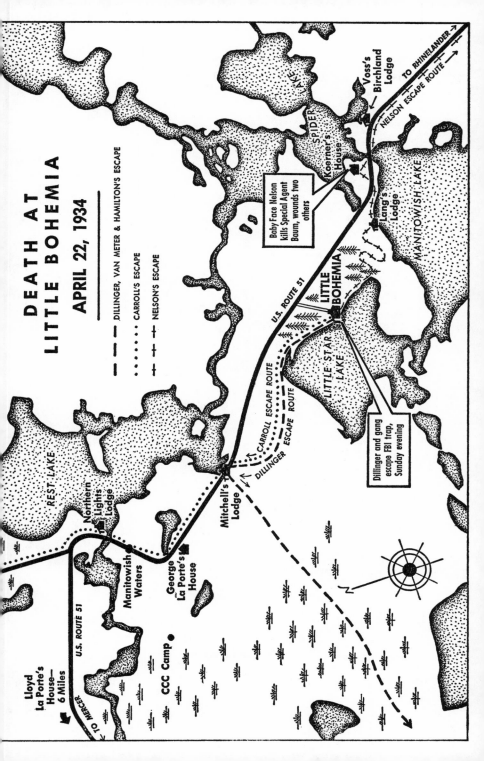

DEATH AT LITTLE BOHEMIA
APRIL 22, 1934

--- DILLINGER, VAN METER & HAMILTON'S ESCAPE
······· CARROLL'S ESCAPE
-+-+- NELSON'S ESCAPE

TO RHINELANDER →

NELSON ESCAPE ROUTE

Voss's Birchland Lodge

SPIDER LAKE

Koerner's House

Baby Face Nelson kills Special Agent Baum, wounds two others

Lang's Lodge

MANITOWISH LAKE

LITTLE BOHEMIA

U.S. ROUTE 51

LITTLE STAR LAKE

Dillinger and gang escape FBI trap, Sunday evening

REST LAKE

Northern Lights Lodge

Mitchell's Lodge

CARROLL ESCAPE ROUTE

DILLINGER ESCAPE ROUTE

Manitowish Waters

George La Porte's House

U.S. ROUTE 51

CCC Camp

Lloyd La Porte's House— 6 Miles

TO MERCER

. . .

About forty-five minutes earlier, Purvis had ordered these two agents to drive to the Voss lodge and telephone the agent left in Rhinelander. They were to report what had happened and check on the progress of the men driving up from Chicago and St. Paul.

They reached Birchwood Lodge about the time Baby Face was stumbling onto the Lang cottage. Once inside the Vosses' they learned a Packard had been stolen in Manitowish Waters —by now Tommy Carroll had driven it several miles up the dead-end lumber trail. Correctly guessing that one of the Dillinger gang was using the Packard for a getaway, the two agents raced back north in their car, the speedy one commandeered in Rhinelander from Tuchalski. They interviewed the local constable, Carl C. Christensen, who agreed to help them trace the Packard. Christensen got into their car and they again headed back for the Voss lodge.

En route south they passed Little Bohemia and a mile further Koerner's, where Nelson had just arrived and was lining prisoners against the wall. Half a mile later they reached the Vosses' and learned that Koerner had called regarding a suspicious car parked near his home. A few minutes before 11:00 P.M. the two FBI men and the constable started back up Highway 51—for the third time—to investigate.

The driver was Special Agent Jay Newman, a Mormon lay preacher. He wore glasses. Constable Christensen, elected only a month previously, sat on the right, Special Agent Carter Baum in the middle. Baum was a big, good-natured young man of twenty-nine who, like Newman, had spent many tedious hours on the Dillinger chase, following false leads. This was probably another. After all, their second-in-command, Purvis, was still convinced the main body of the gang was trapped at Little Bohemia.

They saw the parked Lang car and stopped. Newman told Baum to take down the license number and then they turned off the highway into Koerner's lane to check on the driver. When Constable Christensen saw the Ford in front of Koerner's he remarked that it looked like George La Porte's and as they drew closer they could see it was filled with occupants.

Newman stopped just to the right and rear of La Porte's car, lowered the left-hand window, and said, "I'm looking for Mr. Koerner."

Baby Face Nelson leaped from the other car, quickly covering the two agents and constable with his automatic pistol. He told them to get out. As Newman opened the door and stepped on the running board, Nelson said, "I know you bastards are wearing bulletproof vests so I'll give it to you high and low!" He shot Newman in the forehead. The agent fell. Though semiconscious, he began crawling. Christensen opened the other door and started out but Nelson fired rapidly and the constable toppled into the ditch. Before Baum could reach for his gun, Baby Face shot him.

By this time Koerner had dashed back to his house, locking the door behind him. La Porte's friend could only duck down in the back seat but Wanatka dove into a snowbank.

Nelson seemed to have gone crazy. He either reloaded or grabbed another gun and began shooting up everything that moved. He fired at Wanatka, then loosed a burst at the ditch in the direction of Christensen, who already had eight bullets in him. Baby Face looked around for new targets, saw none, and jumped into the FBI Ford. He swung it around La Porte's car and circled back toward the highway. Newman, by a miracle alive though hit squarely in the forehead, regained consciousness long enough to empty his gun at the Ford, but the bullets missed and now Nelson was heading south in a car that could travel 103 miles an hour.

Wanatka felt his legs to make sure he wasn't hit. He touched his neck; there was no blood. Newman tottered to the Koerners' and banged on the kitchen door. But Koerner, fearing it was a trick of Nelson's, wouldn't let him in.

Wanatka ran back toward Little Bohemia for help.

Half a mile down the highway at Birchwood Lodge his wife heard about the mysterious car near the Koerners', and the report that Dillinger had held up the Mitchells. She thought, "The next stop will be here. They're looking for me."

Her hysteria was contagious and soon she convinced her sixty-six-year-old mother, her sister, and niece to escape into the woods with her. When they got to the shore of Spider Lake they saw lights across the bay at the Koerners' and heard shots. They turned and ran through the towering trees until they came to an abandoned shack. They hid inside.

In the past few days Mrs. Wanatka had lived through far more danger than most women see in a lifetime. Now she had reached the breaking point. She laughed, screamed, and cried hysterically. Mrs. Voss, swept by her sister's fear, was suddenly sure this was just the kind of hideout Dillinger was looking for and the four women plunged deep into the woods, finally dropping exhausted on the snow-patched ground. After some time they heard Henry Voss call, "It's all over with, come on back!"

But it was not over for Nan Wanatka. For many years she would live in terror, afraid some associate of Dillinger would murder her or her family in revenge.

Her husband was so winded by the time he arrived at Little Bohemia he could hardly put up his hands when ordered to do so by an agent.

Purvis asked what had happened.

"All your men are dead," panted Wanatka. "At Koerner's."

Outwardly calm, Purvis asked him how to spell his name and address.

Wanatka thought he was crazy. "Did you come for me or Dillinger?" he asked with as much amazement as anger.

Purvis seemed not to hear but kept looking back at the lodge. No one, including the three girls, had come out since Wanatka had emerged and tear gas was still pouring from its windows. By now a crowd of self-appointed deputies had arrived with weapons and were adding to the confusion with an occasional shot at the building.

Wanatka and one of his bartenders took it upon themselves to drive back to Koerner's to see if they could help the wounded. The house was still locked; everything was quiet and deserted. Only Baum lay in the road—dead. They lifted

him gently into the truck. Then Wanatka pocketed the agent's
.45 automatic and drove the body to the CCC camp.

By the time Wanatka returned to Little Bohemia it was
dawn, but the firing had not stopped. An eighteen-year-old
boy aimed a shotgun at the lodge and said, "I'm going to get
the award. I'm going to shoot Dillinger."

Wanatka said the next one that put a bullet into his house
would get hit over the head with his own gun. Exasperated, he
pulled out Baum's .45 and shouted to the agents, "Dillinger
left last night!"

Gas from the house was even affecting those outside, filling
their eyes with tears. In the silence could be heard the faint
voice of one of the girls in the basement, "We'll come out if
you stop firing," and a moment later the three girls, eyes streaming, stumbled out. Marie Conforti carried Rex, the bull pup.
The girls didn't know if anyone else was inside.

Six agents now charged through the front door; they
checked both floors and found no one. Then they ran outdoors
and put their heads under a pump.

The battle of Little Bohemia was over.

PART SIX

•

CHAPTER 15

The Narrowing Corner

1

Not long after midnight newspapers in Chicago, Milwaukee, Minneapolis, and St. Paul were sending reporters and
photographers to Little Bohemia by car, train, and air. No
crime story in America had ever caused such excitement.
Reporters Frank Sinclair and L. C. Eklund and a photographer from the *Milwaukee Journal* and a staffman of the Milwaukee Associated Press bureau were the first to arrive,
their plane landing at dawn in a farmer's field near Mercer.
As news of the gangsters' escape spread, local residents
were calling the affair a fiasco, assuring the *Journal* men

that Dillinger would have been easily captured if they had known what was going on earlier. Guards at two bridges, they said, would have completely bottled up the gangsters.

A petition—eventually signed by thirty-five persons—was circulated in the area asking for the suspension of Purvis and charging him with "wanton recklessness" and Newman and Baum with "criminal stupidity."

Criticism of the FBI was widespread. Two Republican senators accused the FBI of bungling the whole affair and it was reported that Director Hoover would be demoted or discharged unless Dillinger was soon caught. Attorney General Cummings excused the failure to catch the gang with a unique suggestion: "If we had had one armored car there in Wisconsin, our men would have driven right up to the house where Dillinger was. The terrible tragedy then would not have happened." He requested airplanes, cars, and more men to combat crime.

Senator Royal S. Copeland, chairman of the committee on racketeering, assailed the combined forces of the law. "There has been a pathetic failure of co-operation between federal, state, and local authorities," he said.

Will Rogers wrote, "Well, they had Dillinger surrounded and was all ready to shoot him when he come out, but another bunch of folks come out ahead, so they just shot them instead. Dillinger is going to accidentally get with some innocent bystanders some time, then he will get shot."

The skirmish at Little Bohemia began to be pictured as a major battle and Dillinger as such a national peril that a dozen Midwest communities even voted funds to buy their police departments machine guns and fast cars. John Dillinger had become a benefactor, in spite of himself, of those enforcing the law.

The guns and cars were certainly long overdue, but of far greater significance in the fight against crime was the effect Dillinger had on the President and Congress. President Roosevelt summoned the chairman of the House Judiciary Committee, Hatton Summers, to the White House. Until now the twelve anti-crime bills sent to Congress by Cummings had been held up because the committee felt they "did violence" to states' rights. When Summers emerged from his talk with the President he said his committee would report out the bills the next day.

2

The gang was fleeing in three different directions. Carroll, after finding he had driven his stolen Packard up a dead-end lumber road, abandoned it and was continuing on foot some twelve miles due north of Little Bohemia.

Baby Face Nelson was also on foot, the same distance due south. He had turned his 103-mile-an-hour Ford down a side road into a sea of mud.

Dillinger, Hamilton, and Van Meter had freed their hostage with a "so long" and were heading for St. Paul. The police of that area, warned of their probable approach, were guarding the main roads leading in and out of the city. On the morning after the shooting, Deputy Sheriff Norman Dieter and three other lawmen were posted at the famous spiral bridge over the Mississippi, twenty miles below St. Paul. According to information from Wisconsin, the gang was escaping in three cars—two Fords and a Packard. Dieter's mission was to capture Dillinger in case he had somehow entered the city and was trying to sneak out. Consequently he was only checking those cars heading south.

At about 10:30 A.M. Dieter happened to notice a Ford bound north toward St. Paul. Even though no one suspected Dillinger would enter the city from this direction, Dieter had a hunch. The car had a Wisconsin license; there were three men inside and the one in the middle had a handkerchief tied around his head. The lawmen jumped into their car as the Ford started to climb the spiral bridge.

The man with the handkerchief was Hamilton. Van Meter was driving. Dillinger sat beside him.

By the time Dieter's car got on the bridge, a slow-moving

cattle truck was between him and the gangsters and when the lawmen reached the other side of the Mississippi, Dillinger was out of sight. But ten miles later they caught up with the Ford, which was traveling at a conservative thirty-five miles an hour. They drew closer and checked the license number. It was on their list—but for the Packard. The lawmen were almost sure the numbers had become switched by mistake but they didn't want to take a chance of killing innocent people, so Dieter fired his rifle at a rear tire.

Van Meter stepped on the accelerator as Dillinger punched out the rear window of the Ford with the butt of his automatic and began shooting. The lawmen replied and in the next few miles a dozen bullets ripped into the Ford, one plunging into Hamilton's back.

Finally Van Meter got a lead of several hundred yards and, after rounding a sharp curve, suddenly turned off onto a dirt road. The lawmen roared straight ahead.

The gangsters now had to change their plans; obviously St. Paul was being too closely watched and they would have to find sanctuary in Chicago. And it would have to be soon. Hamilton was seriously wounded.

First they had to find another car; theirs was full of holes. They parked near an intersection three miles south of South St. Paul and waited. At about 12:40 P.M. they saw an auto coming from the city. It was another Ford and in it were Roy Francis, his wife, and their infant son, of South St. Paul, taking their usual noonday ride. Van Meter deftly cut them off.

Dillinger, gun in hand, walked up to Francis. "I'm sorry," he said. "But I'll have to take your car."

Dillinger got into the driver's seat with Hamilton beside him while Van Meter squeezed in back with the three Francises. Francis had no idea who he was but his wife, a magazine fan, recognized him. She said nothing.

Van Meter asked Francis what he did.

"I work at the power company."

"You're lucky to have a nice job and a family."

Several minutes later Hamilton said, "I've got to have a drink."

Dillinger drove up to a gas station and bought a bottle of soda pop for Hamilton and one for the baby.

But Mrs. Francis wouldn't let her son have his. "He's just had his lunch," she said disapprovingly.

Dillinger had the car filled with gas, patiently waited for two cents change, and drove off. After about a mile, he stopped, let out the Francises, and headed for Chicago.

At that same time Baby Face Nelson was walking through the woods toward the Lac du Flambeau Indian Reservation. By late afternoon he came upon a small frame shack. Out front Ole Catfish, a full-blooded Chippewa in his late sixties, was building a fire to make maple sugar.

Nelson told him he'd better put out the fire.

"I don't put out no fire."

"You'll burn up the whole woods."

"Indians don't burn up no woods," said Catfish.

Nelson showed his gun. "Do you know who I am?"

Catfish, who had never even heard of Dillinger, let alone Nelson, said he didn't care. Baby Face put out the fire and told Catfish he was going to have a guest for a few days.

That evening the three girls captured at Little Bohemia, their eyes still puffed from tear gas, were transferred to Madison and locked up in cells at the Dane County jail. Armed deputies picketed the building. At midnight there was a sudden alarm that Dillinger was coming and the girls were taken to a nearby church, where they were hidden in the pews until dawn.

3

By Tuesday morning the Little Bohemia story was international. An editorial in the *London Express* read:

Hull said a few words yesterday about Wall Street which will help you understand the atmosphere of the country in which Dillinger works. When a community lets a pack of man-eating tigers dwell in its midst, it is easy for a lone wolf like Dillinger to slip under the fold gate. . . .

The Roosevelt revolution, shaking up the whole structure of the American government, has upset organized crime which fattened on corrupt officialdom.

Capone had got that business down to a fine art. Nobody has followed him because conditions have been changed. In the present confusion of the economic crisis it is the lone raider type you would expect to flourish. Hence, Dillinger.

In Germany, the *Zwoelf Uhr Blatt* declared that no voice in America should be raised against Hitlerism so long as Dillinger was loose. It advised America to follow the Nazis' "deep sense of responsibility" and sterilize gangsters.

In America, of course, Dillinger continued to inspire numerous human interest stories. His name was written in as "slicker candidate for constable at large" in the St. Paul municipal election and in Minneapolis a man with an unkempt beard burst into a café, waving a pistol, and proclaimed he was the outlaw. Several hundred people in Kankakee, Illinois, jammed streets around a hotel when police got a tip Dillinger was inside with a dangerous weapon. Dillinger turned out to be a candy salesman, the weapon a knife for slicing candy.

The public became so confused by the myriad reports of his whereabouts, it was ready to believe almost anything. Even the law wasn't sure what was really happening. Purvis announced he believed the Barker-Karpis gang had also been at Little Bohemia. The capture of Dillinger, he said, might also bring about the solution of the Bremer kidnaping.

4

Three nights after his arrival at the Catfish cabin Baby Face Nelson told Ole Catfish he was leaving. He had helped boil maple syrup and played with the Catfish children but now food was running short.

At about 6:00 P.M. the two men started on foot down the old railroad bed, then walked up a dirt road toward the town of Lac du Flambeau. After three and one-half miles they found a car parked near a lake where its driver, a Postal employee was fishing. Nelson pulled out a gun, demanded the car keys, threw some money on the ground, and drove off.

By the next dawn Nelson was only 140 miles from Little Bohemia and he had burned out a connecting rod in the stolen car. Posing as a CCC boy, he asked a farmer to drive him to Marshfield, Wisconsin. The farmer, who thought Nelson was about sixteen, agreed to do so for $20.

On the way Baby Face said, "What you looking at me for so much? Are you scared? Maybe you think I'm Dillinger."

The farmer laughed.

A few minutes later Nelson went into the Marshfield Hardware and Auto Company and asked for a car with "a good motor and good rubber." The salesman hesitated because the customer looked so young, but finally sold him a 1929 Chevrolet.

It took Dillinger and Van Meter almost two days to drive Hamilton to Chicago. The wounded man, weak from loss of blood, was left in a saloon, while Dillinger and Van Meter made the rounds of underworld doctors. The answer was always no. Too many people were looking for Dillinger.

It wasn't until April 27, five days after the Little Bohemia shooting, that Dillinger happened to hear about Dr. Moran. His office in the Irving Park Hotel was now the clearing house for the Bremer ransom and when Dillinger, the world's most wanted man, walked into the biggest money-passing operation in America, it was like sticking a sputtering fuse in a powder keg. Moran, of course, went completely to pieces, refusing to lay a finger on Hamilton. But Dillinger, in turn, refused to leave empty-handed. The tipsy doctor grew abusive, then frenzied. Finally in desperation he actually disclosed the name and address of the man who had arranged the Bremer hideout.

Dillinger and Van Meter loaded their wounded companion into the Ford they had stolen in St. Paul and drove to the little town that had featured so prominently in two major kidnapings. But the Bensenville man was just as terrified as Moran and hastily passed them on to Volney Davis in nearby Aurora.

Here at last they received help of sorts. Hamilton's wound was cleaned. It was an ugly color; gangrene had obviously set in. Dock Barker, who lived only a few blocks away, agreed that the Dillinger gang should not be turned away and promised to try and find a real doctor. In the meantime Rabbits did what she could to ease Hamilton's suffering.

Purvis's wild guess that the Dillinger and Barker gangs were connected had belatedly come true.

As soon as Dillinger left his office, the nervous Dr. Moran imagined he was out of danger, but already a chance remark had led the FBI to one of the money passers. This man, while getting change for a $100 bill from the Bremer ransom, had casually told a teller at the City National Bank and Trust Company that he was a bookie. As a result, Hoover's agents made a systematic check of every bookmaker in Chicago until they found the right man. The bookie admitted he had passed the bill but denied knowing it was ransom money and, without prompting, revealed the names of those who had hired him.

On the day after Dillinger was turned out of Moran's office, FBI agents questioned John J. "Boss" McLaughlin, the silver-haired politician Ma Barker had selected to head the operation. McLaughlin protested his innocence. Wasn't he a prominent politician, a close friend of many leading Democrats? In spite of threats—and promises—he was arrested. Now it was his wife's turn to protest. She sent telegrams to Attorney General Cummings and President Roosevelt and a protest to Assistant Attorney General Keenan that her husband was being subjected to threats and abuse by FBI agents at the Bankers' Building to try to make him confess to the Bremer kidnaping.

That evening Dr. Moran's nephew, an errand boy for his

uncle, who was putting him through medical school, drove to Aurora and reported the arrest of Boss McLaughlin. Dock Barker and Dillinger conferred and agreed that if McLaughlin talked, the FBI would soon know the address of the Aurora hideout. Since Hamilton, who was still unattended by a doctor, could not be moved, the two leaders decided to barricade the apartment against a possible raid. All that night Dillinger, Van Meter, Dock Barker, Davis, and two lesser members of the Barker gang guarded the windows and doors with machine guns.

There was no raid. The next morning one of the Barker gang said they'd taken enough chances already and should escape at once to Ohio. But Dock Barker insisted they all stay until Hamilton could be moved. It was a useless gesture. Two days later he died and was buried in a nearby gravel pit. While the other gangsters, shovels in hands, watched, Dillinger pronounced a strange benediction. "I hate to do this, Red," he said, pouring lye on Hamilton's face and hands to prevent identification, "but I know you'd do the same to me."

Dillinger convinced Van Meter they should now return to Chicago, where they had a clever lawyer with numerous contacts. Besides, who would imagine they'd have the nerve to return? Dillinger's reasoning was good but he made one incredible mistake. He drove into Chicago in the same bloodspattered Ford he had stolen in St. Paul and abandoned it on the north side. This was the most advertised car in America and before nightfall everyone knew Dillinger was in town. Chicago's 8,000 policemen were ordered to be on the alert and Stege's Dillinger Squad joined the FBI in raids on numerous underworld hideouts.

By that time a London paper was telling its readers, "Even red Indians joined the hunt today with bows and arrows," and Will Hays, President of the Motion Picture Producers and Distributors of America, was announcing he would ban any movie based on the exploits of Dillinger as "detrimental to the public interests."

Will Rogers was also still commenting on the situation.

"Republicans coming out pretty strong now against administration," he wrote. "Looks like if the Democrats don't get Dillinger [they] may lose this fall's election."

A few days later, on May 5, ten of the twelve anti-crime bills were approved by the House of Representatives, the name of Dillinger often spurring the brief debate. It was obvious the bills would pass the Senate just as quickly. Then it would be a federal crime to assault or kill a federal officer; to rob a federal bank; to flee from one state to another to avoid prosecution. FBI agents were also given broader powers of arrest and the right to carry arms at any time. At last they had the tools to fight the underworld on more equal terms.

But Cummings and Hoover, not content even with these measures, convinced the President that gangsters such as Dillinger existed largely because the public was not fully cooperating in the war against crime. Roosevelt made a personal appeal to the nation: "I ask citizens, individually and as organized groups, to recognize the facts and meet them with courage and determination. . . . Law enforcement and gangster extermination cannot be made completely effective while a substantial part of the public looks with tolerance upon known criminals, or applauds efforts to romanticize crime."

In spite of the new laws and the concern of the President himself, America's most wanted criminal still had only a $25 reward on his head—for violating parole.

CHAPTER 16

"This Sure Keeps a Fellow Moving"

1

THE FBI HAD DRIVEN DILLINGER INTO DEEP COVER. THE SAME was about to happen to Clyde Barrow and Bonnie Parker. Hoover's agents tracked them from state to state, always getting a bit closer. By early April, Special Agent L. A. Kindell had discovered that the third member of the gang was young Henry Methvin. More important, he also knew the Barrows occasionally visited Methvin's father, Ivan, in Louisiana.

Ivan Methvin had recently moved from the family home. Kindell trailed him to the Arcadia area, some eighty miles east of the Texas-Louisiana border, then called on Henderson Jordan, the Arcadia sheriff, and asked his help.

Until now the history of co-operation between the FBI and local police agencies had been frequently disappointing. The police often felt the special agents were mere "Boy Scouts" who took too much credit, while the FBI occasionally distrusted—with reason—local lawmen.

Here, however, from the first moment there was complete co-operation and mutual respect between Sheriff Jordan and Kindell. For ten days the sheriff traveled through the backwoods until he learned that Mr. Methvin had rented a farm not far from Arcadia. While Kindell and Jordan were setting a trap, a third man joined the operation: Captain Frank Hamer of the Texas Highway Patrol. An ex-Texas Ranger, six foot three, he had reportedly killed sixty-five outlaws and was known as the fastest draw in Texas. He had been given a special assignment by the general manager of the Texas Prison System: track down the Barrows, who had killed a guard while freeing Methvin and Hamilton from the prison farm.

Jordan and Agent Kindell were delighted when Hamer, who had tracked the killers through nine states, asked to work with them. It was the beginning of a remarkable team effort, with Agent Kindell as co-ordinator.

Three weeks after the Little Bohemia shooting, Bonnie and Clyde forced Methvin's father to move again, this time to an abandoned house deep in a pine forest. By now Mr. Methvin was so terrified that he secretly met the lawmen and agreed to help trap the Barrows if his son, virtually their prisoner, were not prosecuted in Texas.

Mr. Methvin suggested a plan. Henry had told him that if the gang ever got separated, they were supposed to meet near the abandoned house. Methvin said he would tell Henry to escape, without arousing suspicion, and when the Barrows appeared at the rendezvous they could be captured.

On the evening of May 21, when the Barrow gang once more visited the abandoned house, Ivan took his son aside and told him of the plan. Henry, willing to do anything to be free of his nightmare life, said he would "disappear" at the first opportunity. It came the very next morning after the gang drove to Shreveport and Henry was ordered to go to a store for supplies.

When he didn't return, Bonnie and Clyde thought he had been scared away for some reason, so they returned to the abandoned house and waited. Finally Clyde instructed Mr. Methvin to check the rented farm. Perhaps Henry had become confused and gone there instead. Mr. Methvin was told to meet the Barrows the next morning on the road between Sailes and Gibsland and make a report.

As soon as Bonnie and Clyde drove off, Methvin got in touch with Jordan. The sheriff, in turn, telephoned Kindell's office but the latter was out of town on an emergency assignment and could not be reached. Jordan now phoned Captain Hamer to come at once to Arcadia.

The lawmen drove back and forth between Sailes and Gibsland looking for the best place to ambush the Barrows, eventually selecting a wooded section where the road cut through a small hill. At about 3:00 the following morning, May 23, a party of six law officers hid their cars near the ambush area and squatted in the dew-soaked weeds behind an embankment.

By dawn they were cold and hungry. The minutes passed slowly. At last they heard a truck coming. Jordan, recognizing the elder Methvin, motioned him to park and then instructed him to take off the truck's right front wheel as if the tire were flat.

Jordan told the other five lawmen that he wanted to take Bonnie and Clyde alive. "But if they reach for their guns let them have it." Armed with a Browning automatic rifle, three automatic shotguns, and two rifles, the six men lined up behind the embankment. They had a perfect field of fire.

At nine o'clock several cars passed. Fifteen minutes later a Ford V-8 appeared over the rise and approached the ambush. Clyde, wearing sunglasses, was driving in his socks. Bonnie was wearing a red dress and red shoes. Under the rear seat were hidden fifteen sets of license plates. They carried their usual heavy armament: a shotgun, eleven pistols, a revolver, three Browning automatic rifles, and more than 2,000 rounds of ammunition. On the rear seat were Bonnie's overnight case, a saxophone, and sheets of music.

Her masterpiece, "The Story of Bonnie and Clyde," was not in the car. Upon completing it she had sent it to a Dallas newspaper to be published after her death. These were the final verses:

> The road gets dimmer and dimmer,
> Sometimes you can hardly see,

Still it's fight, man to man,
And do all you can,
For they know they can never be free.

If they try to act like citizens,
And rent them a nice little flat,
About the third night they are invited to fight
By a submachine-gun rat-tat-tat.

They don't think they are too tough or desperate,
They know the law always wins,
They have been shot at before
But they do not ignore
That death is the wages of sin.

From heartbreaks some people have suffered,
From weariness some people have died,
But take it all in all,
Our troubles are small,
Till we get like Bonnie and Clyde.

Some day they will go down together,
And they will bury them side by side.
To a few it means grief,
To the law it's relief,
But it's death to Bonnie and Clyde.

Clyde recognized Ivan standing in the road and brought
the Ford to a stop between the parked truck and the six
concealed lawmen. "Got a flat?" he asked and Methvin
nodded. "Did you find Henry?"

Methvin said he hadn't, then asked Bonnie for a drink.

At that moment Sheriff Jordan heard a heavy rumble. A
truck, with two Negroes in the cab, was approaching. When he
saw it would soon pass between the ambush party and the
Barrows, Jordan stood up and shouted, "Put 'em up, Clyde.
You're covered!"

Clyde shifted the car into first, grabbed a shotgun, and opened the door to shoot. Bonnie reached for a pistol.

The six lawmen fired. It was a shattering broadside. The approaching truck stopped with a shriek of brakes and its two occupants fled into the woods.

Barrow's head fell back and Bonnie slumped forward. The Ford rolled down the hill, bounced across a ditch, and plowed into the embankment. The lawmen ran down the road, weapons ready, but the Barrows were dead. A shotgun, with seven notches carved in the stock, rested in Clyde's lap. Bonnie's head was between her knees. In her lap was a pistol with three notches.

Though Bonnie's last poem was prophetic, it was incorrect on one point. They died side by side but she and Clyde were buried in different graveyards miles apart.

The role played by the Methvins in the ambush was never revealed by law officials for fear of possible reprisals against the informers though some of the details came out at court trials. Henry Methvin was not prosecuted by either Louisiana or Texas, but he was brought to Oklahoma and, after two trials, convicted of complicity in the murder of the Commerce sheriff. Unable to pay for the defense, Methvin gave his lawyer, J. J. Smith, permission to publish full details of the case, including his personal relationship with the Barrows. Smith—now a temporary judge in Miami, Oklahoma—waited until both Methvins died before revealing the story here.

2

After Dillinger thoughtlessly abandoned the blood-stained Ford in North Chicago, he and Van Meter found a new hideout in Calumet City and disappeared so completely that rumors began to filter through the underworld that Dillinger had fled the country. Then police were informed that he had "definitely" left for England.

On May 4 the Chicago police asked Scotland Yard

to check all vessels arriving from the United States and Canada. Simultaneously the Department of Justice notified Canadian authorities that Dillinger might be fleeing on a British ship and commanders of all Canadian Pacific steamships were urged to search their vessels.

The following day the steamer *Duchess of York*, out of Halifax, was carefully searched when she landed in Glasgow. Though Dillinger was not found, a rumor spread that he had slipped through the cordon and was heading for London, where he supposedly had many underworld connections.

But those lawmen who had been trailing Dillinger for some time—such as Leach, Reynolds, Stege, and the FBI—knew better and continued the hunt throughout the Midwest. In addition, Governor Henry Horner of Illinois decided something should be done about the ridiculous $25 reward for Dillinger's capture and proposed that five Midwestern states each post a $1,000 reward "to provide an additional incentive" for his capture. Governor George White of Ohio said he would approve such a reward. So did the governors of Michigan, Minnesota, and Indiana.

Perhaps at first Dillinger was flattered that five governors were putting a $5,000 bounty on his head. If so, he undoubtedly soon regretted that several million people, inspired by this large sum, now had an active interest in spotting him. And this would be a simple matter since his face was on the front page of many newspapers almost daily.

During the long vigil at Aurora, Dock Barker must have told him of Moran's plastic surgery. In spite of the ineffective job the drunken doctor had done on Freddie Barker and Karpis, he had somehow convinced everyone he'd performed miracles. Dock Barker and several other members were going to submit to similar operations as soon as they settled in Ohio.

Whatever the inspiration, Dillinger asked Piquett if he knew a doctor who could change his face and fingerprints. The lawyer did know just such a man, Dr. Wilhelm Loeser, a German-born surgeon who was a "magician with the knife"; but it would take several weeks to complete all the arrangements. First he had to return to St. Paul and defend Billie Frechette in her trial for harboring. He told Dillinger not to worry. Billie would be free before long.

A few days later, Dillinger decided to add to the confusion of those hunting him. He wrote a letter to Henry Ford and gave it to a messenger for posting in Detroit.

> Hello Old Pal:
>
> Arrived here at 10 AM today. Would like to drop in and see you.
>
> You have a wonderful car. Been driving it for three weeks. Its a treat to drive one.
>
> Your Slogan should be.
>
> Drive a Ford and watch the other cars fall behind you. I can make any other car take a Ford's dust.
>
> > Bye-Bye
> > John Dillinger

Trying to make lawmen think he was in Detroit was probably only one reason for writing the letter. It must also have appealed to his sense of humor. It was like taking pictures of the police or telephoning Leach and Reynolds— another gibe at authority.

A week later Billie Frechette and the doctor who tended Dillinger's leg wound were sentenced to two years for harboring him in the Twin Cities. But when Piquett returned to Chicago he had apparently lost none of his confidence, assuring Dillinger he was filing an appeal which was bound to free Billie. He also said everything was almost ready for the plastic surgery.

Dr. Loeser would perform the operation in two days, assisted by a "very capable young Irishman." The financial arrangements were simple. Dillinger would pay Piquett a flat fee of $5,000 and the lawyer would "take care" of his assistant, Arthur O'Leary, and the two doctors. His own fee would be one third.

On the evening of May 27 Dillinger arrived at a weather-beaten two-story shack on Chicago's north side. He was on time but, since no one was there to meet him, he began restlessly pacing the sidewalk. A few minutes later a car drew up— in it were Piquett and O'Leary, a self-possessed young man with a hard, assured manner.

Piquett explained that the house was owned by a former speakeasy operator, James Probasco, who needed money to keep his tavern going. The operation would take place in a bedroom and Dillinger would recuperate in a back room. Probasco's price was $35 a day. Naturally this was an extra not covered by the $5,000 fee.

The next day O'Leary brought the two doctors to the frame house. Loeser was tall with stooped shoulders. After practicing almost thirty years in Chicago he had been convicted of violating the narcotic laws and sent to Leavenworth. Now he needed money badly. The assistant, Dr. Harold Cassidy, was pale and nervous. Though young, his face looked dissipated and his hands shook. Loeser examined the gangster's heart and asked if he wanted a local or general anesthetic.

"General," said Dillinger and told Loeser to remove three moles between his eyes and fill in a depression on the bridge of his nose. He also wanted Loeser to remove a scar on the left side of his upper lip and the dimple from his chin.

He took off some of his clothes and lay down on a cot. While Loeser went to the bathroom to wash his hands, young Cassidy formed a makeshift mask from a towel and administered ether but in his nervousness he gave too much too quickly and Dillinger stopped breathing. Cassidy lost his head and started shouting.

By the time Loeser got there Dillinger's face was blue. He had swallowed his tongue. Loeser grabbed a forceps and pulled the tongue out, then kicked the gangster's elbows into his chest and began giving artificial respiration.

When Dillinger finally began to breathe again the two doctors removed the moles between the eyes—Loeser working on one side, Cassidy on the other. Then they cut the cheek along the ear and the edge of the jaw and transplanted some of the flesh to the dimple on the chin. Finally they tightened up the cheeks with kangaroo tendons.

Five days later Piquett told the doctors, who were both still shaken by the first operation, they had to return for the second: the obliteration of Dillinger's fingerprints. The lawyer also said a friend of Dillinger's, Homer Van Meter, wanted the same surgery.

The following evening Piquett and Van Meter arrived at Probasco's to find Dillinger staring unhappily at his swollen face in a mirror. A few moments later the two doctors arrived and Dillinger accused them of "botching the job." Loeser explained logically that this was the way every patient looked after facial surgery. Dillinger angrily retorted that, except for being "messed up," his face was the same.

At this critical moment Piquett put a reassuring arm around Dillinger's shoulder and said, "John, you look wonderful."

"You really think so?"

Piquett said a few minor corrections should be made—this always had to be done, he explained—but he convinced Dillinger that the doctors had done an exceptional job. Secretly he thought his client looked as if he'd been in a dog fight.

Dillinger, placated, handed over the balance of what he owed Piquett.

Loeser, feeling more apprehensive than he had the first time, applied a caustic preparation to Dillinger's finger tips. Next he made the corrections suggested by Piquett, taking a wedge of skin near the ear and touching up the area around the dimple.

Van Meter had already paid Piquett $5,000 for his operations and he eyed Loeser menacingly before reluctantly allowing himself to be given an anesthetic. The two doctors removed a bump on the bridge of his nose, then shortened the nose by removing the tip and decreased the thickness of his lower lip. Finally they attempted to remove the blue and red anchor tattooed on his right arm.

When Loeser returned the following night Van Meter put on an exhibition that made Dillinger's display seem mild. Shouting that his face was a "goddamn mess," he even grabbed a machine gun. An absorbed spectator was Baby Face Nelson, who had dropped in to see the doctor's handiwork since he was also thinking of surgery. Having always detested Van Meter, he sat back sipping a bottle of beer as if he were enjoying a floor show.

Loeser again patiently explained that it took several weeks to recover from surgery. At last Van Meter, like Dillinger, was pacified and the doctors made a few minor facial corrections and worked on his fingers.

Piquett gave the two doctors less than he had promised, arguing that his clients had not been completely satisfied. O'Leary also was forced to take a cut, since things had not gone smoothly. The lawyer, of course, didn't refund any of the $10,000 he'd received from the two gangsters. He decided $5,000, not one third as originally agreed, was more equitable compensation for all the trouble he'd experienced.

The only members of the gang now with Dillinger after the Little Bohemia shooting were Van Meter and Nelson. Hamilton was dead and Tommy Carroll had returned to territory more familiar to him. The day after Van Meter's final operation, he arrived at the Evening Star Tourist Camp, a few miles east of Cedar Rapids, Iowa, on the Lincoln Highway. With him, registered as Mrs. Leonard Murdock, was his wife Jean, sister-in-law of Karpis and Pat Reilly. Jean and the other two girls captured at Little Bohemia had just been released from the Madison jail and placed on eighteen months' probation. "The court is satisfied that while these girls are technically guilty," Judge Patrick Stone had said, "they didn't do anything to aid in the concealment of Dillinger."

Hoover's reaction to this was indignation. Crime, he insisted, could be uprooted only if those who aided criminals were also punished. But Judge Stone later said he had freed the girls because he thought that they might lead the law to their gangster sweethearts. As a matter of fact the girls did immediately rejoin their men, but no one trailed them.

The following morning Carroll and Jean headed for Waterloo, Iowa. Several hours later a call came to the Waterloo police station from an excited gas station attendant. While servicing a new Hudson, he had lifted up the front floor board to put water in the battery—under the floor mat were extra sets of license plates.

Detectives Emil Steffen and P. E. Walker got descriptions of the car and the two occupants and searched the streets in vain for an hour. They were just putting their car in the police garage when they saw the wanted Hudson parked across the street next to an alley. The car was locked and empty but Steffen noticed a robe covering something— perhaps a machine gun—in the back seat. A little after noon a man and girl came out the rear door of a restaurant into the alley.

"I'm an officer and I'd like to talk to you a minute," said Walker, grasping Carroll by the shoulder. As Carroll drew a gun from his pocket, Walker swung. Carroll slipped and fell. His gun dropped under the car but he grabbed it and darted down the alley. Walker fired. In the meantime Steffen had pushed Jean to the sidewalk to prevent her from getting in the car. Now he jumped into the alley and shot three times at the still running Carroll. The ex-boxer dropped, wounded four times. He was taken to the hospital, and died a few hours later.

Dillinger was still recuperating at Probasco's when he read of Carroll's death. That same day he also learned Billie Frechette had left St. Paul for an undisclosed prison. (She was taken to the Federal Detention Jail in Milan, Michigan, and put in a cell not far from Kathryn Kelly's.) Overpowered by a wave of guilt and self-pity, he told Van Meter he was a jinx to all his friends. First Shaw had been caught; next his partners in Kentucky and East Chicago; then Copeland and Dietrich in Chicago; and the three girls at Little Bohemia.

Now Green, Hamilton, Carroll were dead; Pierpont and Makley would soon be executed; and Billie was as good as dead—in prison.

He lapsed into a deep depression and would sit for hours in the frame house without saying a word. Finally he wrote a letter to his father, sending it to Mooresville by a messenger. It was nostalgic, recalling the family reunion. "I enjoyed seeing you and the girls so much," he wrote. "I have been over lots of country, but home always looks good to me. Tell that little Francis to keep smiling." He didn't say he had recently met an elderly couple—a Mr. and Mrs. Joseph G.—who promised to drive him to Mexico as their son for a fee of $10,000. He merely remarked, "This sure keeps a fellow moving. I will be leaving soon and you will not need worry any more."

About a week later Dillinger's face was healed and he immediately headed for home. Convinced, in spite of the evidence of his mirror, that he could not be recognized, he visited friends and family—though it is doubtful if he actually went to the farm—without trying to conceal himself. He stopped at Mary Kinder's. When she came to the door, he grinned and said, "Guess who?"

"You look like you got mumps or something, Johnnie," she said.

He laughed, then asked if Miss Levy had succeeded in getting a new trial for Pierpont and Makley. Mary said there was no hope; the boys were going to be electrocuted. He was quiet for a moment and finally said in a serious tone she had never heard him use before, "Mary, of all the gang, you're the only one that's lucky." He grinned crookedly. "My time's coming, but I don't know when it'll be."

4

In spite of the risks Dillinger had been taking, the police still had no idea where he was. He had dropped out of sight so completely that it was again widely believed he had escaped to England. In fact so many "reliable sources" indicated he was hiding in London that Scotland Yard mobilized its entire flying squad, and "Q" cars were requisitioned from London's twenty-three divisions.

On June 19 an innkeeper at Stratford-on-Avon heard four of his customers using "strange slang" expressions such as "chief" and "okay." One looked so much like Dillinger that he phoned police, "I have Dillinger here. His whole gang." They were four American Rhodes scholars on their way to Oxford.

Three days later, Mrs. Audrey Hancock inserted a notice in the classified columns of an Indianapolis newspaper: "Birthday greetings to my darling brother, John Dillinger, on his 31st birthday. Wherever he may be, I hope he reads this message."

A year before he had been an unknown parolee. Today throughout the world his name was synonymous with crime. That same day the FBI designated him their Public Enemy Number 1 and a day later the Department of Justice offered a $10,000 reward for his capture and another $5,000 for information leading to his arrest.

Before Billie Frechette's incarceration Dillinger had read every newspaper story about himself, even sending some home. Now publicity only made him more aware of his danger.

The trip to Mexico became almost an obsession but he had little cash after paying for the surgery. He would need $10,000 for his passage and at least another $25,000 for living expenses—originally his goal had been $100,000 but he had come to realize in the past weeks that this was now an impossible figure. He decided to make one final robbery—the "one big haul" every thief dreamed of—then head south.

Van Meter found the perfect bank: the Merchants National of South Bend, Indiana. The local post office, he assured Dillinger, made large deposits and they should get at least $100,000 and probably much more. Of course, he and Dillinger couldn't rob the bank alone. They needed three or four more men.

Nelson came to mind, but by this time Dillinger was not at all anxious to endure more of his arrogance and temper. Moreover Baby Face had become almost childishly sulky ever since the reward of $10,000 was offered for Dillinger's capture and only half that sum for himself.

But Dillinger could find no one else willing to join the gang—the spotlight of publicity was too dangerous—and, in spite of misgivings, he was forced to approach Baby Face. Nelson not only accepted but said he could find a wheelman and a torpedo. A date was set: June 30.

With these arrangements made, Dillinger relaxed. He began enjoying himself again and, on the face of it, was the carefree Dillinger of old. He revisited the Century of Progress; he went to wrestling matches and ball games. He even found a new girl.

The streets of South Bend were crowded at 11:30 A.M., Saturday, June 30. It was a beautiful summer morning—warm and clear. About twenty-five customers were lined up at the windows of the Merchants National Bank located near the corner of Wayne and Michigan Streets.

Across from the bank a banner assured State Theater customers it was many degrees cooler inside. The feature picture was *Stolen Sweets* with Sally Blane and Charles Starrett. Directing traffic at the busy intersection was a big, good-natured policeman, Howard Wagner. He was twenty-nine years old and it was his last day at this post. Tomorrow the man he'd relieved would be back from his vacation.

The assistant postmaster came out of the post office, carrying $7,900—far less than Van Meter had predicted—for deposit at the bank. Trailing him in a police car were two detectives, Edward McCormick and his partner, who had been doing this for several weeks, following a tip that the post office was going to be robbed. As soon as they saw the postal employee walk into the bank they drove to a nearby restaurant and ordered pork chop sandwiches.

Alex Slaby, a young bachelor, drove his Ford down Michigan, turned right on Wayne, and parked near the corner.

As he was scanning his shopping list, a brown Hudson double-parked next to him and its four occupants got out. One looked familiar but Slaby couldn't quite place him. When two of the men walked in front of Slaby's car to the sidewalk he noticed they had guns hidden under handkerchiefs and realized they were robbers.

He turned and studied the man he half recognized. He was short and stocky, and wore overalls and a straw hat. His shirt seemed a little bulky as though he were wearing a bulletproof vest. Dillinger poked a gun through Slaby's window and said quietly, "You'd better scram," then followed the first two men toward Michigan Street.

Slaby, a small man of about 120 pounds and an amateur boxer, got out of his car. He noticed that the motor in the bandits' Hudson was running, the radio playing a popular song, and started to reach for the ignition keys when a voice said, "What're you doing?" Slaby turned and saw a short, squat young man—with a boyish face.

"Nothing." Slaby somehow managed to look bored and casually crossed the street to call up the police.

Baby Face let him go and walked to the corner of the intersection, trying to hide a machine gun under his jacket. His job was to guard the car. Dillinger and the other two had turned left at the corner and were already nearing the bank. At a slight nod from Dillinger, Van Meter stopped in front of a shoe store. His mission: to guard the front entrance of the bank with a .351 rifle.

Dillinger and the other bandit, a friend of Nelson's, met the fifth member of the gang, a fat man who had driven to South Bend in a second car, and these three now entered the bank.

Dillinger called out, "This is a holdup." He and the fat man—his identity is still in doubt—went behind the cages. The customers, frightened by the sight of guns, surged toward the back.

Suddenly Nelson's friend—his identity is also still in doubt—loosed a burst from his machine gun at the ceiling that would have made Baby Face proud. Near panic broke out as the terrified customers dashed toward the directors' room.

The machine gunner, obviously pleased with himself, smiled at Delos Coen, the cashier, who had been standing at his desk talking to Perry Stahly, a prominent businessman and director of the bank. They both were sure the man with the machine gun was Pretty Boy Floyd.

Some pedestrians thought the firing from inside the bank was a premature Fourth of July celebration; others that the rifle-carrying Van Meter, also dressed in overalls and straw hat, was a clown advertising something.

When Patrolman Wagner heard the noise he started across the trolley tracks toward the bank, traffic whistle in hand. Van Meter raised his rifle and fired. The patrolman staggered back across the intersection and fell on the pavement. Hundreds of shoppers scrambled for safety; others stood petrified, unbelieving.

Harry Berg ran out of his jewelry shop with a revolver and shot at Baby Face Nelson. Saved by his bulletproof vest, the little gangster spun and fired wildly. Berg ducked safely back into his shop but one of Nelson's bullets hit a man's leg, veered up and lodged in his abdomen, while another shattered the windshield of an automobile parked across the street, spattering the driver with glass.

Joseph Pawlowski, a sixteen-year-old sophomore at Central High School, was sitting in a car parked a block below the intersection. At the first sound of shots he ran up toward the bank. When he saw Nelson shooting recklessly into the crowd he was shocked that no one was doing a thing to stop the gunman. The youth jumped on Nelson's back.

Baby Face must have wondered what was wrong with the citizens of South Bend. First a jeweler had fired at him, now some madman was actually grappling with him. He twisted savagely, flung Pawlowski against a plate-glass window, and from ten feet began shooting at his assailant. The window behind the boy shattered as a bullet pierced the palm of his right hand. He passed out.

Patrolman Sylvester Zell and another officer on traffic duty a block away saw people running south. As they were crossing the street diagonally, a burst of machine-gun fire went over their heads, striking the canopy of the State Theater. A man in an office over the theater shouted, "Look out, Zell. It's a holdup!" The two patrolmen ducked behind cars and cautiously approached the bank.

At that moment Dillinger and his two assistants were coming out the front door with three hostages—Coen, Stahly, and Bruce Bouchard, the youthful manager of the Radio Service Company. Though Bouchard's hands were raised he was sure he looked like a gangster because he was smoking a cigarette. He had tried to spit it out but it was stuck to his lower lip. Finally, when it burned his lip, he managed to eject it with his tongue.

One block away Detective McCormick and his partner were just finishing their pork sandwiches. As soon as they heard the restaurant radio request all police cars to proceed to the Merchants Bank they ran to their car but made little progress because of the tangled traffic. "I can run faster than you can drive," shouted McCormick. "Give me the rifle and you drive to the corner." In the excitement the other man picked up a sawed-off shotgun. McCormick grabbed it without looking and ran.

He saw Dillinger bringing out the hostages, and raised his weapon. To his disgust he discovered it was a shotgun. With a rifle he knew he could have picked off every bandit but he couldn't fire the shotgun for fear of hitting one of the hostages.

Another lawman did shoot; he aimed at Dillinger but hit his shield, Coen, in the left leg. The banker fell on the pavement unconscious. Another police bullet tore into Stahly's side.

"I'm shot," he said.

"Keep going," said the robber—who Stahly thought was Floyd—punching him with a gun.

Seconds later a blast of bullets came from the south. Several went between Stahly's legs and one shredded the left leg of his trousers. But one of the bullets in this volley must have hit the bandit just behind Stahly—he began to swear.

When they reached the curb near the corner of Michigan and Wayne Avenues, Stahly saw the getaway car. "Floyd" jabbed him in the back with a gun and said, "You're going with us." The bandit grabbed for Stahly's arm.

"You've got your money," said Stahly, swinging away. "Make your getaway."

Just then the fat robber, now in the driver's seat of the bandit car, shouted, "Come on, get in here!"

"Floyd" ran to the car, then suddenly turned and fired at Stahly. The bullet whistled past Stahly's head, barely missing his left ear. By now Dillinger and the other robbers were bolting toward the getaway car and Detective McCormick at last had an open shot. But as he raised the shotgun, a bystander blocked him. "Get the hell out of there," warned the detective.

"To hell with you too."

McCormick leveled the gun and pulled the trigger. The roar must have deafened the bystander. "Oh, my God," he screamed. He fell, then scurried on hands and knees into a clothing store.

The police and bandits began a fire fight. A bullet tore harmlessly through Bouchard's pants' leg; another struck the heel of his new shoes.

Van Meter, lucky in so many other encounters, was finally hit in the right side of the head. He staggered and, as he was falling, Dillinger grabbed him and helped him into the car. The Hudson, by now riddled with police bullets, started jerkily, almost ramming a car driven by a local dance teacher; then it turned, tires screeching, and raced to the south. Police gave chase but their cars were not fast enough and they had no sirens to clear their way through the crowds.

Late that afternoon the Dillinger gang abandoned the shot-up Hudson on U. S. Highway 24 near the Indiana-Illinois border, transferred to another car and proceeded to Chicago. Van Meter, bleeding badly from the head wound, was half-carried into the Probasco house. The ex-speakeasy proprietor telephoned Dr. Cassidy and told him to come at once.

As usual Nelson divided the money in neat little piles—and they were little piles. Dillinger's face fell when he saw that each share was not the $20,000 Van Meter had calculated but only $4,800. All were upset but the disappointingly small take affected Dillinger most. His share brought his total stake to just about what he must pay to be taken to Mexico—with nothing left over for himself!

There would have to be still another bank robbery. And each new one was becoming more and more hazardous. As little as eight months ago, the police of Greencastle hadn't fired a single shot. Now even citizens were a menace: that noon an amateur boxer had tried to steal their car keys, a jeweler had given battle with a pistol, and a boy had jumped on Nelson's back. What could they expect the next time?

But South Bend had paid for its bravery. Wagner, the affable traffic policeman, died ten minutes after his arrival at the hospital and six citizens, including the sixteen-year-old Pawlowski, were wounded.

Jeweler Berg did business as usual that night in spite of a shattered plate-glass window. A sign outside read: "Not hurt. Open for business."

CHAPTER 17

Deadfall

1

Two weeks before the South Bend robbery Dillinger had met Polly Hamilton, an attractive twenty-six-year-old waitress in a Chicago restaurant, recently divorced from a Gary policeman. Since Dillinger had given up all hope by then of ever seeing Billie Frechette again, Polly became his girl friend.

The day after the robbery, Dillinger picked up Polly at the restaurant. The other waitresses teased her as they had a dozen times about going around with someone who "looked like Dillinger." Polly, as usual, laughed—in spite of the remarkable resemblance.

To her he was Jimmie Lawrence, a Board of Trade clerk. He was polite, spoke quietly, and was generous. He had already bought her a diamond ring and given her $50 to fix her teeth.

Polly rented a room from a friend, Anna Sage, who had an apartment on the north side. Mrs. Sage was a husky, square-faced woman of forty-two with a strong foreign accent. Born Ana Cumpanas, she had migrated from Romania some fifteen years previously and, after settling in Gary, started a house of prostitution, becoming locally famous as Katie from the Kostur

Hotel. She was so successful she opened another parlor in East Chicago. Though convicted twice for "operating a disorderly house," Indiana Governor Leslie pardoned her both times. Then McNutt came into office and her luck changed. He refused to pardon a third conviction and now the Immigration Bureau was about to deport her as an undesirable alien.

Also living in the apartment was her twenty-three-year-old son, Steve Chiolak. Several times he and his girl accompanied Dillinger and Polly Hamilton to the movies or a night club. Dillinger always acted carefree, impressing his companions as easygoing, considerate, and likeable. He was so mild-mannered that Chiolak even thought him a bit sissified.

By the middle of July Dillinger was a familiar figure in Mrs. Sage's neighborhood. He bought an $8.95 striped white shirt at the Ward Mitchell Company; he ate fresh strawberry sundaes at the corner ice cream parlor; he dined at the Seminary Restaurant and would often visit the bookmaker, operating in the loft above the Biograph Theater. Just across the street he occasionally patronized the Biograph Barber Shop. When Louis Scelfo, son of the owner, first shaved him he saw that Dillinger's eyebrows and mustache were penciled black and decided his customer was a bit queer.

Now for the first time since leaving Michigan City, Dillinger was living like an ordinary citizen. His contacts with criminals were so rare that the underworld began to think he was dead. In St. Paul Pat Reilly told a reporter, "You can take all the rumors about John Dillinger robbing banks a few days ago with a lot of salt. Because I have it pretty straight that he was killed just after he left Little Bohemia. . . ."

In spite of such stories, the great man hunt continued. Never before had so many lawmen and private citizens, spurred by the large rewards, been on the alert for a criminal. Dillinger knew others were looking for him too—the underworld. The Judas prize was too tempting to resist.

Until recently Dillinger, like men in battle, undoubtedly had thought he was not going to be killed. Almost every successful criminal shared this fantasy; companions could die but because of cleverness and luck he would somehow be spared.

But his recent retreat into a prosaic life indicated that perhaps, for the first time, he was afraid of death. If this was true, he was at last awakening from his dream world.

Even so, he still could not stop flouting the law. One evening he not only strolled into the headquarters of the Chicago police station on South State Street with Mrs. Sage but even asked the desk sergeant for a nonexistent girl prisoner.

A few days later he went to Wrigley Field to see the Chicago Cubs play. When he saw Piquett standing next to a policeman near the main gate of the ball park he couldn't resist the impulse and walked over, said, "Hello, Counsel," then casually walked away.

In these brief skirmishes he was again the old Dillinger— superior to all men—and it is significant that there was a witness each time who could appreciate his impudence. Mrs. Sage had just learned who he was.

But the satisfaction from these moments was fleeting, and by the middle of July he decided to go ahead with the trip to Mexico even though he had little more than $10,000, barely enough to pay for his transportation. Mexico was no longer a romantic dream but a desperate escape. He made tentative plans to leave with the elderly couple in a week, on Monday morning, July 23.

2

After the Little Bohemia incident, Hoover sent Special Agent Sam Cowley to take over the Special Squad in Chicago but Purvis remained head of the field office with its many responsibilities.

The Director had been following all developments in the Dillinger hunt on an hourly basis and told Cowley just before he left for Chicago, "Stay on Dillinger. Go everywhere the trail takes you. Take everyone who ever was remotely connected with the gang. Take him alive if you can but protect yourself."

The contrast between Purvis and Cowley was sharp. Purvis was small, excitable, quick. Cowley was big, heavy-set, somber. He moved slowly, deliberately; but his judgment was sound. Like Jay Newman, who had so narrowly missed death at Little Bohemia, he came from Utah and had been a missionary of the Mormon Church. He was a serious, dedicated man, and he drove the men on the Dillinger detail so relentlessly they at first complained to each other. Then they realized Cowley was working himself even harder. When the last man left the office Cowley was still bent over his desk as if pure labor and concentration alone would bring Dillinger to heel.

But a situation that had no connection with Cowley or the FBI was about to bring the case to its climax.

John Dillinger felt that Anna Sage was the least of his worries, even though she probably was the only one of his present companions who knew his identity. He could relax with her; there was no need to pose and he trusted her completely. She was an older woman and when she had finally discovered who he was, her attitude had seemed sympathetic—almost like a mother's.

The large rewards did tempt Anna Sage but there was a far greater temptation: she had finally realized that her knowledge of Dillinger's identity might possibly save her from deportation. She visited Sergeant Martin Zarkovich of the East Chicago, Indiana, police department, an acquaintance of many years.

Mrs. Sage told Zarkovich that Dillinger had been visiting her apartment and if her deportation proceedings were dropped, she would co-operate with the law. Zarkovich passed on the proposal to his superior, Captain Timothy O'Neill, Chief of Detectives assigned to the Dillinger case after the murder of Officer O'Malley. Since O'Neill had no jurisdiction in Chicago, he knew he would have to get the co-operation of some law agency there.

He told his superior, the chief of police, "I've got a lead on the Big Case. I'll need some men and we'll be out of town a few days." It was no novelty to work with lawmen of other

cities and his superior assigned a detail to accompany O'Neill
and Zarkovich on their mission. It was Friday, July 20.

That same day Captain John Stege of the Chicago Dillinger Squad was visited by two out-of-town police officers.
Sergeant Frank Reynolds and Lieutenant John Howe both
heard them tell Stege they knew how and where to trap Dillinger. But they would only give this information if the Chicago police agreed to kill Dillinger in the ambush. Stege,
controlling himself, replied that he would give anyone, even
John Dillinger, a chance to surrender and then ordered the
out-of-towners to leave his office before he had them thrown
out.

The following afternoon Sergeant Zarkovich and Captain
O'Neill telephoned Purvis and said they had some information
about "the Man." They wanted to discuss the matter at a secret
place.

Purvis passed on the request to Cowley, who set up an appointment for 6:00 P.M. in his room at the Great Northern
Hotel. At this meeting the East Chicago policemen told Cowley
and Purvis about the visits of Dillinger to the Sage apartment
to see Polly Hamilton. Before revealing other details, said
Zarkovich, Mrs. Sage insisted on talking privately with the chief
of the Chicago office. Cowley called Hoover, told him the details, and a meeting with the informer was approved.

At about 9:00 P.M. Zarkovich and Purvis arrived at the
rendezvous, a point diagonally across the street from the Children's Memorial Hospital. In another car just behind them
were Cowley and O'Neill. Some thirty minutes later Anna Sage
walked up to the Purvis car. She went past, looked around as
if suspecting a trap, then returned and got in the car.

They drove to a secluded place on Lake Michigan. She
told Purvis she hadn't known who Dillinger was at first but
when she thought she recognized him and showed him a newspaper picture of himself, he had readily admitted his identity.
Before telling Purvis any more she wanted assurance that the
FBI would assist in her fight to prevent deportation back to

Romania. He said his authority was limited but he did agree to do what he could to enable her to remain in the United States.

Satisfied on this point she also wanted his word she'd get the reward. Purvis said he couldn't make any definite promise, he could only guarantee it would be a substantial fee.

She thought a moment, then agreed to betray Dillinger. She was pretty sure he was going to take Polly and herself to a movie the next day, Sunday. They'd probably go to the Marbro Theater.

Once more Cowley called Hoover, who insisted Dillinger be taken alive, if possible. The agents were to be armed only with pistols and would not even draw unless "absolutely necessary." Hoover didn't want innocent bystanders hurt.

Cowley and his assistant, Virgil Peterson, now went to the Marbro and made detailed notes on all entrances, exits, and fire escapes.

3

Sunday, July 22, dawned hot and muggy. The air was heavy, full of moisture. By 11:30 A.M. the temperature was 101.3 degrees and deaths from prostration were being reported at an alarming rate. Seventeen had died the day before in Chicago and twenty-three would die that day. A hundred thousand were on the lake front, hoping for a breeze, as they watched the *Herald and Examiner*'s fifteen-mile marathon swim. People streamed from town to the beaches and parks in an exodus of holiday proportions.

As in the Little Bohemia case, every available agent in Chicago was alerted and by midmorning the offices in the Bankers' Building were stifling from the gathering crowd. A few agents felt this was just another of the countless false alarms they had answered in the past months, but as soon as Cowley began to speak, it was obvious the hunt was approaching its real climax.

He explained that Dillinger and two women were going to the Marbro Theater sometime that day. After they entered the theater, men would be stationed at all fire exits and on both sides of the front entrance. Purvis and Zarkovich, the only ones who knew Mrs. Sage, would be placed at either side and, no matter which direction the trio turned after leaving the theater, there would be someone who could give the signal that Dillinger was approaching.

The plan had one astounding aspect: perhaps because of a decision made exclusively by the FBI, or perhaps at the insistence of the East Chicago police for private reasons, America's Public Enemy Number 1 was to be captured in Chicago without the knowledge of the Chicago police. Even Stege's Dillinger Squad and Howe's Scotland Yard detail were not to be notified.

After Cowley had gone over the plan twice and made sure every man had examined the map of the Marbro Theater, Purvis spoke. "Gentlemen," he said, "you all know the character of John Dillinger. If . . . we locate him and he makes his escape it will be a disgrace to our Bureau. It may be that Dillinger will be at the picture show with his women companions unarmed—yet, he may appear there armed and with other members of his gang. There . . . will be an undetermined element of danger in taking Dillinger. It is hoped that he can be taken alive, if possible, and without injury to any agent . . . yet, gentlemen, this is the opportunity that we have all been waiting for and he must be taken. Do not unnecessarily endanger your own lives. If Dillinger offers any resistance each man will be for himself. It will be up to each of you to do whatever you think necessary to protect yourselves in taking Dillinger."

The five East Chicago officers were now introduced so the agents would know them on sight and Zarkovich described how Dillinger's face had been changed by the operation. By midafternoon every man knew exactly what he had to do.

Time dragged in the stifling rooms. At 5:30 P.M. Anna Sage called. Dillinger, she said, would take Polly and her to

a movie that night—probably at the Marbro or the Biograph.
"I'll call when I know something definite," she said.

This was an unexpected development. Cowley knew nothing about the Biograph, except that it was a moment's walk from Mrs. Sage's apartment. He sent two agents to the Biograph to draw a map of the exits and main entrance. The tense vigil continued. Finally at 7:00 P.M. Mrs. Sage telephoned again.

"He's here," she whispered. "He's just come. We'll be leaving in a short while. I still don't know if we're going to the Biograph or Marbro." She hung up.

Since Purvis knew Mrs. Sage, it was decided that he sit in a parked car outside the Biograph so he could report in case Dillinger walked into that theater. Zarkovich and Special Agent Charles B. Winstead, who weighed only 135 pounds but was an expert marksman, would cover the Marbro. Cowley and the main body would wait in the Bankers' Building, ready to converge on either place.

Purvis and his companion, Agent Ralph Brown, parked just left of the theater entrance. Purvis, neatly attired as usual, wore a single-breasted blue jacket, white trousers, white shoes, and a straw hat. For an hour the two men watched the theater fill up until Purvis began to feel certain they had either arrived too late or that Dillinger had gone to the Marbro. Just then Anna Sage and a couple walked by. Dillinger wore dark glasses, gray trousers, a white-striped shirt, a gray-flecked tie, and a straw hat. Polly Hamilton hung on his arm.

Mrs. Sage and Polly waited while Dillinger bought tickets. Under the marquee lights the older woman's orange skirt looked red—blood red.

As soon as they entered the theater, Brown phoned Cowley; then Purvis bought a ticket and went into the air-conditioned auditorium. It was a first-class neighborhood house, clean and well-managed. Purvis impulsively started down an aisle but his eyes were not yet accustomed to the dark and he hurried back to the foyer. After a moment he could see and anxiously peered into the orchestra. Almost every seat was filled and it was impossible to find Dillinger. Not daring to go down the aisles again, he returned to the ticket office and learned that the feature, *Manhattan Melodrama*, had just started and would run ninety-four minutes; the entire show lasted two hours and four minutes.

He went back to the car, briefed Brown, and scurried back to the cashier to reaffirm the times. She wondered how often he had to be told. Purvis then went up to the ticket taker, peered past him into the foyer, and returned to the car.

At the Bankers' Building Cowley was phoning the latest developments to Hoover, who had been pacing the library at his home in Washington. They discussed the possibility of capturing Dillinger inside the Biograph but vetoed it because of the danger of gun play in a crowded auditorium. He would be taken, as previously planned, when he walked out.

Cowley ordered his men to take their positions at the Biograph. Zarkovich and Agent Winstead at the Marbro were instructed to report at once to the north side theater. By the time Cowley arrived at the Biograph, Purvis had questioned the cashier a third time and again nervously peeked into the foyer. The cashier was now worried since the theater had been recently robbed. Could it be another holdup?

Cowley was calm, curt. He told Purvis to stand in a doorway just left of the theater's front entrance. When Dillinger and the women came out they would probably walk in that direction to return to Mrs. Sage's apartment. As they passed, Purvis would light a cigar as a signal of identification. Some ten feet away Agent H. E. Hollis would be chatting with Brown who sat in the parked FBI car; and a few yards farther, in another doorway, another agent would be stationed. About a hundred feet beyond was an alley, a short cut to the Sage apartment, which also led to the back of the theater. At the mouth of this alley two agents were to head toward the theater as soon as they saw Purvis light the cigar. Thus Dillinger would be trapped from both sides.

Cowley placed two of the East Chicago policemen and two agents to the right of the entrance in the unlikely event the trio turned in that direction after leaving the theater.

Across the street from the theater were Cowley, Zarkovich, five agents, and Captain O'Neill of the East Chicago police. They would go into action in case Dillinger somehow escaped the two converging forces. There were also agents at every fire exit and in the alley. No matter what happened, apparently, the FBI was ready.

But nobody could know exactly when Dillinger would come out. It could be in a minute; or in several hours. Would he turn right or left or go out through a fire exit? Purvis was the most visibly nervous. He bit off the end of his cigar and began to chew it.

About this time the theater engineer in charge of the air-conditioning unit went outside to take temperature readings. When he saw men loitering in the alley and one standing ominously on the catwalk above the boiler room he hurried to the office of the theater manager, Charles Shapiro, and said he was scared. Perhaps it was another holdup. Shapiro escorted the frightened engineer to the boiler room and told him he'd be safe inside if he kept the door locked.

The manager wasn't worried about another robbery. Why would thieves lurk at the rear of the theater? Their objective would be the ticket window. Just then the cashier beckoned to him. She was as nervous as the engineer. She pointed across the street to a man sitting on the bakery steps. Half a dozen others were also lounging nearby, and a little, jumpy man had asked her three times about the length of the show.

Shapiro checked with the ticket taker. As soon as he learned Purvis had gone into the foyer, returned and peered back several times, he locked himself in his office and called the Sheffield Street police station. "I want you to send a plain-clothes squad," he said. "It might be a holdup."

At about 10:20 P.M. a city patrol car entered the other end of the alley and slowly approached two men standing near the mouth. A detective jumped out and aimed a shotgun at Special Agent Ray Suran.

"Find out who he is before you shoot him," called the detective at the wheel.

Suran convinced the Chicago officers he was a federal

agent on assignment "after a fugitive," and the police car backed up, then disappeared.

Two more Chicago plain-clothes men were just walking into Shapiro's office. The manager closed the door and told them about the suspicious "characters" outside and how they were placed. When the detectives asked him to point them out, Shapiro said he wasn't that crazy. The two plain-clothes men went outside, turned right, walked up to an agent, and asked who he was and what he was doing.

Inside, *Manhattan Melodrama* was approaching its end. William Powell, the prosecutor, had convicted his friend, Clark Gable, of murder. He offered Gable life imprisonment but the gambler-killer said he'd rather die at once than stay in prison all his life. The picture ended as Gable walked to the electric chair.

At 10:30 P.M. some of the crowd, not waiting to see the added attractions, began filing from the theater. Dillinger and his two companions were among the first, and they came out just as one of the four men placed to the right of the entrance was showing his credentials to the Chicago police.

Fortunately the trio turned left toward Purvis and didn't notice the fuss.

Purvis had torn a match from a book as soon as the first customer emerged from the theater. The cigar shook in his mouth; his eyes ached. He glanced intently at every passer-by. Suddenly he saw Dillinger flanked by the two women. As Purvis struck the match and lit the cigar, Dillinger looked directly but incuriously at him.

Dillinger passed the agent in the next vestibule, who thought, "That's Dillinger with the straw hat and glasses," and quickly stepped across the sidewalk to the right of Dillinger. Hollis and Purvis also closed in from behind with drawn guns. Suddenly Dillinger reached into his right trouser pocket and sprinted toward the alley in a partial crouch.

By now Dillinger had a Colt automatic in his right hand. Paying no attention to Purvis's squeaky command to halt, he continued toward the alley. He must have known he had been betrayed—and by a woman.

Hollis and two other agents fired at the fleeing figure. One bullet went through Dillinger's left side. Another tore into his stooped back and went out the right eye. Dillinger dropped, his feet still on the sidewalk, his head in the alley. Purvis leaned over, spoke to Dillinger. There was no answer.

Anna Sage and Polly Hamilton had vanished. He was alone.

Across the alley Mrs. Etta Natalsky was shouting to her brother, "Oh, Morrie, they shot me!" One of the bullets that passed through Dillinger had struck her leg. Another woman, Theresa Paulus, who had followed Dillinger from the theater, was screaming and running with her dress pulled up. She had been hit by a stray bullet; blood was streaming from her left knee. She crossed the alley and collapsed.

There was excitement but no panic in the neighborhood. Violence was no rarity here; it was only a few blocks from the garage made famous by the St. Valentine Day's Massacre.

Cowley and Purvis went into the theater manager's office and only then did the latter realize both buttons of his coat had been torn off. He never knew when his gun had come into his hand.

Shapiro, convinced it was a holdup, had shouted to his assistant manager to get the ticket magazines and money and bring the cashier into the office. When Purvis and Cowley identified themselves the theater manager was angry and said the FBI should have alerted him so he could have helped.

Purvis smiled affably and asked permission to call Washington. Shapiro, still protesting indignantly, told him to go ahead. Cowley and Purvis gave Hoover a detailed report. Hoover congratulated them: "Fine work!"

Shapiro, suddenly realizing his engineer was still locked in the boiler room, asked one of the ushers to tell him all was clear.

Dillinger was put in an ambulance, then five agents climbed aboard. The ambulance carried him to Alexian Brothers Hospital but Dillinger was already dead and he was taken to the receiving room of the Cook County Morgue.

Here a young doctor, Charles Parker, was waiting with

a cart. Parker wheeled Dillinger's body into the elevator, then to the basement, and in minutes the room where corpses were undressed and washed was crowded with morgue and law officials. It reeked with the smell of formaldehyde and dead bodies. Agent Maxwell Chaffetz pushed his way through the group curiously staring down at Dillinger and began checking the gangster's scarred fingerprints with his Identification Order. In spite of Dr. Loeser's attempts to obliterate the whorls, Chaffetz soon knew that the right man had been killed. He refused to tell anyone around him what he'd ascertained, but found a phone and called Cowley. "It's Dillinger," he said quietly. "There's no question in my mind at all." As he was leaving the morgue, an excited woman offered him money for a lock of Dillinger's hair.

Reporters collected at the locked basement door, noses pressed against the glass, trying to see what was going on inside, where one of their colleagues had managed to take charge of the entire proceedings. They thought the young doctor who had wheeled the boy downstairs was the coroner. Parker was a doctor, certainly, but no coroner. More to the point, he was also a member of the press, helping to support himself during the Depression by gathering hospital news items for the *Chicago Tribune*. When the paper phoned him that Dillinger was dead, Parker had gone to the morgue and simply told the attendants he would help them out.

Trying to act as official as possible, in spite of the straw hat cocked jauntily on the back of his head, he now supervised the undressing of the corpse. He noticed Dillinger's legs were exceptionally sturdy and powerful; his feet neat, almost womanish; his arms slender. In his pockets were several keys, a watch containing Polly Hamilton's picture, and $7.70.

A few minutes later Sergeant Frank Reynolds of the Dillinger Squad arrived. He was so happy to see Dillinger dead that he shook the corpse's hand.

Hundreds of curiosity seekers—nicknamed morbids by the morgue attendants—pressed into the first floor of the building, offering money for a glimpse of the body. Thousands, drawn by radio broadcasts, were also crowding around the entrance to the Biograph. A car parked nearby with Indiana license plates was being dismantled by those who mistakenly thought it was Dillinger's. Others were dipping handkerchiefs and pieces of paper into the tiny red pool in the alley. Some women were even soaking the hems of their skirts with blood.

A representative of the *Indianapolis Star* brought the news to the farm at Mooresville. The elder Dillinger, barefoot, wearing a shirt and overalls, was dazed. "Is it—true?" he stammered. "Are—you really sure there is no mistake?" He was assured it was the truth. "Well—well, John is dead," he said. "At last it has happened—the thing I have prayed and prayed would not happen." He wept.

Because of the oppressive heat Dillinger's sister, Audrey, was sleeping on the lawn of her home in Maywood with the rest of the family. When she was told, she cried, then said, "He was just like a son to me."

The next day congratulations poured in at the Bankers' Building. The one Cowley treasured was a letter from Hoover:

Dear Sam,

I wanted to write and to repeat to you my expressions of commendation and pleasure last evening upon the excellent results which you attained in the Dillinger hunt . . . to you, as one of those who has actively participated in the planning and direction of this hunt, must go a major portion of the credit. Your persistence, patience and energy have made it possible for the Division of Investigation to attain this success, and I am proud of and grateful to you. . . .

But again the FBI did not escape some criticism. At Little Bohemia they had been blamed for Dillinger's escape; now they were being attacked and even belittled for killing him. In addition to numerous letters to newspapers from indignant teen-age admirers of Dillinger, there was harsh censure from more responsible sources. A Virginia editor wrote, "Any brave man would have walked down the aisle and arrested Dillinger . . . why were there so many cowards afraid of this one man? The answer is that the federal agents are mostly cowards." The campaign of vilification gathered such momentum that Hoover felt it necessary to furnish information from the FBI's secret files two years later to Washington newsman Rex Collier to prove that the shooting of Dillinger was justified.

The day after the killing, Dillinger's name still monopolized the nation's headlines with stories of a Woman in Red, who had betrayed him. The FBI refused to comment, but when the Chicago police picked up Mrs. Sage for questioning she admitted she was one of the women at the Biograph. She said she'd occasionally entertained Dillinger and Polly Hamilton in her apartment but denied knowing anything about the trap. Regarding the large reward she said she had not thought of that.

After an inquest, Dillinger's body was put on display in the morgue and thousands passed by in a line a quarter of a mile long. The majority were women. One was heard saying, "I wouldn't have wanted to see him except that I think it's a moral lesson." A fat blonde, after a trip to the basement, put on new lipstick and said, "I'm disappointed. Looks just like any other dead man. But I guess I'll go through once more."

A mob followed the body when it was transferred to the McReady Mortuary. A barker passed through the crowd shouting, "Here you are, an original guaranteed swatch of Dillinger's blood on a handkerchief." He sold so many that one onlooker commented that Dillinger's blood must have flowed from one end of Lincoln Avenue to the other.

The circus was far from over. Dillinger's brain, removed for examination, somehow got "mislaid" and there was a series of charges and denials, culminating in a groundless story that the Dillinger family was going to sue the city.

Two days after the shooting, Mr. Dillinger rode in an old black hearse from Mooresville to get the body. It was his first trip to Chicago. The crowd of 5,000 was so eager to see everything that the six husky men carrying Dillinger in a wicker basket had to fight their way to the hearse.

When the body arrived at the E. F. Harvey Funeral Home six hours later, five hundred Mooresville citizens were waiting.

Once more Dillinger was put on display, and in the next few hours the Harvey lawn and flower garden were trampled as townspeople and visiting morbids filed past Dillinger's body in an endless line.

Everyone had his own idea of what Dillinger had been and what he should look like. He was a Robin Hood, a villainous murderer, a misunderstood young man, a stupid hoodlum. Some of those who knew Dillinger best filed past four and five times. They were puzzled. This didn't look like the man they knew: he was too big, too small, too heavy, too thin. Each had created such a personal image of the man that he could not accept what he now saw as the real John Dillinger.

Rumors began to spread that the wrong man had been killed. Dillinger's older sister, Audrey Hancock, hearing of these stories, told Harvey she could positively identify her brother by a scar on his leg. Harvey uncovered the leg and she said, "There is no question in my mind. Bury him." But others were not satisfied and the more the family insisted the more the rumors grew. It was the beginning of a myth.

There was another rumor that the family, suspected by some of possessing Dillinger's "fortune," had paid $7,000 for a special lavender casket. The following morning he was put into a simple casket, costing $165. He was dressed in a new gray suit; it was too big and the sleeves almost covered his hands.

Dillinger seemed to be as mobile in death as in life. Because of the growing confusion at Harvey's the body was again moved to the home of his sister in Maywood. Police set up a fence to keep back the crowds but a disturbance soon broke out when guards chosen by the family swung clubs at newspaper and newsreel photographers who converged on the house.

Tourists from as far as California lined up, hoping to see the body. Only a man named Ralph Alsman, who had been arrested many times because he was the exact double of Dillinger, and a few others were admitted into the house.

It was inevitable that Hamilton, Van Meter, and Baby Face Nelson were reported en route to Maywood to pay last respects to their leader, and all three gangsters as well as Billie

Frechette and Pierpont were positively identified by bystanders. The only one of the gang to visit the Hancock home was
Mary Kinder, who stayed with the family throughout the or-
deal.

The police were afraid of a riotous scene at Crown Point
Cemetery and asked the family to announce the burial for the
following day even though it would actually take place that
very afternoon. After agreeing to this precaution the family
surprisingly permitted the public to enter the Hancock home
and file past the body. An unruly crowd pushed into the house
as if storming a ball park, one drunk almost tumbling into the
coffin.

Finally the house was cleared and only close friends and
relatives heard the Reverend Charles Fillmore, who had also
officiated at the burial of Dillinger's stepmother fourteen
months before, read the service in the front parlor. The solemn
atmosphere was marred by the drone overhead of three planes
carrying photographers and the shouts of police trying to
keep back the surging sightseers.

"We should eliminate the cause of these gangsters in our
schools, churches, and home life by educational processes,"
said Fillmore. "Given the proper encouragement, who knows
but that today John could have been a great preacher?"

Immediately afterwards a procession of twenty cars
headed for Crown Point Cemetery in spite of protests against
burying the gangster in the same cemetery with President
Benjamin Harrison, three vice-presidents, two governors, and
James Whitcomb Riley. The foreman at the gate admitted only
cars with flags but some others sneaked in. A number of these
brought their lunches. Outside, an estimated 5,000 pressed
against the high iron fence. They had been waiting hopefully
for hours, even though the burial had been announced for the
next day.

Because of the threatening weather a tent was over the
grave. As the mourners gathered around for the final rites,
there was a clap of thunder, then a torrent of rain. The mourners hurried back to their cars but ten minutes later the rain
stopped and Dillinger was lowered into the ground. Again

there was a great clap of thunder and rain poured onto the plain rose-colored coffin.

Dillinger's sister and half sisters cried. The elder Dillinger stood hatless, with the rain beating against his face. He had been offered $10,000 for his son's body and had turned it down but said he would listen to "propositions for other things John had."

After Dillinger was buried, the rumors continued that the wrong man was in the grave. His father, fearing that someone might dig up the body to make sure, ordered three feet of earth over the coffin removed. Cement, laced with scrap iron, was poured into the hole. The tombstone, through the years, was hacked by souvenir hunters until it finally had to be replaced but no one, as yet, has dug through the cement barrier.

The fable that Dillinger was not the man killed outside the Biograph persists today. Some Mooresville citizens who viewed the body still insist it was not Dillinger. In the summer of 1961 one said, "I saw Johnnie not long ago in a motel up in Michigan." Another, "Johnnie drove through town only a few days ago. He smiled at me."

The myth and the man, in death as in life, are hard to separate. The mythical Dillinger was first created by Matt Leach and then exaggerated and embellished by newspapers. Yet the myth was not mere fiction, for the man himself was possessed by it and lived up to it finally; and at times, such as when he escaped from Crown Point, he even exceeded it.

John Dillinger—both man and myth—was created by his times. But even though he was not what most of his contemporaries imagined, he has remained—understandably—the symbol of the modern outlaw.

EPILOGUE

•

"Nothing Can Be Worth This . . ."

1

A WEEK AFTER JOHN DILLINGER'S DEATH HIS FATHER, HUBERT, Audrey, and her husband appeared on the stage of the Lyric Theater in Indianapolis to give fifteen-minute shows between the performances of *I Give My Love*. The advertisement read: "Hear From Their Own Lips Incidents in the Life of the Late John Dillinger, Jr.—and of His Visit to the Kindly Old Father's Home April 8, When the Entire Nation Was Searching for Him." Later Mr. Dillinger lectured in a carnival and also spent several summers at Little Bohemia talking about his son to crowds at the museum set up by Emil Wanatka. It is said that few women left one of the old man's talks dry-eyed. Some fondled the suit of clothes Dillinger had worn at Little Bohemia, and Mrs. Wanatka even observed one visitor kissing the coat sleeve.

But the Dillinger case was by no means closed with his death. A few hours after the funeral, James Probasco, in whose house the plastic surgery had taken place, was arrested by the FBI and brought to the Bankers' Building for questioning. The next morning, moments after being fingerprinted, Probasco suddenly jumped out a window. He fell nineteen stories to the alley, narrowly missing a passer-by.

Though he died before he could implicate Piquett, O'Leary, and the two doctors, these four were arraigned and brought to trial for harboring Dillinger. Only Piquett pleaded not guilty; the others testified against him. When his lawyer fainted, Piquett defended himself and was never more histrionic. After claiming it was illegal to punish him for doing only what a good lawyer should do for his client, he talked about his aged mother and father and "the little girl from home"—his wife—and finally, with a catch in his throat that was undoubtedly genuine, begged the jurors to give him "a break" if they could do it "without stretching things too far." Then, for the first time in his legal career, he slumped gloomily as if there were no hope.

When the jury returned after two hours' deliberation and the foreman said, "We, the jury, find the defendant not guilty," probably no one in the courtroom was more surprised than Piquett.

But he was tried again—this time for harboring Homer Van Meter, who was not his client—and sentenced to two years in Leavenworth. Dr. Loeser was returned to Leavenworth to serve the remainder of the three-year sentence from which he had been paroled, and the other two, because of their cooperation, were given suspended sentences.

The man responsible for Piquett's imprisonment was trapped in a St. Paul alley a month and a day after Dillinger's death. Following what was claimed to be an auto salesman's tip, the police chief, a former police chief, and two detectives shot down Homer Van Meter in a gun battle. The sum of $923 was found in his pockets and only $400 in his money belt. What happened to the more than $10,000 an underworld associate later said Van Meter had in his money belt is still a mystery.

Only weeks later, two other close friends of Dillinger—Pierpont and Makley—also faced the guns of the law. Imitating what they thought Dillinger had done at Crown Point, they carved pistols out of soap and attempted to escape from the death house of the Ohio State Prison in Columbus. They overpowered one guard and were beating on the door leading out of the death house with pieces of a wooden table when a riot squad began firing through the bars. Makley was killed. Pierpont was wounded and a few days later told Mary Kinder, who he pretended was his wife—"We thought we'd do some good but we didn't." In less than a month he seated himself in the electric chair with a slight, sardonic smile. Only a few hours previously, he had written his lawyer, Jessie Levy, that he alone knew the secret of the Michigan City break. "Today I am the only man alive who knows the 'who's and how's' and as my end comes very shortly I'll take this little story with me on the last walk. . . ."

But there also was one woman who had heard it from his own lips, Mary Kinder, and she would be silent for many years.

Now, except for Clark, who was serving a life sentence at Columbus, there was only one important member of the Dillinger gang alive—Baby Face Nelson—and he had replaced Dillinger as the FBI's Public Enemy Number 1.

On the afternoon of November 27, little more than four months after Dillinger's death, two special agents who were trailing a suspect in the Bremer kidnaping on Chicago's north side checked in with the main office only to be told by Cowley, now an inspector, that Nelson had been seen near Lake Geneva. They were ordered to drop their own case and head for Wisconsin at once. Cowley would follow in a few minutes.

As Special Agents William Ryan and Thomas McDade started out the Northwest Highway, Ryan wrote down the li-

cense number of the suspected car, Illinois 639578, pinning it
over the sun visor. Some forty miles from the city they reached
Fox River Grove. After about a mile a Ford sedan with Illinois
plates approached from the north and they strained to see the
license. As it passed, both agents said simultaneously, "578!"

"There's two men and a woman in it," said Ryan. He told
McDade, who was driving, to turn around.

Nelson, at the wheel of the Ford, noticed them. "What're
those two fellows taking a gander at us for?" he asked John
Paul Chase, who was sitting in the back seat with a Browning
automatic rifle. But before Chase could answer, Nelson also
made a U-turn.

McDade saw the Ford head back toward them and as it
passed this time he read the entire number—639578.

"They've turned around again," said Ryan. Nelson's Ford
was now trailing them.

"Let's keep ahead of them," suggested McDade, fresh out
of the FBI training school.

"No," said the more experienced Ryan, who had been at
Little Bohemia and the Biograph. "Let 'em come up and we
can get a look at them." He pulled out his pistol, a Super .38,
and put it between his legs.

McDade watched the Ford draw closer as they went
through Fox River Grove. A mile later it suddenly pulled
alongside the FBI car. Nelson—he wore a cap and sunglasses
—leaned across his wife Helen, who was sitting next to him,
waved his right arm, and shouted, "Pull over!" He told Helen
to get down, then said, "Let 'em have it!" Chase aimed the
rifle over her squatting body and fired.

McDade, six feet four, tried to slide down so his head
would be lower than the back window. Ryan began shooting
through this window, his shells ejecting into McDade's face.

Nelson was firing with his left hand and his shots went
wild. Chase, aiming carefully, wondered what was keeping
the agents alive. He didn't know that his dumdum bullets were
mushrooming as they went through the windshield of their
own car.

McDade, who had pushed the FBI car up to seventy-five

miles an hour, saw the side road leading into Barrington not far ahead and shouted, "Where are they?"

"They've fallen back." Ryan told him to turn off so they could phone the office.

McDade tried to make the 90-degree turn but when he saw he couldn't, released the wheel, and the car bumped across a field. Ryan jumped out one door, McDade the other. They waited at the side of the road, pistols ready, but Nelson didn't appear after several minutes and they figured he had turned off on another road.

They had no idea another FBI car was now chasing Nelson. Inspector Cowley and Special Agent Herman Hollis—one of the three men who had fired at Dillinger near the Biograph —had been driving up to Wisconsin when they encountered the running gun fight. They made a U-turn and were soon chasing Nelson.

Less than a mile from Barrington, Baby Face heard his motor sputter—one of Ryan's bullets had hit the water jacket. He jammed on the brakes, swung right into a gravel road, and stopped. Helen jumped out and ran into a field. The FBI car, unable to stop, speeded almost fifty yards past with a screech of brakes. With bullets thudding into their car, the two agents jumped out. Hollis, armed with a shotgun, hunched behind the car. Cowley, clutching a machine gun, leaped into the ditch.

Nelson and Chase were shooting from behind their auto. Finally Nelson impatiently grabbed a machine gun and said, "I'm going down there and get those sons of bitches."

A group of men planting trees several hundred feet away were horrified to see Baby Face walk toward the FBI car, upright, his gun blazing from the hip—like a movie gangster.

Cowley fired from the ditch as Nelson shot at him. One of Cowley's bullets hit Nelson in the side. But he didn't fall; he kept sweeping the ditch with bullets until Cowley dropped, fatally wounded.

Hollis was firing his shotgun. Half a dozen slugs tore into Nelson's legs but he plodded forward. Hollis dropped the empty shotgun, pulled out a pistol, and ran for the protection of a telephone pole. Before he reached it a bullet from Nelson's machine gun hit him in the head, killing him.

Nelson, mortally wounded, staggered to the FBI car and backed it up to his Ford. After Chase had transferred their weapons, Nelson said, "I've been hit. You'll have to drive." Chase headed the car back toward Fox River Grove just as Helen ran from the field and jumped in. The next morning Nelson's body, stripped nude to prevent immediate identification was found in a ditch some twenty miles away.

It was the end of the Dillinger gang.

The other gangs that had been ravaging the Midwest the past two years were also near extinction. Five weeks before Nelson's death, Pretty Boy Floyd and Adam Richetti, who had murdered four lawmen and Frank Nash at the Kansas City railroad station, were trapped by the FBI on an Ohio farm (a year previously the man who had hired them, Verne Miller, had been found in a ditch near Detroit riddled with bullets). Richetti was captured but Floyd put up a fight and was badly wounded. When Melvin Purvis bent over and asked if he was Pretty Boy, he refused to acknowledge the nickname and said, "I'm Charles Arthur Floyd." Another agent, wanting to know if he would confess to the Kansas City massacre, was answered with obscenities. "I won't tell you nothing," said Floyd, then died.

At Richetti's trial in Kansas City, Mrs. Lottie West, the Travelers Aid case worker, testified—though most of the other witnesses refused. Richetti ended his life in the gas chamber.

The Barker gang was fast disintegrating. A few days after Dillinger's death, Dr. Moran got drunk at the Casino Club near Toledo and told several of the gang, "I have you guys in the palms of my hands." He left the club with two mob members, who took him on a boat ride in Lake Erie, and never was seen again. Fred Barker later told an associate, "Doc will do no more operating. The fishes probably have eat him up by now."

Early in 1935 the FBI began to close in on the gang. On the night of January 8 Dock Barker was captured as he was coming out of his Chicago apartment. His only remark to the arresting agents was, "This is a helluva time to be caught without a gun." That same night, in another part of the city, two other members of the gang were trapped. One, the ex-golf professional surrendered; the second, Russell Gibson, was killed when he tried to shoot his way to freedom.

Eight days later, fourteen agents—the majority from the Special Squad in Chicago—converged on a house on the shores of Lake Weir, Florida. They had come because of an alligator. According to the captured golf pro, Ma Barker and Freddie were living near a lake which was the habitat of an alligator named Old Joe. Karpis and Freddie Barker, towing a live pig behind their motor boat as bait, had tried to shoot it with machine guns. On a map found in Dock Barker's effects, a circle had been penciled around Lake Weir—and the agents determined this was the home of Old Joe.

About 5:30 on the morning of January 16 a squad of agents crept close to the cottage that was reported to be Ma's hideout. Then Special Agent in Charge E. J. Connelley, who commanded the Special Squad after Cowley's murder by Nelson, demanded that Ma and Freddie come out and surrender. Someone inside the house said, "All right, go ahead," and fired at Connelley. The agents replied with tear gas bombs, rifle and machine-gun fire. After some forty-five minutes of silence from inside the house, Connelley walked up to the front while Willie, a colored handyman who worked for Ma, went inside to find out if the Barkers were injured or dead. Finally Willie stuck his head out of a second-story window and yelled, "They're all dead."

A .45 pistol was found near Fred Barker's body and the dead Ma Barker was clutching a machine gun.

Three days later the FBI brought Bremer to Bensenville and he positively identified the house where he had been held captive. In the next year twenty-five people—including members of the gang, their girls, and those who had helped them—were convicted in connection with the kidnaping. Six—including Dock Barker, Volney Davis, and Harry Sawyer—got life and others received sentences totaling a hundred years and a day.

Now there was only one leading member of the gang free—Alvin Karpis. Upon learning of the death of Ma and Freddie, he had fled Florida with his wife Dolores, sister-in-law of Tommy Carroll and Pat Reilly; but four days later they were trapped in an Atlantic City hotel by local authorities. Dolores, who was pregnant, was wounded in the leg and captured but Karpis escaped. When J. Edgar Hoover personally apprehended him about a year later, he pleaded guilty to the kidnaping of William Hamm and was sent to Alcatraz for life.

2

Today many of the leading characters of the Dillinger days—lawmen as well as criminals—are dead. Machine Gun Kelly died at Leavenworth in 1954 but not before writing to Urschel, the man he helped kidnap, ". . . these five words seem written in fire on the walls of my cell: 'Nothing can be worth this.' This—the kind of life I am leading. This is the final word of wisdom so far as crime is concerned."

Dock Barker served less than four years of his life term at Alcatraz; he was killed in a reckless attempt to escape The Rock. Today Ma Barker and all her sons are buried together—outcasts in death as in life—in an isolated corner of a country graveyard on a lonely hill near Welch, Oklahoma. Their markers are decorated only by a few faded artificial flowers.

John Dillinger, Senior, was almost eighty when he died in 1943 and was buried next to his son at Crown Hill. Dillinger's associate in his first crime is also dead; in 1937 Ed Singleton fell asleep on a railroad track and was run over.

Anna Sage died in Romania in 1947. She got $5,000 from the FBI for her services but a request to stay deportation proceedings was denied. In a last appeal she went to Indianapolis and asked Governor McNutt to set aside the Indiana conviction which had caused all her trouble.

McNutt called in Donald Stiver, head of the Department of Public Safety. "Don," he asked, "did this woman give any information to Indiana that led to the arrest, apprehension or killing of John Dillinger?"

"No," said Stiver.

"Madam," said McNutt coldly, "there's your answer." Later that same day McNutt refused to give an Indiana reward to Sergeant Zarkovich, who had acted as Mrs. Sage's go-between with the FBI. "It is a sordid picture," McNutt told newsmen and then bitterly criticized the sergeant for failing to co-operate with Indiana officials in the Dillinger case.

Matt Leach's bitterness was aimed at a different target—the FBI. He claimed that it was not a special agent but a member of the East Chicago police who had actually killed Dillinger. He also claimed to have evidence that Dillinger was unarmed when he was shot and that $7,000 had been taken from his pockets and given to the widow of the East Chicago policeman murdered by Dillinger. Leach's feud with the FBI broke into the open a few years later during the Brady case when J. Edgar Hoover complained to Stiver that Leach was counseling citizens not to co-operate with the FBI. On September 4, 1937, Stiver requested Leach's resignation, citing thirteen charges based on his lack of co-operation with the FBI. Twelve days later Leach was formally dismissed by the Indiana State Police Board.

He spent the next years writing a book, feeling that only by revealing the inside facts of the Dillinger case would his honor be vindicated. But it was never published. While returning from New York, after discussing its publication, he and his wife were killed in an accident on the Pennsylvania Turnpike.

Another hunter of Dillinger also died a violent death—but by his own hand. Melvin Purvis, who resigned from the FBI the year after Dillinger was killed, shot himself in 1960. The man who tried to send Dillinger to the electric chair, Robert Estill, was reported dead by a Chicago newspaper some years ago. Like so many things in the case, it wasn't true. He died in 1961, only a few months after being interviewed for this book.

John Stege of Chicago's Dillinger Squad is also dead, but

Frank Reynolds, now a captain, has remained on the Chicago police force—and is still capable of using his .38.

Billie Frechette, after serving a two-year sentence at Milan, joined a carnival and told thousands of eager listeners about John Dillinger. "He liked to dance and he liked to hunt. . . . I think he liked gravy better than anything else. He liked bread and gravy." She then dropped out of sight, to reappear briefly again when her husband, a minor hoodlum, was arrested in Chicago several years ago.

Mary Kinder also joined a "Crime Does Not Pay Show," touring as far east as New York City. When a member of the audience once asked if she was the Woman in Red, she replied, "If I was, I wouldn't be up here. I babied them boys. I was a mother to them." At one of the interviews for this book she said she was not ashamed of her life with the gang. "I did wrong going with them—and I ruined my name. But I'm not sorry of a thing I did of which I'm not. They showed me a wonderful time. I was good to them and they were good to me. No, I'm not sorry of a thing I did."

She now lives in Indianapolis. So do Harvey Hire, Fred Brewer Whiteside, and many others who vividly remember Dillinger.

There are still inmates doing time at Michigan City who knew John Dillinger well. Each of these men was asked why he became a criminal and why he kept stealing after being paroled. William Shaw, Dillinger's first professional partner in crime, who probably shared some of his needs and feelings, wrote:

. . . The closest thing I can give for answer is that I want the nice things in life and not work for them. What caused me to start stealing, I can never answer. As you guessed, I have given it considerable thought. I never wanted for anything when I was young, as my parents took good care of me—but even then I wanted to steal. I guess I was borned to be a hoodlum. . . . I have lived a life of crime and misery and wouldn't take a fortune for my experience. Rest assured it's nothing to be proud of. Thirteen months freedom in the last twenty-eight years—it's not very glamorous, is it? I guess everyone has a different reason for their life of crime.

Whatever the reasons, society still hasn't found any satisfactory answers to the problems of those who seem doomed to steal. Crime has not decreased since the Dillinger days. In fact it has increased several hundred percent and now costs America $60,000,000 a day.

Notes

THE MAIN SOURCES FOR EACH CHAPTER ARE LISTED WITH EX-
planatory details. Though millions of words were written in
newspapers and magazines, there were relatively few reliable
books to draw from. The professional criminal has been neglected as a subject of serious study. Books which proved of
great value for numerous chapters, and will not be listed
again, are: *Persons in Hiding* by J. Edgar Hoover; *Ten Thousand Public Enemies* by Courtney Riley Cooper; *The FBI
Story* by Don Whitehead, and *The Dry and Lawless Years* by
Judge John H. Lyle.

There was, however, a wealth of documentary material
from city, county, and state police files. Police reporters—like
Nate Bomberg of St. Paul and Rex Newman of Joplin, who
have spent most of their lives not only following crime but
interpreting and understanding it—gave me access to much
invaluable material.

CHAPTER ONE

The early life of Dillinger in Indianapolis is based on interviews with Fred Brewer Whiteside, Leroy and Dorothy

Carney, Paul Corbin, E. F. Murphy, Laura Presnell, Mr. and Mrs. Cecil Thomas, and others who wish to remain anonymous. The Mooresville days come from interviews with Mr. and Mrs. Robert Clift, Paul Henderson, Mrs. Wallace Hadley, Grafton Kivett (Beryl Hovius' attorney), Ace Edwards, Elmer F. Harvey, Dorothy Hobson, Delbert Hobson, Gordon Whittaker, Homer Zook, John William McCleary, A. F. Miles, and others.

Most official Dillinger records are missing. His once voluminous file at Michigan City is now slender. Even the page from the 1924 Morgan County Marriage Record noting his marriage to Beryl Hovius has been stolen. His "packet" at Pendleton could not be found when we first visited that institution but was finally unearthed months later.

CHAPTER TWO

Ward Lane, warden of Indiana State Prison at Michigan City, and John W. Buck, superintendent of the Indiana State Reformatory at Pendleton, made all records available and gave me free access to their institutions with permission to interview guards, civilian employees, and inmates. The conditions and attitudes which helped make Dillinger a professional criminal do not exist today. Though penology in America is admittedly in its infancy, Indiana can be proud of the progress it has made in the past thirty years.

The section on Pendleton is based on interviews with newsman Tubby Toms; former superintendent A. F. Miles; J. F. McManus, his secretary; Robert Hardin, present reformatory psychologist; C. B. Hite, a guard in charge of Dillinger on yard detail; R. E. Slater, his supervisor in the shirt factory; Ernest Ellingwood, his teacher; and Will "Machine Gun" Kelley, one of his closest friends. A series of articles entitled "I Remember When" by Mr. McManus in the reformatory newspaper, *The Reflector*, was very helpful. Kelley, who was also a good friend of Van Meter's, spent two full days in an Indianapolis motel taping his recollections. When he finished he gave me his almost new Remington so the book could be typed on it. He died eight months later but left behind an unpublished manuscript, *Cathedral in the Sand,* the story of his many years in crime and prison.

CHAPTER THREE

Part of the Barrow story comes from Rex Newman, police reporter of the *Joplin Globe.* Newman reached the garage apartment soon after the Barrows escaped and found the poem Bonnie was writing, other poems, and numerous snapshots. Also useful were the reports of Chief of Detectives Ed Portley, who wrote a long definitive article on the Barrows in the February, 1945, issue of *Master Detective.*

Information on the Barkers came from Newman, former FBI agents, Roger Devlin of the *Tulsa Tribune,* and a number of informants, some of whom were involved with the gang and insist on anonymity.

The story of crime in St. Paul was told by newsmen T. Glen Harrison, Ray Schneider, and Nate Bomberg; Mike McGinnis, former detective in the city police; Ray Noonan, superintendent of the Minnesota Bureau of Criminal Apprehension; State Senator Claude Allen; John Connolly, former city attorney, John J. Verstraete, Jr., of Minnesota Mining and Manufacturing, and many others. William Hamm and W. W. Dunn were interviewed.

The Kansas City Massacre: interviews with Mrs. Lottie West, Roderick Turnbull of the *Star,* and Sergeant Fred Ennis of the Kansas City, Missouri, Detective Division; also reports from the city police department.

CHAPTER FOUR

Interviews with William Shaw, Mary Kinder, and five other early associates of Dillinger who wish to be nameless; Horace Grisso, Mata and Maud Taylor of the New Carlisle bank; Mrs. Fred Fisher, Mrs. Frank Kellenburger (Mildred Wilson), and Mrs. Russell Sines of Monticello; Mrs. Lysle Haines (Margaret Good) and Mrs. Marjorie Hoppes of the Daleville bank. The most important sources on Matt Leach were two former state policemen—Harvey Hire (presently Chief U. S. Probation Officer in Indianapolis) and Art Keller—and newsmen Joe Shepard and Tubby Toms. The story of Dillinger's lone encounter with his parole officer came from Frank Hope. Muncie information was supplied by Leon Parkinson of the *Press* and Bob White, who, as a young police reporter, wrote the first stories on "Desperate Dan." Dayton material was supplied by the city police department and Detective Russ Pfauhl. Dillinger's letters in this and other chapters: from the Dayton police department, Indiana State Prison, Pendleton Reformatory, and others.

CHAPTER FIVE

Barrows: see Chapter three.

Main sources for the Kellys were former FBI agents and E. E. Kirkpatrick, who wrote two books on the Urschel kidnaping: *Voices from Alcatraz* and *Crimes' Paradise*. Warden Tracy A. Hand of the Kansas State Prison told a unique story about the escape of Harvey Bailey and ten others from that institution on Memorial Day, 1933. Several weeks before the crash-out, Hand resigned as deputy warden of the prison to take a job in a nearby city. A few minutes after Bailey and his associates escaped over the wall, taking with them the warden and a guard, Hand's phone rang.

"Can you come to the Pen?" asked a worried voice. It was one of the inmates, Charlie Collinson. "We're having trouble!" When Hand said he didn't work there any more, Collinson explained what had happened—and that the deputy warden and several carloads of guards had given chase. "There doesn't seem to be anyone here in charge of the place. I'm afraid of what might happen." Hand hurried to Lansing and when he found the inmates milling aimlessly in the yard, took charge.

While visiting the scene of this escape, I noticed a sign in a cell house put up by an inmate: Crime Don't Pay But the Hours Are Sure Good.

Albert Bates wrote two letters from Alcatraz to Urschel revealing some interesting details of the kidnaping:

I received the sum of $94,250.00 for my "end," and when I left the room to clean up a bit on the back porch I saw Bailey was still there, although he had told me four days previous that his friends would call for him not later than Saturday. I had warned him that the place was "hot" on account of our past activities in Texas and our connections with detective friends, Messrs. Weathersford and Sweeney of Ft. Worth. I was in a hurry to get the job over with so I did not converse much with anyone. I gave Bailey $500.00 out of my pocket and Kelly did likewise. . . .

. . . In my honest opinion the Shannons did not, nor would not, accept any of that money. Kelly may have intended to give them some money later on after he exchanged it for other money. I know they refused time and time again to accept any money from any of us. It would be purely a conjecture for me to say why "Boss" Shannon permitted us to take charge whenever we were inclined to do so—he just seemed to be fascinated with Kelly's line.

Kelly also wrote Urschel from Alcatraz:

. . . I would appreciate any information you might give me regarding the oil prospects in Wise County; especially the prospects around the farm which is four miles south of Paradise. . . .

I have found the secret of how to "do" easy time. I just let myself drift along; the tide of time picks me up and carries me with it. It will leave me high and dry precisely where it chooses and when it chooses; consequently, I have nothing to worry about. . . .

How is your bridge game? Are you still vulnerable? I didn't mean that as a dirty dig, but you must admit you lost your bid on the night of July 22, 1933. . . .

CHAPTER SIX

Interviews:
Lloyd Rinehart and A. J. Krueger of the Massachusetts Ave-

nue bank (now The Jackpot Restaurant), Art Keller, Harvey Hire, Mary Kinder, W. J. Aldredge, and Russ Pfauhl.

CHAPTER SEVEN

Interviews:

Michigan City: Lorenz Schmuhl, Howard Crosby, Mrs. Clara Lamb, Russell Blande, and several inmates. Also helpful was a chapter on the escape from *In for Life,* an unpublished book by Raymond L. Moseley, who has been a convict at Michigan City for thirty-five years.

St. Marys: Chief of Police Gilbert Gerstner; Adrian Weber, cashier of the bank; W. R. Young, a customer, and others.

Lima: Don Sarber, Jr.

Peru: Ambrose Clark, Claude Clark.

Other information from Mary Kinder, Margaret Northern, Lorenz Schmuhl, Tubby Toms, and Joe Shepard. The voluminous testimony at the Lima trials of Pierpont, Makley, and Clark was valuable.

CHAPTER EIGHT

Interviews:

Greencastle: Edwin Seller, a depositor; Kenny Bennett of the *Putnam County Graphic;* and Jack Cejnar.

Chicago: Lieutenant John Howe, Sergeant Howard Harder, Ed Keller, Mary Kinder.

Racine: Cyril Boyard and Mrs. Henry Patzke, Harold Graham, Leslie C. Rowan, Loren S. Bowne, Don Steele, and W. G. Aschenbrener of the bank.

Dillinger Squad: Sergeant (now Captain) Frank Reynolds; Adolph Wagner, *Chicago's American;* and Thomas J. Stapleton, Stege's secretary.

Much of the information on the Touhy case came from Ray Brennan of the *Chicago Sun-Times,* who helped Touhy write his book, *The Stolen Years.*

Also Harvey Hire, Mary Kinder, and Margaret Northern.

CHAPTER NINE

Interviews:

Klutas case: Sergeant (now Captain) Joe Healy. The gun found on Klutas had been bought in Hammond by John Dillinger, who probably gave it to Dietrich.

Bremer case: Edward Bremer, William Behrens (recipient of one of the kidnap notes). I received much detailed information on all aspects of this case from former members of the FBI. The various apartments of the gang in St. Paul, the scenes of the kidnapings, as well as the two houses where Bremer and Hamm were kept captive in Bensenville were visited. Information on Fred Goetz was given by an informant who must remain anonymous.

CHAPTER TEN

Interviewed at East Chicago were bank officials Adam Niederthal, F. Bernard O'Toole, and Maxine Burgess. The bank's president, Colonel Riley, was most helpful. The unanimous opinion of the bankers is that Wilgus came in, not as a result of the alarm "but merely for a routine walk through the bank." The identity of Dillinger's driver is unknown. It could have been Van Meter or even Baby Face Nelson.

The Tucson story came from Frank Eyman (now warden of Arizona State Prison), newsmen William R. Mathews, David Brinegar, Jack Weadock, and Fred Finney; Milo Walker and Frank Keefe, ex-policemen; K. S. Adams, sergeant in charge of the county jail; Mrs. Hattie Strauss; Bruce Hannah and William Benedict. Mr. Benedict said he never got a reward, only several threatening letters. Information on Leach came from Harvey Hire, who accompanied him on the trip, and Joe Shepard and Tubby Toms, who covered the story. Robert Estill, whose bright career was ruined because of the picture with Dillinger, spent a long afternoon reminiscing. G. Reed Thomson, who requested the picture, is still a photographer in East

Chicago. Reynolds himself told of meeting Dillinger at the airport.

CHAPTER ELEVEN

Touhy case: see Chapter eight.

Bremer case: see Chapter nine.

Crown Point: Robert Estill, Robert Volk, Edwin Saager, John Thomas (a vigilante), and Mrs. Lew Baker. The story of the bribed judge was told for the first time by George Hargrave of the Hargrave Secret Service.

CHAPTER TWELVE

Information on the new Dillinger gang came from lawmen whose names cannot be divulged. They got it from one of the principal members of the gang and two associates. Pat Reilly also gave some details in a furtive interview in St. Paul.

Sioux Falls: Leo Olson, Monte Parsons, Robert Dargen, Melvin Sells, Ted Ramsey of the *Argus-Leader*, and bank employees Emma Knabach, Fred Anderson, G. Oliver Nordby, Louis Fannemel, and Bessie Dunn.

Lima trial: Mary Kinder, Don Sarber, Jr., and the testimony.

The detailed information about the Mason City robbery could not have been compiled without the enthusiastic assistance of Earl Hall, editor and publisher of the *Globe-Gazette*. Those interviewed include: Ralph Wiley, Enoch Norem, Mrs. Virgil Allen (Lydia Crosby); Mrs. Don Giesen (Margaret Johnson); Tom Walters; Carl Wright; Mr. and Mrs. Harry Fisher (he is now eighty-eight and alert); Francis De Sart; and Fred Heneman, Virgil Allen, Raymond Keister, Alfred M. Halsor, and Hans Schrader of the bank.

CHAPTER THIRTEEN

This chapter is based on sources already mentioned. Mr. and Mrs. Robert Clift are among those who described the reunion at the Mooresville farm. Other material on the visit came from Jack Cejnar and Mary Kinder. Jess Pittenger described the raid on the Warsaw police station and former Chief of Police J. Willard Welsh told of the visit of Dillinger and Hamilton to Sault Ste. Marie. Ronald Tuxworth and Joe Kelly of Pickford and his two sons George and Joe, Jr., reminisced on Hamilton's early days in the area.

CHAPTER FOURTEEN

In spite of the countless words written about Little Bohemia, the whole story has never before been revealed. Until Mrs. Wanatka agreed to an interview last summer, she had not given any details of the key role she played in the case because of fear of revenge by an associate of Dillinger. Others interviewed were Emil Wanatka, Emil Wanatka, Jr., George and Lloyd La Porte, George Bazso (who now runs the Hillcrest Resort), Mr. and Mrs. James W. Bart (relatives of the Mitchells), Alvin Koerner, Jr., Mrs. Robert Dickerson (daughter of Mr. and Mrs. Henry Voss), Pat Reilly, Carl C. Christensen, and four FBI agents who accompanied Purvis on the foray.

In October 1947 *True Magazine* ran an article by Paul Gallico about the Little Bohemia shooting. In it a reporter of the *Minneapolis Journal* got a tip about Dillinger and flew to Little Bohemia with a photographer. These two, supposedly, were in the bar when the dogs began barking. While I was in the Twin Cities, prior to visiting Little Bohemia, I spent half a day going through every Minneapolis and St. Paul paper in a vain effort to find the real names of the reporter and photographer. A week later I learned in Little Bohemia that the article was a hoax, though Gallico didn't know it.

Purvis's book, *American Agent*, was helpful in this and the final chapter.

CHAPTER FIFTEEN

Frank Sinclair and Lionel Benfer, the first newsmen to arrive at Little Bohemia, gave their personal recollections; William Chapman—Assistant Chief of Police of Lac du Flambeau and a close friend of Ole Catfish, now dead—provided details of Nelson's visit to the cabin and his escape. Norman Dieter described the chase near the spiral bridge, and newsman Miles McMillin told how the three girls captured at Little Bohemia were hidden in a church; Judge Patrick Stone, who tried them, was also interviewed. When I was unable to interview Mr. and Mrs. Roy Francis, Dan Sullivan of the *St. Paul Pioneer Press* volunteered for the job. His excellent story of the episode appeared in the August 6, 1961, issue of the paper. Information about the death of Hamilton in Aurora came from Volney Davis.

CHAPTER SIXTEEN

The story of the ambush of the Barrows is based on an interview with J. J. Smith, of Miami, Oklahoma, and information on the Dillinger and Van Meter operations from the testimony of Drs. Loeser and Cassidy and O'Leary at the Piquett trial. Else K. La Roe in her book, *Woman Surgeon,* describes how John Dillinger came to her office in New York and unsuccessfully tried to force her to operate on his face. He had, she said, a scar "which extended from the outer corner of his right eye to his chin." Dillinger had no such scar.

Mrs. Frank Cargin, proprietress of the Evening Star Camp, described the visit of Tommy Carroll, and Emil Steffen, now Waterloo's Chief of Detectives, told of the shooting in the alley.

Interviewed at South Bend: Sylvester Zell, Joseph Pawlowski, Delos Coen, P. G. Stahly, Irvine "Bruce" Bouchard, Edward McCormick, Alex Slaby, Howard Noble of the *Tribune,* Alvin Shank, a bank employee, and Mrs. Alex Nemeth, a spectator.

CHAPTER SEVENTEEN

The final hours of Dillinger: Louis Scelfo; Gus Gianopulus of the ice cream parlor near Mrs. Sage's; Dr. Jerry Kearns, who performed the autopsy; Dr. Charles D. Parker, now head of Medical Department of Marshall Field's; Fred Lebed, Cook County morgue supervisor; three former FBI agents who were at the Biograph and one who co-ordinated the action at head-quarters; and Charles Shapiro, who told his story for the first time.

The incident of the two out-of-town policemen who visited Captain Stege's office was told by Captain Reynolds and Lieutenant Howe at separate interviews. Other information from E. F. Harvey, Mary Kinder, and Dewey Shoemaker of Crown Hill Cemetery.

At first police thought the picture in Dillinger's watch was Evelyn Frechette's and then Mary Longnaker's. A strong denial of this last identification came from Claude Constable, Mary's husband. He was right; it was, of course, the picture of Polly Hamilton.

EPILOGUE

Barrington interviews: Alfred Trestick, Clarence Lyons, Burton Hoffman, and two former FBI agents who were present. Letters from Bates and Kelly to Urschel are reprinted from *Voices from Alcatraz* by E. E. Kirkpatrick. The end of the Barker gang is based on information from two former FBI agents. Donald O. Stiver told of the visit of Mrs. Sage to Governor McNutt.

Acknowledgments

My wife and I traveled through thirty-four states to gather material for this book. We followed the trail of John Dillinger from the house where he was born on Cooper Street in Indianapolis to the Biograph Theater; to Tucson, Arizona, where his short stay still stirs memories; to the banks he robbed from Bluffton, Ohio, to Mason City, Iowa; to jails where he was imprisoned from Lima, Ohio, to Crown Point; to the Indiana Reformatory at Pendleton and the prison at Michigan City.

We saw the frame house where he underwent plastic surgery (it is now a restaurant), the apartment he escaped from in St. Paul, the farm at Mooresville, and the lodge at Little Bohemia, presently run by Emil Wanatka, Jr. In addition, we also visited the scenes made notorious by Clyde Barrow and Bonnie Parker, Pretty Boy Floyd, Kathryn and Machine Gun Kelly, and the Barkers.

This book could not have been written without the wholehearted co-operation of many people and many organizations. Newsmen who covered the events, former FBI agents, ex-sheriffs, city and state policemen, prison wardens and guards, convicts and ex-criminals, jail and morgue attendants, librarians, bank officials, as well as the hundreds of private citizens who were caught up in the stories, all contributed generously. To list everyone would be impossible, but here are a few:

Barrington, Illinois. *Courier-Review.*

Bensenville, Illinois. Gene Kinkade, present occupant of the Bremer kidnap house.

Bluffton, Ohio. Charles Hilty of the *Bluffton News.*

Carthage, Illinois. Ben Johnston, *Hancock County Journal.*

Cedar Rapids, Iowa. *Gazette.*

Chicago, Illinois. Virgil Peterson, Chicago Crime Commission; Jerry Gamero, Capri Theater; Basil Walters and Ritz Fischer, *Daily News;* Ray Brennan of the *Sun-Times;* Don Maxwell and Stanley Armstrong of the *Tribune;* Major and Mrs. James Haslam; and Arthur E. Hrobsky, Jr., Public Information Consultant for the Superintendent of Police, Chicago.

Columbus, Ohio. E. L. Maxwell, Deputy Warden, Ohio State Prison.

Crown Point: Guy Slaughter, *Lake County Star.*

Dayton, Ohio. James E. Fain, *Daily News.*

Fairbury, Nebraska. L. K. Cramb, *Journal.*

Greencastle, Indiana. *Daily Banner* and Kenny Bennett of the *Putnam County Graphic.*

Hammond, Indiana. James B. Ramos, *Times.*

Indianapolis, Indiana. Jameson Campaigne, *Star;* Otto Frenzel, President, Merchants National Bank; Lucy Gambino.

Joplin, Missouri. Evelyn Goswick, Records and Identification Clerk, Police Department; Rex Newman, *Globe.*

Kansas City, Missouri. Roy Roberts, *Star.*

Leipsic, Ohio. Lawrence, Bernard, and Thomas Ellerbrock, present owners of the Pierpont farm.

Lima, Ohio. Pat O. Riley, *News.*

Madison, Wisconsin. Mrs. Lucile Alstad, U. S. Court Clerk; *Wisconsin State Journal;* and District Attorney William D. Byrne of Dane County.

Mankato, Minnesota. LaDonna Olson, *Free Press.*

Martinsville, Indiana. *Reporter.*

Mason City, Iowa. Earl Hall, *Globe-Gazette.*

Miami, Florida. John D. Pennekamp, *Herald.*

Miami, Oklahoma. *News-Record.*

Michigan City, Indiana. Elwin Greening, *News-Dispatch;* Al Spiers, columnist for the Nixon Newspapers; Warden Ward Lane and Edwin Gabel of the Indiana State Prison.

Milwaukee, Wisconsin. George Tracy and Lionel Benfer, *Sentinel;* Lindsay Hoben, Wallace Lomoe, and Frank Sinclair, *Journal.*

Monticello, Indiana. Bob Fisher, *Herald-Journal.*

Montpelier, Ohio. Jack Bryce, *Leader Enterprise.*

Mooresville, Indiana. *Times.*

Muncie, Indiana. Leon Parkinson, *Press.*

New Carlisle, Ohio. M. Harry Mount, *Sun,* and Tom Reynolds, owner of the New Carlisle Furniture Company, formerly the bank.

Noblesville, Indiana. James T. Neal, *Daily Ledger.*

Oklahoma City, Oklahoma. Charles L. Bennett, *Daily Oklahoman-Oklahoma City Times.*

Pana, Illinois. Don Pauschert, *News-Palladium.*

Pendleton, Indiana. John W. Buck, Superintendent, Indiana Reformatory.

Peru, Indiana. Bill Jackson, *Daily Tribune.*

Port Huron, Michigan. *Times-Herald.*

Racine, Wisconsin. Verne Hoffman, *Journal-Times.*

Rockville, Indiana. William Hargrave, *Republican.*

St. Marys, Ohio. K. C. Geiger, *Leader.*

Saint Paul, Minnesota. Fred Heaberlin, *Dispatch* and *Pioneer Press.*

Sault Ste. Marie, Michigan. *News.*

Sioux Falls, South Dakota. Herb Bechtold, *Argus-Leader.*

South Bend, Indiana. *Tribune.*

Topeka, Kansas. Oscar S. Stauffer, Stauffer Publications, Inc.

Tucson, Arizona. William R. Mathews, David Brinegar, *Arizona Daily Star;* June Jones, *Daily Citizen;* Lieutenant Kenneth Yeazell, city police department.

Tulsa, Oklahoma. Roger Devlin, *Tribune;* E. E. Kirkpatrick.

Warsaw, Indiana. William Mollenhour, *Times-Union.*

•   •   •

Libraries in almost every city visited contributed to the book. Those which were particularly helpful include Minnesota Historical Society (John Dougherty, Assistant Curator); the Indiana Historical Society; and the public libraries of New York, Chicago, Lima, Ohio, and Kansas City, Missouri.

I am grateful to Jack Cejnar—who ghosted a newspaper serial supposedly written by John Dillinger, Sr.—for the photograph of Dillinger and Evelyn Frechette; and to Russell Pfauhl of the R. K. Pfauhl Detective Bureau of Dayton for the snapshots taken at the World's Fair.

I would like to express special thanks to Marian Jager whose lengthy analysis of Dillinger's handwriting was revealing; to Richard O. Peters and the other newsmen of the *Indianapolis Times* for discovering almost forty people who had known Dillinger; to the numerous banks which were so cooperative; to Emil Wanatka, Emil Wanatka, Jr., and Nancy Wanatka for their hospitality at Manitowish Waters; to Henry E. Edmunds, Manager, Research and Information Department, Ford Motor Company, for allowing the use of Dillinger's letter to Henry Ford; to Will "Machine Gun" Kelley and Mary Kinder, who spent so many hours taping their recollections; to the inmates of Indiana State Prison who have patiently answered numerous questions; and, finally, to Dr. Stephen Nordlicht, Assistant Professor of Psychiatry, New York Medical College, for examining the rough draft and clarifying certain psychiatric aspects. Dr. Nordlicht is presently one of a team conducting a global survey of juvenile delinquency for the World Medical Association.

I would also like to thank my wife, Toshiko, who not only did most of the research but interviewed many of the witnesses. I am grateful to my typists, Helen Toland and Edith Lentz, and to Tom Mahoney and John Jamieson for innumerable valuable suggestions. Finally, this book could not have been written without the constant encouragement of my agent, Rogers Terrill, and the creative editing of Robert Loomis, who also gave me the idea.

Index

Books by JOHN TOLAND

Ships in the Sky

Battle: The Story of the Bulge

But Not in Shame

The Dillinger Days

The Last One Hundred Days

Adolf Hitler

Gods of War

In Mortal Combat: Korea 1950-1953

Infamy

Occupation

Rising Sun